YOUR BIRTH YEAR

 **The National Childbirth Trust**

YOUR **BIRTH** YEAR

Understanding the Choices You Have in Pregnancy, Birth and Motherhood

Foreword by Dr Richard Porter F.R.C.O.G

MITCHELL BEAZLEY

contents

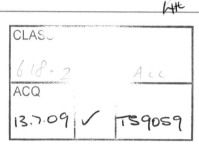

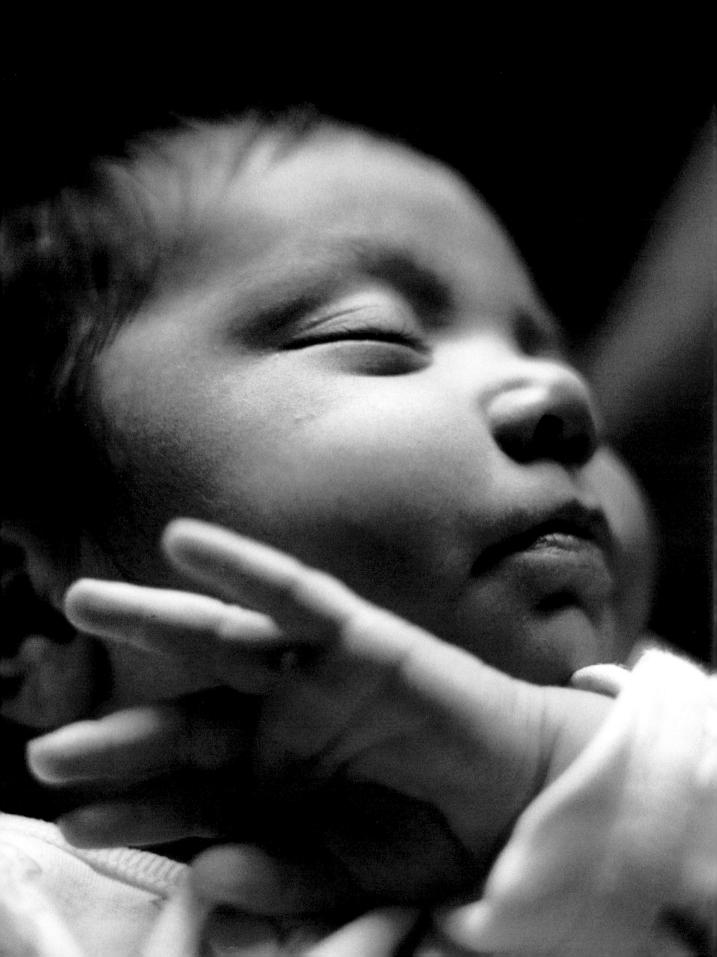

foreword

Pregnancy and childbirth are momentous events, and this book
takes the approach of considering the choices available at all the
points in the journey. It is clearly centred on the people making that
journey – the mother, the baby and the family.

There is a lot of information here, but it is presented in such a
way that all of us, from the 'total beginner' to the 'expert' in the
field, can gain from it.

As we all know, choice is a prerequisite of freedom – and
knowledge is power. And so it follows that those who read this
splendid book will be empowered, and will be better able to exercise
their freedom, during one of the most important times of their lives.

I am delighted that The National Childbirth Trust, for so long a
source of strength for mothers-to-be in this country, should have
produced this book. It is a credit to them. Countless mothers will
gain enormously from reading it, either by dipping into it or by
reading it from cover to cover, and I cannot recommend it too highly.

From girl to mother

journey to birth

from child to adult

conceiving a baby

how birth works

birth stories

journey to birth

Giving birth is often called 'the everyday miracle', and nothing could be more true. The creation of a new human life begins with the mixture of two sets of genes which grow from the meeting of egg and sperm and combine to make a unique human being.

This everyday miracle develops from a microscopic bundle of cells into a fully grown human baby ready to be born. Some cells grow to become legs, while others gradually develop into arms, eyes, hair, lungs, brain. Inside the mother's uterus the baby waits patiently – listening, seeing, sucking his thumb. Meanwhile the mother's body feeds him, filters out harmful substances and keeps the baby safe inside a fluid-filled protective bubble. Then follows the beautifully designed process of labour and birth which allows this baby to emerge from the new mother's body, now able to sustain life alone.

the birth year

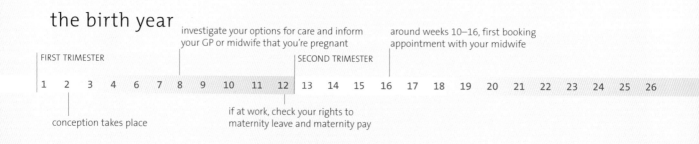

investigate your options for care and inform your GP or midwife that you're pregnant

around weeks 10–16, first booking appointment with your midwife

FIRST TRIMESTER | SECOND TRIMESTER

1 2 3 4 6 7 8 9 10 11 12 13 14 15 16 17 18 19 20 21 22 23 24 25 26

conception takes place

if at work, check your rights to maternity leave and maternity pay

This phenomenal task is accomplished in only nine months. It is nothing less than incredible, and is how each of us began. But of course, for women, preparation for this process started many years earlier. As young girls at the onset of menstruation, we begin releasing eggs ready for fertilization and each month our uteruses prepare for the possibility of a baby.

We are literally made for love: men's and women's bodies are designed for sex, for creating new life – and once pregnant, women's bodies know how to nourish and protect a growing baby (or babies) and how to give birth.

Pregnancy is one step in a journey that began for each of us long ago, and it is a journey common to women across the world. Historically, across all cultures, women have supported each other through the process of pregnancy and birth, with older, more experienced mothers passing on their wisdom to young mothers pregnant for the first time. During the birth itself, women were encouraged and supported by other women who had been through childbirth themselves, and that knowledge gave them strength. Young women grew up surrounded by pregnancy, birth and breastfeeding, so these processes were familiar to them.

This book aims to give you back some of that women's wisdom about pregnancy and birth. There is nothing to be afraid of. You are following the well-trodden footsteps of millions of women on your journey – let them guide your way.

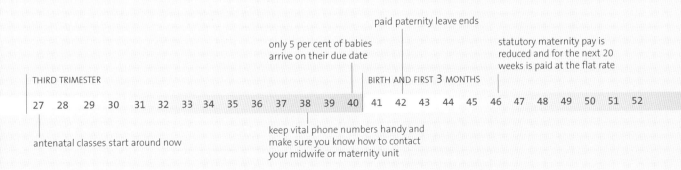

paid paternity leave ends

only 5 per cent of babies
arrive on their due date

statutory maternity pay is
reduced and for the next 20
weeks is paid at the flat rate

THIRD TRIMESTER

BIRTH AND FIRST 3 MONTHS

| 27 | 28 | 29 | 30 | 31 | 32 | 33 | 34 | 35 | 36 | 37 | 38 | 39 | 40 | 41 | 42 | 43 | 44 | 45 | 46 | 47 | 48 | 49 | 50 | 51 | 52 |

antenatal classes start around now

keep vital phone numbers handy and
make sure you know how to contact
your midwife or maternity unit

from child to adult

The transformation of a girl into woman is an extraordinary process. Within four to five years, at any time between the ages of about eight and 14, the average girl grows around 30cm taller, her body becomes adult and her periods start. These physical changes underlie the emotional changes of adolescence.

For girls, the physical maturation of puberty is a complex interaction between the brain, the pituitary gland and the ovaries, and is influenced by social, cultural and environmental factors. It begins with a rapid spurt of growth and usually follows a predictable order, with breast buds coming first and some skeletal growth, followed by the arrival of pubic and armpit hair, the development of rounded breasts and a final growth spurt.

The first period indicates that levels of hormones are adequate to allow the womb to develop.

The ovaries

Ovulation usually occurs about 10 months after a girl's first period, but more than half of these early menstrual cycles do not result in the release of an egg. After around five years, the incidence of cycles where no eggs are released has decreased to about 20 per cent.

All girl babies are born with eggs ready and waiting in their bodies. The eggs lie dormant in the follicles of the ovaries, which in an adult woman are almond-shaped and 3–4cm long. The outer layer of the ovaries contains the egg-holding follicles, which also produce the female hormones oestrogen and progesterone.

Near the ovaries, projecting from the top of the womb on either side, are the Fallopian tubes (named after the Italian anatomist who first described them, Gabriello Fallopio). These are about 10cm long and end in finger-like projections or fimbriae near the ovary. They wave back and forwards to attract the egg, which is released at ovulation, into the opening of the tube. Once inside, muscular contractions and the waving of cilia, small hair-like structures that beat towards the womb, help transport the egg along to the narrower part of the tube, the isthmus, where its transport is held up by about 30 hours. If fertilization occurs, it usually takes place here.

The womb

The uterus or womb is a hollow muscular organ about 7cm long and 5cm wide across the fundus or upper part. The lower part is called the neck or cervix which projects down into the stretchable muscular vagina. Roughly

Fertilization usually takes place in the Fallopian tube as the egg journeys towards the uterus.

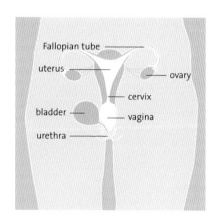

Fallopian tube

uterus

ovary

cervix

bladder

vagina

urethra

every 28 days the womb prepares to receive a fertilized egg as the endometrium or lining thickens to form the site for implantation. If fertilization doesn't occur, the thickened lining is shed and the whole process starts all over again. If the womb receives a fertilized egg, it shelters and nourishes it for nine months before involuntary muscular contractions open the cervix and the baby is ready to be born.

During pregnancy, the womb increases in weight from around 50g to 1kg, stretching and growing in thickness and length to accommodate the growing baby and then shrinking back by six weeks after the birth.

All girl babies are born with eggs ready and waiting in their bodies. From puberty, hormones start to prepare a girl for motherhood. Approximately 10 months after a girl's first period, ovulation occurs, but more than half of these early cycles do not release an egg.

How hormones prepare you for pregnancy

From puberty, every day a few follicles on the ovary restart their development, taking about three months to get to the stage where they are mature enough to respond to 'follicle stimulating hormone' (FSH) – the hormone which is released early in a woman's menstrual cycle.

About 15 to 20 follicles will increase in size and develop protein stores, ready for fertilization, as well as a transparent jelly coat which has an important role in helping sperm to bind and penetrate. The egg-holding follicles also produce the hormone oestrogen in increasing amounts, the more mature producing the most.

By around eight to 16 days into the menstrual cycle, a dominant follicle will form a 2cm bump on the surface of the ovary and the others will wither away. A surge of luteinizing hormone will help this follicle to mature and around 36 hours later it ruptures, releasing its egg which starts its journey to the womb. After taking years to reach maturation, the egg is then only viable for fertilization for about one day.

Back at the ovary, after the follicle collapses it fills in to form the *corpus luteum*, or 'yellow body', which produces the hormone progesterone. Meanwhile, oestrogen has changed the composition of the cervical mucus which becomes copious, clear and receptive to sperm penetration and has prepared the womb to receive a fertilized egg. It has stimulated the glands in the lining of the womb to encourage arteries and veins to grow. The lining thickens ten-fold in a few days. Progesterone finishes the job of blood vessel growth and stimulates the glands to produce nutrients ready for the nourishment of the fertilized egg before it implants.

All this is to no avail if fertilization doesn't take place. The *corpus luteum* shrinks back, levels of progesterone fall, the womb lining sinks lower, the glands regress, and the spiral arteries and veins are coiled tighter and compressed, cutting off their blood supply. Eventually the superficial layers of the lining of the uterus are shed in a 'menstrual period'.

This second phase of the cycle from ovulation to menstruation, lasts about 14 days – a helpful predictor of ovulation if your periods are regular.

The protective pelvis

A woman's reproductive organs are held safely within the protective circle of the bony pelvis. The pelvis is a bowl-like structure (the word means basin in Latin). You can feel the bones that form it. The ilia or hip bones at the sides are what you feel when you put your hands on your hips, The sacrum is the triangular section which ends in the coccyx or tail bone at the back; the ischia or sitting bones are at the base. You can feel these if you put your hands under your bottom when you are sitting. The ischia sweep up from either side, in a shallow curve in a woman, to form the pubis at the front.

During birth, your baby has to negotiate a tunnel that bends back towards the tailbone and then turns forward under your pubic arch. Being in an upright position or on all-fours during labour gives your lower spine and sacrum the freedom to move, allowing your baby room to descend.

Your pelvis is the heaviest part of your bone structure. The strong, protective circle holds a woman's reproductive organs safely.

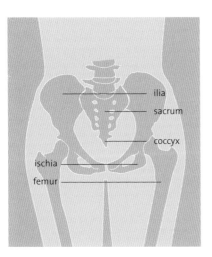

ilia

sacrum

coccyx

ischia

femur

How is it for boys?

There is no difference between male and female development during the first six weeks of life in the womb. If the Y chromosome is present, however, the 'unisex' genital of the embryo will develop into a testis at about six weeks. In a female embryo, no development occurs at this time – instead the enlargement happens at about 12 weeks when the outer part of the genital develops into an ovary.

In a boy baby, testosterone is produced by the testis and this hormone remains in your baby's bloodstream to complete the development of his male genitals. After birth, a boy baby still has high levels of testosterone in his body for a while and it is believed that this has the effect of delaying male brain development both before and after birth; the knock-on effect also means that puberty occurs later in boys.

Sexual development for boys begins and ends, on average, two years later than puberty for girls. At some time between the ages of 11 and 13, levels of the hormone testosterone increase in a boy's body, resulting in a growth spurt which stretches arms and legs. Penis and testes start to grow from around the ages of 11 to 13 and a boy is able to ejaculate semen about a year after this, although at first the ejaculate contains no sperm. At age 14, testosterone levels are at their peak, which is on average when the larynx enlarges and a boy's voice 'breaks'.

The sperm is one of the smallest human cells. Shaped like a long-tailed tadpole, its 23 chromosomes, including the X or Y chromosome that will determine the sex of the new baby, are carried in its 'head'. The head also contains digestive enzymes that will help the sperm burrow into the egg. Unlike the female egg, which is passively washed along the Fallopian tube, sperm can move actively, propelled by their 'tails'.

Ejaculation

The ability to produce sperm is something a boy can do from puberty and it continues throughout his adult life. Although the amount, and the quality, of sperm diminishes from middle-age, men in their 80s and even 90s have fathered children. At times of sexual activity, men produce more sperm. In fact, every second, a man can make on average, 1000 sperm but the quantity goes down with very frequent ejaculations.

Over a lifetime, a man may produce as many as 12 trillion sperm. Each one is about 1/25th of a millimetre long, the 'tail' being ten to fifteen times as long as the 'head'.

Having been released into the vagina at ejaculation, semen initially coagulates which helps the sperm stay put and buffers them against the acidic vaginal environment. The alkaline seminal fluid also nourishes the sperm, as does the watery cervical mucus produced by the woman at ovulation. This means sperm remain able to fertilize an egg for up to five days.

During the first six weeks of life in the womb, there is no difference between male and female development. The testes of a male baby start to develop at six weeks, producing testosterone, which completes the development of his male genitals.

conceiving a baby

During the nine months of pregnancy, a baby develops from one single cell – formed from the fused nuclei of one sperm and one ovum – into your moving, breathing, sleeping, waking, crying, feeling, recognizable offspring.

When two adults make love and a man ejaculates, between 40 and 500 million sperm are released. However, most sperm never even enter the woman's womb, and only a hundred or so reach the Fallopian tubes within a few hours of sex. The sperm are chemically attracted to the egg and progress through the womb stimulated by a substance that makes their 'tail' movements whiplash-like so they can swim upstream into the Fallopian tube. Once there, they bore into the egg. The first one to penetrate the outer layer fuses with the egg membrane beneath. Immediately, changes in the membrane prevent other sperm entering. This is 'fertilization' and the process of an egg and sperm uniting is known as 'conception'.

From single cell to full-term baby

Fertilization takes 18 to 24 hours, and the first cell of a unique human is called a 'zygote'. The joined-together sperm and egg contain the genes responsible for passing on various characteristics from the parents. The zygote now begins to divide and takes four to six days to travel down the Fallopian tube to the womb. At first, cells divide around every 15 hours, but that cell-division slows down and at birth the baby has around 60 billion cells that have divided around 40 times.

During the first three weeks of development the cells separate into the layers from which all future organs and tissues develop. From weeks four to eight the embryo starts to look like a tiny human being. Week nine to birth is mostly a time of growth, development and refinement.

As many of us are not aware of exactly when conception took place (although we might have a good idea) pregnancy is officially dated from the first day of your last period, and it is assumed that conception takes place at the end of the second week. This puts the average length of pregnancy at 280 days (40 weeks), at which stage the baby is 266 days old (38 weeks).

The baby's life-support system

The early embryo is contained in an outer sac called the chorion, which sends out tiny branches that grow into the thickened, blood-filled lining of the womb. These grow and branch throughout pregnancy and develop into the placenta. Inside these branches are small, thin-walled blood vessels and through these substances are transferred – for example, nutrients and oxygen from the mother and waste products from the baby. The development of this placenta is vital for the survival of the baby.

Loosely joined to the chorion is the inner 'amnion'. This is a sac that produces fluid to cushion the baby, allow easy movement, keep body temperature constant and provide protection from many bacteria. However, some smaller bacteria and viruses are able to cross the placenta – as are drugs, carbon monoxide from smoking and other harmful substances.

By the end of the pregnancy (described as 'at term') the placenta is about 18–20cm thick. The umbilical cord contains blood vessels, gets longer as pregnancy progresses and becomes your unborn baby's first 'toy'. It's normally between 50cm and 60cm long at term.

Your pregnancy week by week

Week 1 The thickened lining of your uterus is shed as a fertilized egg has not implanted, and menstruation occurs. The uterus then prepares to receive a fertilized egg and the endometrium (the lining of the uterus) starts to thicken all over again.

Week 2 At ovulation, a new egg is released from the ovary and starts on its journey to the womb.

Week 3 Egg and sperm have met in a Fallopian tube and fertilized. The resulting single-celled zygote begins journeying to the womb. By the time it reaches the womb, a blastocyst, or hollow ball of cells containing an inner cell mass, has been formed. The blastocyst, about 0.1mm across, implants in the lining of the womb, usually at the upper end.

Week 4 Cell division in the blastocyst is frequent. The beginnings of the umbilical cord appear, and the placenta starts to form.

Week 5 Three layers begin to form: the ectoderm, mesoderm and endoderm, which will give rise to all the tissues and organs of the body. (For example, the nervous system comes from the ectoderm.) The digestive tract, brain, heart and nervous system begin developing and the beating heart is the embryo's first movement.

Week 6 At around 27 days old, the embryo is a shrimp-shaped little being, a bit less than a quarter of an inch long and visible for the first time to the naked eye. It has a definitive head and tail. The arms buds are beginning to form, followed by leg buds.

TWINS

One in 70 births in the UK results in twins. Around two-thirds of these are non identical (dizygotic), and the rest are identical (monozygotic). Non-identical twins result from multiple ovulation and two fertilized eggs implanting while identical twins come from one fertilized egg, which either splits early at the two-cell stage or, most commonly, at a later stage. Non-identical twins have separate chorions, amnions and placentas, as have identical twins who have split at the two-cell stage. Twins that result from splitting at the later stage share chorions and placentas and either have their own private amniotic sac or they share all three.

ECTOPIC PREGNANCY

Fertilization occurs in the wider area of the Fallopian tube. The fertilized egg then proceeds down the tube to the womb where it will implant. However, if the Fallopian tube is blocked in any way and the egg cannot reach the womb, the fertilized egg will then implant in part of the tube. This is called an ectopic (or tubal) pregnancy. The main causes of blocked tubes are infections such as pelvic inflammatory disease and scar tissue from surgery. The majority of ectopic pregnancies implant in a Fallopian tube. Occasionally an ectopic pregnancy may be found on the ovary or in the abdominal cavity.

Week 7 There is rapid brain development and head enlargement. In a five-week embryo, a more mature and rhythmic heartbeat replaces the earlier form. Facial prominences appear and eyelids have begun to form a protective layer over the eyes. The embryo has elbows and finger areas. Ridges indicate the position of the primitive kidneys.

Week 8 The tiny skeleton has been fully formed, at this stage not of bone but of cartilage. The head is proportionally large, the joints of the arms appear and the beginnings of fingers are evident. All five distinct toes are in place, although there is webbing between them, and the legs have developed knees. The external ear is formed.

Week 9 The embryo has in miniature the foundations for all the organs needed as an adult. The fingers are partially separated and the liver is prominent. At this point, he can make very simple movements of a single arm or leg joint, or wrist, elbow or knee. If the baby's hand or foot touches something in the uterus, the fingers or toes will curl.

Week 10 The embryo is well developed into a fetus – the name given after eight weeks of development. The head is still very large and the eyelids are closing. Fingers have separated and the beginnings of toes are visible. A little arm and leg movement occurs, and bones form in the legs. The sex is not yet identifiable, although genitalia are visible.

Weeks 11–14 The fetus now looks like a tiny baby and growth accelerates. By week 12 he can open his mouth in response to touch, suck his fingers and starts swallowing. At around 11–12 weeks he will start yawning and at 12 weeks can extend his fingers.

Weeks 15–18 There is rapid growth and co-ordinated limb movements not yet felt by the mother. In girl babies, the ovaries have appeared. The baby's sex can be identified and the eyes and ears are closer to normal positions. Eye movements begin between 16 and 18 weeks and the baby will make sound vibrations in the womb.

Weeks 19–20 You may begin to feel your baby kick or roll over because your growing womb has now reached your abdominal wall. The baby can step, and hold himself erect. From the 20th week there are slight differences in the baby's activity between morning and night, with the busiest being towards midnight. The baby's skin is covered in protective waxy 'vernix' held in position by downy hair, which prevents the skin becoming waterlogged. Brown fat, a special fat easily processed by the body to produce energy, is laid down.

Weeks 21–25 Your baby's hearing has developed well enough to recognize your voice. Teeth buds have formed under the gums, hair is starting to appear on his head and the lungs are beginning to mature. The baby can grasp and, in fact, they are often seen on ultrasound screens holding their umbilical cord. After 24 weeks, fetuses are sufficiently well developed to have a good chance of survival providing they receive expert specialist care.

Weeks 26–29 The baby's nostrils have opened, the lungs are capable of breathing and the central nervous system can control breathing. The eyes are open and toenails are visible. The baby is able to blink and does so in response to external sound. He often moves the eyes as if looking for something to see. White fat is deposited and skin-wrinkles smooth out. The muscles are becoming well developed and you will probably feel kicks and punches as he tries them out, sometimes even turning head-over-heels.

Weeks 30–34 Babies are perfectly formed at this stage and by week 32 their heads are fully in proportion with their bodies. They have delicate eyebrows and eyelashes and their eyes are now open. The pupils of the baby react to light. The skin is smooth and the arms and legs are chubby. Your baby is starting to develop an immune system to fight off germs as the placenta has been taking up antibodies from your bloodstream. Babies will borrow their mothers' immunity to a whole range of diseases until they can develop their own immunity, which is boosted after birth by colostrum and breastmilk. Sleep and waking becomes more differentiated, and when awake the baby opens his eyes, is alert and kicks.

Weeks 35–37 Your baby has a firm grasp and his fingernails cover the nailbeds – babies can sometimes scratch themselves in the womb. He turns his head towards light and the circumference of his head and abdomen are about equal. The skin appears bluish-pink.

Weeks 38–39 The baby is well rounded, with good skin tone. There is now very little room for manoeuvre in the womb and you may feel your baby's feet pressed hard up against your diaphragm under your ribs and odd energetic kicks may take your breath away.

Weeks 40–42 By 40 weeks or 'at term', your baby has grown to seven times taller than he was at 12 weeks and is nearly 200 times heavier. Close to term, babies often make vigorous squirming movements as they try to stretch not only their arms and legs but also their spine. The average full-term baby is about 55cm long and weighs 3300g. Nobody quite knows what starts labour. One theory is that hormonal 'messages' go back and forth between mother and baby until a biochemical switch is triggered and birth begins.

see also

how pregnancy affects your body	70–1
early discomforts	96–9
later discomforts	100–3
pregnancy at risk	104–7

how birth works

We give birth instinctively – before it starts, you cannot know how you will react. Going into labour involves being open-minded and being prepared to trust your body to go with an involuntary process that is both hard work and painful. But it is pain with a purpose, not the pain of injury, and if you understand the process of birth, the pain becomes meaningful.

Every woman is different and every labour is unique. A woman will never experience the same labour twice, no matter how many children she bears. When friends tell you their stories, or you read accounts or watch videos, remember that your birth experience is not likely to be the same.

Labour is divided into three stages just to help midwives make judgements about its progress, but the lengths of individual labours vary widely. There are, however, some landmarks that will happen to all of us in a certain order. During the first stage, the cervix (exit) at the neck of the womb must soften and begin to open (dilate), getting wider until it is wide enough for the baby to leave the womb. In the second stage, your baby will travel down the birth canal (vagina) to be born. The third stage is when the afterbirth (placenta) must then be expelled.

The first, second and third stages are sometimes further divided into:

- pre-labour (or the 'latent' phase)
- early labour (until the cervix is 3cm to 4cm dilated)
- active labour (4cm to 10cm)
- transition (preparing to push)
- pushing
- birth
- delivery of the placenta

Remember that your body is designed to do the work of labour and you will have the love and support of a friend or partner and your midwives as companions on this journey.

The first stage of labour

Often the first sign of labour starting will be regular tightenings or contractions. These can feel like period pains (anything from mild to quite severe), like backache or twinges and aches inside your womb, bottom and hips. How can you tell early labour from the 'practice' Braxton Hicks contractions you may have had over the past weeks? The 'real' contractions become gradually stronger, longer, and closer together as time passes. They tend to build to a peak of intensity and then die away. You may have anything from about 5 to 30 minutes between them.

Or you may have a 'show'. In pre-labour, the neck of the womb starts to soften and thin out over your baby's head and the plug of mucus which has sealed it up during pregnancy can come away, bringing with it a little blood. You may notice a pinkish discharge.

Finally, you'll know you are in labour if your waters break (that's the bag of amniotic fluid surrounding your baby in the womb). There may be a distinct 'pop' and then a gush of warm fluid, or you may just notice a gentle trickle.

All these are signs that the cervix (the neck of the womb) is beginning to dilate. This dilation can take a short time, or hours, every birth is unique. The dilation rate gradually increases until, finally, when the cervix is almost fully open, the contractions are less than a minute apart. However, every labour is different. Your contractions could also be five minutes apart all the way

THE WOMB IN LABOUR
In order to squeeze the baby out, the womb has three layers of elastic, spiralling muscles. During labour, contractions begin at the top of the womb, which has the highest density of muscle fibres, and travel in a wave downwards and inwards towards the cervix, becoming less strong. The muscle fibres of the upper womb do not return completely to their full length between contractions and gradually get shorter and thicker with each contraction. Thus, the less-active lower womb is pulled up towards the shortening upper part.

Sitting on a birth ball makes it easier to rock your pelvis as you breathe through a contraction, and holding onto something (wall bars, chair back, partner) means you can lean forward to find the most comfortable position.

through. You could have a long contraction followed by a short one. Contractions are involuntary, but distractions can cause them to slow down.

Transition

Transition is the bridge between the first and second stage of labour. It can last a matter of seconds or minutes, or, occasionally, hours. Sometimes, the stages simply blend together. Sometimes at this point, there is also a lull in contractions – known as the 'rest and be thankful' stage – just before you feel the urge to push.

The second stage

The second stage of labour, the 'pushing' phase, can last anything from a few minutes to a couple of hours (or even longer). It begins when the baby's head moves out of the womb into the birth canal. As the baby's head starts to stretch the pelvic floor, you will find the urge to push irresistible. As you breathe in before pushing, the diaphragm is lowered and the abdominal muscles contract, assisting the contractions. During a contraction the baby's head advances forwards, and between contractions it slips back slightly.

Some women find the second stage of labour less painful than the first. At this point, dilation of the cervix is complete and progress is faster. Getting into the right position helps greatly. If you are lying on your back, you will have to push your baby through the L-shaped bend of the birth canal, against gravity. If you're upright, on all-fours, or lying on your left-hand side if tired, you will find pushing easier.

During the second stage, as your baby's head passes through the pelvis the pressure on certain nerves sometimes causes cramp or shooting pains down your legs. As his descent continues, his head which has been tucked chin to chest turns further and his neck extends so that the back of his neck turns under your pubic bone in front. This may take some time and turning is usually complete before the back of the head shows at your vaginal opening – which is called 'crowning'.

Stretching of the vulva is now at its maximum. When you feel a burning pain, or numbness, around your vagina, try to stop pushing and pant to help ease the head out gently. With further contractions the baby's head will come out and then turn again so that the head is in line with the shoulders: first one shoulder, then the other is born.

Some mothers want to hold their new baby immediately and put him to the breast, but don't worry if you feel too tired or disoriented to do so.

The third stage of labour

After the birth, the elastic-walled womb contracts and, as it does so, the shortening muscle fibres tighten around the mother's blood vessels, literally binding them off. The placenta is not elastic and it is sloughed off the

'I really felt "in tune" with my body and that I was doing the right stuff. I used the gas for a couple more contractions, then Maria said she could see the head and asked if I wanted to touch it, which I did.'

'wrinkling' wall of the womb. Fibrinogen, a protein that helps with blood clotting, is then deposited in a mesh over the site of the placenta. Delivering the placenta usually happens within an hour or so of birth. Meanwhile, your baby begins to breathe independently and after anything up to 10 minutes or so, the umbilical cord will stop pulsing. (The placenta and cord continue functioning until breathing is fully established, guaranteeing the baby a supply of oxygen.)

The third stage of labour can be 'natural' or 'managed'.

With a 'natural' third stage, the baby's umbilical cord is not cut. You put your baby to the breast and encourage him to suckle. This stimulates your body to produce more oxytocin which makes your uterus contract and push the placenta out.

When the third stage is 'managed', you will be given an injection of syntometrine (synthetic or artificial oxytocin) as your baby's shoulders are being born. As soon as he's born, the cord is clamped in two places and cut in between so that he is no longer attached to you. The syntometrine makes your womb contract strongly to expel the placenta.

Your newborn baby's most developed sense is touch. His ears are still full of amniotic fluid to protect him from the loud noises outside your womb, but he will still be able to hear and recognize your voice.

giving birth in your own home – a first baby

A first-time mother's birth story

'My midwife and I agreed on the local maternity unit for my first birth. After my antenatal class, I looked around the unit. It was lovely, but the thought of having to get into a car and travel to hospital when I would be in pain was terrible. At the next class I said I could see why people chose home birth. The teacher asked if I was considering it and gave me a couple of books to read. I saw that there was no reason why I shouldn't give birth at home; it seemed a positively sensible choice. I discussed it with Steve and our only misgiving was that if I gave birth in hospital I would have more recuperation time. However my husband is eminently capable and in fact, I wouldn't want anyone else looking after me. That left me with just two fears: the neighbours and the upholstery!

'I saw that there was no reason why I shouldn't give birth at home it seemed a positively sensible choice.'

On the day

'Four days before my due date my waters broke. The midwife Annie came out and checked I was OK and then left. She hardly got home before the contractions started. I expected to be baking cakes in between contractions; so going straight into active labour was a surprise. I had a bath and Steve made the bed with some plastic and a charity shop sheet!

'We called Annie and I knelt against the bed swaying my hips during contractions. The midwives laughed when I asked if I was in second stage – and when I said that I was going to hospital to get some drugs. I remember being annoyed that the baby's heartbeat was calm, because if it hadn't been, I would have got a lift straight to some painkillers! As I became tired, the midwives encouraged me onto the bed to rest. After a while I got back onto my knees leaning on the headboard. I soon needed to push but resisted it – it was going to hurt! I lay on my side, with one leg on Rosie's shoulder.

'Alegria was delivered onto my breast, and Steve cut the cord. She latched on almost immediately, and my happiness was complete. The midwives made Steve find the camera, and took a couple of shots for me to remember that moment by. Annie and Rosie cleared up and left. They were great and I was lucky to have them. Steve rang relatives and I had a bath with Alegria.

'The days afterwards were easy. On the first day we had a lot of visitors but after that, one a day. The doctor arrived and found me, breastfeeding. *"So, you had her at home?"* was his surprised comment.

'I tell everyone what a good idea home birth is. The reaction is *"how brave!"* but for me, brave is getting into a taxi in labour – not brave – mad! As for my fears, my neighbour asked if we'd had the baby because all she could hear was laughter, and there isn't a spot on the upholstery!'

a man's experience of home birth

'After some investigation, and then chatting to our antenatal teacher and community midwife, it was clear that there were some definite advantages to having a baby at home. Instead of running the risk of hitting a birth rush-hour and having to share your midwife with others, we would get not one but two midwives all to ourselves.

'My biggest concern was the recuperation period. In our hospital you get that nice three-day cooling-off period at being a parent. A little bit of time to ease yourself into it. Midwives helping you out with feeds and nappy-changing, and most importantly uninterrupted sleep for the father at home. It was clear that this was not going to happen with a home birth, and that the midwives would be out of there ASAP leaving you to cope on your own.

'They were however very clear about the fact that they would be taking away *all* of the "waste".

'It would take too long to recount all the happenings of that night. Needless to say like all men wherever it happens I had that feeling of helplessness. Wanting to help out and share the pain but just not being able to. At one point we were both kneeling, leaning against the bed, Kathryn was recovering from a contraction and I was rubbing her back. Suddenly she looked down at the floor and cried out "Where did you get that pillow?" In the heat of the moment I had not realized that she had been kneeling on the hard floor for an hour whereas I had whipped a pillow off the bed. Well, that can really hurt your knees, can't it?

'After about seven hours of heroic effort the time was nearly upon us. Now was my moment and I was sent to get the towels. In hindsight, I did panic a bit and instead of bringing the old, ordained towels I picked up the best, fluffiest towel in the house. On my return Kathryn was in the throes of another contraction, this time not tempered by the Entonox. *"Not that one!"* she screamed through clenched teeth, and I could see in her eyes that she was already regretting allowing her DNA to get involved with something from my shallow end of the gene pool.

'But it all went well in the end. Baby born, photos taken, midwives removed *all* the waste, and it was time to say our goodbyes. This was the bit I was dreading. Just the three of us in the house. No support, no one to take over, no one to give advice. And do you know what? That was the best part. We all snuggled up on the bed together (the sheets had been changed) and we just revelled in the fact that we were a family.

'And there was a definite feeling that if we can do this with little outside assistance then it was always going to be so, and it was all going to be all right.'

The same story from a father's viewpoint

'We all snuggled up on the bed together and just revelled in the fact that we were a family.'

Choices for your care

planning your care

the role of your midwife

choosing an independent midwife

other birth supporters

antenatal classes

choosing where to have your baby

home birth

water birth

birth centre or midwifery unit

natural birth in hospital

birth stories

planning your care

Choosing where your baby will be born, and who is going to care for you during pregnancy and birth, are important decisions that you will have to make during your pregnancy.

For most women, the first health professional they see when they become pregnant is their family doctor or general practitioner (GP). It is the GP who helps women access their maternity care. While some GPs are very knowledgeable about local maternity services, others are not aware of all the choices women now have.

The choices you do have will depend on your local area, but at the very least you should be able to choose between a consultant unit at your nearest hospital and a home birth. Some areas may have several hospitals with maternity units, some with a midwife-led unit alongside, or there may be a separate midwife-led birth centre. Most maternity provision in your area will be run by the NHS

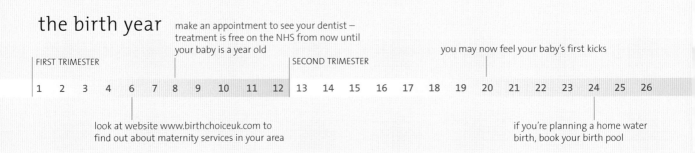

the birth year

make an appointment to see your dentist – treatment is free on the NHS from now until your baby is a year old

you may now feel your baby's first kicks

FIRST TRIMESTER

SECOND TRIMESTER

1 2 3 4 6 7 8 9 10 11 12 | 13 14 15 16 17 18 19 20 21 22 23 24 25 26

look at website www.birthchoiceuk.com to find out about maternity services in your area

if you're planning a home water birth, book your birth pool

but in many regions of the UK, you will also be able to hire the services of an independent (private) midwife. Some maternity hospitals also provide private care. For information on local options look at the www.birthchoiceuk.com website. For a private midwife, look at www.independentmidwives.org.uk.

At the beginning of your pregnancy, the maternity care system can seem like a maze. Some simple facts can help you:

- Pregnancy and birth are normal natural processes; for a healthy woman and her baby, medical assistance is not usually necessary.
- Continuity of care throughout your pregnancy and birth, together with continuous support during labour have been shown to reduce reliance on medical pain relief and other interventions.[⊙] (For full references, please see references on page 248)
- Midwives are trained to care for women during labour and birth and typically will attend a woman in labour. Unless there are complications, no other health professional need be present.
- If you wish, you can arrange your midwifery care directly with local midwives, rather than through your GP by contacting the Supervisor of Midwives at your local hospital.

Great advances have been made in obstetrics to deal with complications in pregnancy and emergencies. However, most women with the right support and environment can give birth without the need for medical assistance.[⊙]

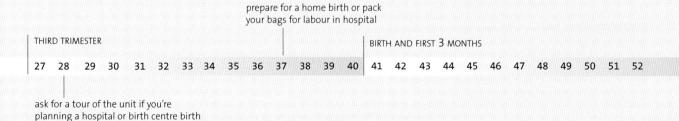

prepare for a home birth or pack
your bags for labour in hospital

THIRD TRIMESTER														BIRTH AND FIRST 3 MONTHS												
27	28	29	30	31	32	33	34	35	36	37	38	39	40	41	42	43	44	45	46	47	48	49	50	51	52

ask for a tour of the unit if you're
planning a hospital or birth centre birth

the role of your midwife

The word 'midwife' means 'with woman'. Midwives are specialists in normal birth, and are qualified to look after a pregnant woman and her baby throughout the antenatal period, through labour and birth and for up to 28 days after the baby has been born.

Few women are aware that they do not need to access their maternity care through a GP, and they do not need to see an obstetrician (a medical specialist in childbirth) either, while they are pregnant or giving birth. As long as everything remains normal, midwives can provide their total care. If complications arise, a midwife will refer you to a doctor who is trained to deal with special situations.

What is a midwife?

Within the NHS there are both hospital midwives and community midwives.

- Hospital midwives are based in a hospital unit, and staff the antenatal clinic, labour ward and postnatal wards.
- Community midwives often work in teams and provide a degree of continuity of care. They see women antenatally either in the woman's home or at a clinic. When the woman goes into labour they are available for a home birth, or they may come into the labour ward to be with the woman in labour. Once the baby is born, they visit the woman at home until they are ready to be signed off from NHS care – generally 10 to 28 days after birth.

Community midwives also provide postnatal care for women who have been looked after during labour by hospital midwives.

There are also private midwives who work independently of the NHS (see useful organizations page 245).

What care can I expect?

You will see a midwife regularly throughout your pregnancy and she will let you know how to contact her, if you need to. Your first visit will be at around 10–16 weeks of pregnancy. This is known as your 'pregnancy welcome visit' or, more often, your 'booking appointment'. Your midwife will spend quite a long time finding out all about you and your pregnancy. She will ask you questions about your medical history, any previous pregnancies and also about your current pregnancy (see box). If this is a midwife you will be seeing regularly, this is an opportunity for you to get to know each other and for her to find out about your hopes for the pregnancy

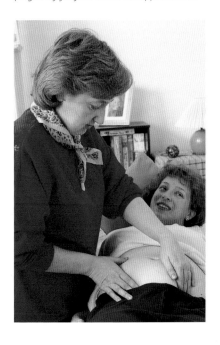

If you book a home birth, your midwife may be able to visit you at home during pregnancy for your antenatal appointment.

and birth. She will answer all your questions and should also be able to help you with any concerns.

Your midwife can also advise on diet, exercise and dealing with minor discomforts of pregnancy. She will also discuss screening tests, including ultrasound examination, with you so that you and your partner can decide whether you will have any of these tests.

At antenatal appointments the midwife will, with your consent, routinely take your blood pressure, test your urine for glucose and protein (see box), and feel your abdomen to see how the baby is growing. She will write everything down in your maternity notes. You will be given a copy of your own maternity notes to look at and to take to subsequent appointments.

When the baby has grown enough, your midwife may listen in to the baby's heart rate with a hand-held device that uses ultrasound waves (if you are happy to have ultrasound, later in pregnancy the baby's heart rate may be heard using a Pinard stethoscope). Once the baby is big enough for you to feel movements, your midwife will ask if the baby is active. Towards the end of pregnancy it will become more important for your midwife to establish which way the baby is lying in the womb. At certain points blood tests will be done with your consent (see box).

These checks form the basis of every antenatal appointment a woman will have and they become more frequent as pregnancy progresses.

During labour

If you have booked a home birth, your midwife will come to see you at home when you go into labour. If you are having a hospital birth, some community midwives do home assessments before you go into hospital, but often you will have to make your own way to hospital at some point during your labour, before you get seen by a midwife.

During labour, your midwife's job is to support and help you. She is also there to support any birth partners you have. Her role includes helping you to give birth in the way that you would like, and to monitor your health and that of the baby. She can help you to get into positions which are comfortable and that help labour progress, and she can suggest ways of coping with contractions. If the midwife feels concerned at any point that things are not progressing normally, she will liaise with medical staff.

If you are being looked after by a team of midwives, you may already know the midwife who is with you during labour. To be cared for during birth by a midwife you have got to know beforehand is helpful. If your labour is long, you may experience a change of shifts, when your midwife will go off duty and be replaced with another who is just starting her shift.

After your baby has been born, your midwife will help you, and your partner, if present, to get comfortable and feed the baby. Both you and the baby will be checked regularly to make sure everything's fine.

Your midwife will ask you about your current state of health; lifestyle habits (whether you smoke or drink) your medical history and your partner's medical history. She will also ask about any previous pregnancies and the date of your last period.

She will check your blood pressure and take your height and weight. If you are 10 weeks pregnant or more, and there's a query about dates, the midwife may palpate (feel) your tummy to see if she can feel the fundus (top of the womb). This gives an indication of gestation. An internal vaginal examination is not necessary unless there's a specific reason for it.

Urine: you will be asked to give a urine sample. This is tested to see whether you have any sugar or protein in your urine and for signs of any infection.

Blood tests: different areas have different policies. In general, several 'bloods' are taken to:

- identify your blood group
- check your rhesus factor
- rule out anaemia
- check your immunity to rubella (German measles)
- make sure you're not producing any unusual antibodies
- screen for syphilis and hepatitis
- measure your blood glucose level.

You will be offered HIV testing with counselling and certain genetic disorders such as sickle cell anaemia and thalassaemia may also be checked. Some places screen automatically for neural tube defects too.

Ultrasound: you may be offered an ultrasound scan, or given a return appointment for a scan, which you do not have to take up.

'She held my hand, encouraged me to blow and not push and breathed with me. She knew just what kind of support I needed.'

After the birth

In the days and weeks following the birth, you will be visited at home by a midwife who will examine you and the baby to make sure that you are both adjusting well. In some areas, the midwife may stop visiting once your baby is 10 days old, but in other areas she may carry on visiting for up to 28 days after the birth. She will ensure that the baby is feeding well and beginning to gain weight, and that you are recovering well from the birth.

How do I get continuity of care?

Research shows that to receive care from the same person throughout pregnancy, labour and the postnatal period provides a better birth experience for a woman, than being looked after by lots of different people.[⊙] One way of getting continuity of care is to book a home birth. Some women

Making sense of your notes

Your baby's position (or presentation and lie)	Recorded as Ceph or C or Vx (cephalic, vertex or head down); Br (breech or bottom down); Long (longitudinal or vertical); Tr (transverse or across your body); Obl (oblique or diagonally). OA = Occiput Anterior (head down, facing your back); OP = Occiput Posterior (head down, facing your front); OL = Occiput Lateral (head down, facing your side). L or R written in front of these indicates which side of your body your baby is lying on. OA is the most favourable position for your baby to be in.
How much of your baby's head is in your pelvis	NE, NEng, Not Eng (not engaged or 'free') means that baby's head is above pelvis. 1/5, 2/5, 3/5, 4/5 refer either to how much of the head can be felt above your pelvis or to how much of it is in your pelvis (ask your midwife which). Your baby is engaged once 3/5 of the head is in your pelvis. E or Eng = Engaged.
Your baby's movements	FMF = Fetal Movements Felt; F = Felt FMNF = Fetal Movements Not Felt; NF = Not Felt
Your baby's heartbeat	FHH = Fetal Heart Heard; H = Heard FHNH = Fetal Heart Not Heard; NH = Not Heard
Urine test results	Prot or Alb (protein or albumin) and glucose are what are tested for. NAD means Nothing Abnormal Detected; Nil means none found (normal); Tr (trace) means that a small amount of protein or glucose has been found; +, ++, +++ indicate that greater amounts have been found.
Your blood pressure	The average blood pressure for adult women is 110/70. Blood pressure above 130/90 is considered high but if the blood pressure was particularly low at the beginning of the pregnancy, lower levels may be considered to be excessive later on.
Swelling (or oedema)	Oed. Amount recorded as +, ++, +++

book one even if they are not sure that is what they want, and they make their final decision later on during their pregnancy or even in labour. You are also more likely to receive continuity of care at a birth centre.

If you are planning to give birth in a hospital unit, it's not always so easy to get to know your midwives. If you arrange to have 'shared care' with your GP and the hospital, the majority of your appointments will be at the GP's surgery. While this can be very convenient, your GP will not attend the birth and it also means you are unlikely to know the midwives at the hospital when you go in to give birth.

Some hospitals operate a team midwifery system, usually run by community midwives. If you have only one local hospital, you can ask whether it is possible to have midwifery-led care, and to be looked after by a small team of midwives. Where you have several maternity units to choose from, you may need to ask several of them. Some hospitals have teams which operate only in certain areas which may limit your choice. If in doubt, phone up your local community midwives and discuss it with them.

What training has my midwife had?

Some midwives will have trained as nurses before becoming midwives, but now it is possible to qualify as a midwife without qualifying as a nurse first of all.

Student midwives are based at university, and are studying for either a diploma or a degree in midwifery. The course contains a mixture of theory and practice. Courses vary across the country but are designed to prepare a student for the responsibilities of being a midwife.

Once qualified, a midwife must be able to care for women throughout pregnancy, birth and during the postnatal period too, as well as care for newborn babies. She must also be able to detect problems and summon medical help if needed, and be trained in emergency procedures herself. She also has a role in health education and preparation for parenthood, such as teaching antenatal classes.

Midwives also have to keep up to date in order to keep their registration, which is reviewed every three years. This includes having to work a minimum number of hours as a midwife, and attend study events.

It is important that you and your midwife have a good relationship. You need to work together and she needs to support you in the choices that you make. In order to help you give birth, your midwife will need to be respectful, responsive, unintrusive and accepting. This will help to give you a feeling of safety and allow you to relax, which in turn will allow the hormones of labour to work, undisturbed.

Childbirth may be the most powerful life experience a woman undergoes. With a midwife's full support she can tap into enormous reserves of strength during the birth process and learn that she is capable of so much more than she realized – a valuable discovery as she becomes a mother.

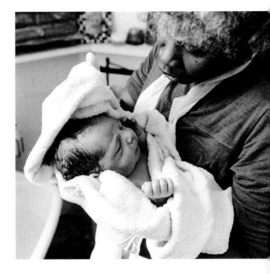

One of the best ways to ensure continuity of care is to have a home birth. Your midwife will stay to keep an eye on you and your baby and will often tuck you, your partner and your new baby up into bed for a well deserved rest before she leaves.

'She was superb throughout: minimal fuss, minimal monitoring and maximum care. She helped me birth Adam slowly enough so I didn't tear and all credit goes to her because he was a 9lb baby!'

choosing an independent midwife

Independent midwives are fully qualified midwives who have chosen to work privately, rather than to be employed by the NHS. Working independently allows them the freedom to practise the midwife's role to its fullest extent, enabling them to be truly 'with woman'.

The art of midwifery is to trust in the birth process, helping to create a supportive environment where a woman can relax and find her inner strength and power to give birth. The woman is entitled to choose where she wants to have her baby and midwives can work with women giving birth at home, in hospital, or in small midwifery-led units and birth centres. They can work under the umbrella of the NHS or be self-employed.

Although independent midwives are not confined by rules governing the NHS or the guidelines of their local Trust, they are still regulated by law and must practise within the rules laid down by the relevant Acts of Parliament. They are subject to the same supervision as NHS midwives, are required to keep up to date with their practice and are only allowed to act within their sphere of competence as midwives.

There are currently approximately 70 independent midwives practising outside the NHS in the UK. They often work in partnerships or have close connections with other independent midwives, so that they can provide seamless care to the women who use their services.

Independent midwives form relationships of trust with pregnant women, which then help women to feel safe and supported when they go into labour. Many independent midwives have become very experienced in areas of childbirth which are usually dealt with by obstetric management these days. These include breech birth, twins and vaginal birth after caesarean (VBAC). The majority of births attended by independent midwives are home births but they can also attend planned hospital births.

Why choose an independent midwife?

Women choose independent midwives for many reasons:

- They want to feel that they are being looked after on an individual basis, with all their needs taken into account.
- They like the continuity of care provided by one or two midwives with whom they can develop a close relationship.
- They want to be sure that they will know who's at the birth.
- They want to feel they have someone they can call on if they have any worries at all during their pregnancy.

- They want their antenatal care to take place in their own home, or at a time to suit them and their families.
- They can get the type of care they may not be able to access through the NHS, due to low staffing levels or inexperienced midwives: for example, a home birth or a water birth.
- They know that being at a higher risk of complications (for example, breech birth, twins or a previous caesarean birth) who want to avoid an obstetrically managed birth or a caesarean.
- Women who have previously experienced a traumatic birth and unsatisfactory maternity care, who want a normal birth without medical intervention and think that this may not happen using the other local maternity services available.
- They would like extra care and support after they have had their baby, and more help with breastfeeding. Independent midwives can give an excellent service in this area.

It is possible to book the services of an independent midwife at any stage during your pregnancy, no matter how close you are to your due date. Some independent midwives are willing to give free consultations to women who are considering all their birthing options.

What else should I know?

Before deciding to book with an independent midwife, there are several issues you may wish to consider:

- **Cost** – independent midwives charge for their services. The amount will depend on where you live and the type of service they provide. You can book their care for the postnatal period too, for example. Some independent midwives will accept payment in installments.
- **Place of birth** – most independent midwives attend births at home. There is one independent midwifery service in the UK which has its own birth centre. If you are planning a hospital birth or need to be transferred to hospital, you will need to consider the role of your midwife. Some hospitals issue 'honourary contracts' so that independent midwives can continue to act as your midwife in hospital. Other hospitals however, will not do this and discussions of the legal situation are ongoing. If you transfer to one of these hospitals with your midwife, you will be attended by a hospital midwife, and the independent midwife will remain with you but only as a birth companion or advocate.
- **Insurance** – at the time of writing it is impossible for independent midwives to hold professional indemnity insurance. Independent midwives will be happy to discuss the position with you.

You can find out more information about independent midwives, including those working in your local area from the Independent Midwives Association (www.independentmidwives.org.uk).

'Having an independent midwife was fantastic, I had a fabulous birth and superb support both post- and antenatally, and I would encourage anyone to save / beg / borrow to pay for an IM. They are worth every penny. If only the hospital in our area could provide a service even one tenth as good then I am sure that we would see an increase in uncomplicated happy births and healthier, happier children and mums.'

other birth supporters

A woman in labour generally has a need for companionship and emotional support from a person or people she trusts and feels comfortable with. Research findings have shown one-to-one continuous empathic support has a strong positive effect on the physiology and outcome of labour.[○]

A BIRTH PARTNER'S ROLE IS TO:
- provide empathic support
- be a listening ear
- be positive and encouraging about the woman's ability to go through the process of birth
- keep her refreshed with sips of water
- help by sponging her brow, etc
- make her as comfortable as possible.

All this helps a woman become relaxed enough to increase her levels of oxytocin (the hormone produced in labour) and endorphins (natural pain relieving substances) and to reduce adrenaline – the 'fight or flight' hormone produced by anxiety that inhibits labour.

'My husband massaged my back from when we went in at 10am until I had Matthew at 8pm and never wanted to smell the lavender oil again, but he was brilliant and I could not have done it without him.'

Research over the past 25 years has shown that the constant presence of a supportive birth companion is one of the most effective forms of care that women can receive in childbirth.[○]

Constant support is associated with a shorter labour, reduced use of medical pain relief, fewer forceps/ventouse deliveries and caesareans, and fewer babies needing resuscitation after the birth. Women who had the benefit of uninterrupted support during childbirth, have found labour better than expected and generally to be a more positive overall experience.[○]

A birth support partner could be the woman's partner, a family member, a friend, trained lay women (such as a doula – see page 39), student midwife or midwives. Religious and cultural beliefs are important considerations for some women as in some cultures it is thought shameful for a man to be present during childbirth.

A woman needs to come to her own decision about what the appropriate support may be for her. Some fathers, in particular, just do not feel comfortable attending a birth. Some people have a fear of hospitals or are terribly squeamish and the emotions can be overwhelming.

Having their mother present also may not be appropriate for some women as the dynamic of the mother–daughter relationship may throw them into the 'child' role when vulnerable in labour, and not bring out the strength they need to access to give birth.

Some women will prefer not to have people close to them present in labour: they may feel less inhibited with a professional support person such as a doula. Trials have shown that 'the continuous presence of an experienced support person who had no prior social bond with the labouring woman' has beneficial effects on childbirth.[○]

A woman could ask a few people close to her to be her birth supporters and leave the final choice open until the day arrives: she may not be sure who she wants with her until labour begins, when she will have a heightened sensitivity about who to invite.

It is important others understand this and respect her choice – for labour to progress, a woman needs to be as relaxed as possible and to feel happy about putting her own needs first.

What does a birth supporter need to do?

It is a tremendous privilege to witness the entry of a new human being into the world and few fail to be deeply moved by the experience. To be asked to be a birth supporter can be very exciting. Some may feel nervous, especially if they are the woman's partner. They may wonder how they will cope especially when they see her in pain if she becomes very distressed, or if things don't go according to plan. It is natural to want to stop another's suffering – feelings of helplessness may come up and a birth supporter may worry that they are not doing enough.

Support during early labour

While the contractions are mild, support people can maintain their normal daily activities. Women may wish for time alone to relax and prepare themselves. They can be encouraged to rest and eat and drink to preserve and build energy reserves.

It may be hours before regular, stronger contractions occur that signal the arrival of established labour, and important changes in the woman's behaviour will indicate this.

Entonox, or 'gas and air', gives effective pain relief through a mouthpiece – but being supported by another person also helps deal with contractions.

'I think I would have been too scared to do it without my sister, she was brilliant, and we both cried when he was born.'

Support during strong labour

When labour is advancing and the hormones are flowing unimpeded a woman usually becomes less communicative and goes 'into herself'. She will show signs of withdrawal – such as wanting to rest, sinking towards the floor, closing her eyes, stopping conversation between contractions and showing a need for concentration as contractions begin to increase in intensity.[⊙]

Supporters need to mirror her behaviour by quietening down, avoiding chat and slowing down their movements. Conversation, soothing words, massage, or even trying to get eye contact may then be felt as intrusive.

Anticipate her needs: if her mouth appears dry, offer her sips of drink with as little disturbance as possible; if she appears cold and shivery, wrap a

When the hormones are flowing unimpeded, as the labour advances, the labouring woman becomes less communicative and 'goes into herself'.

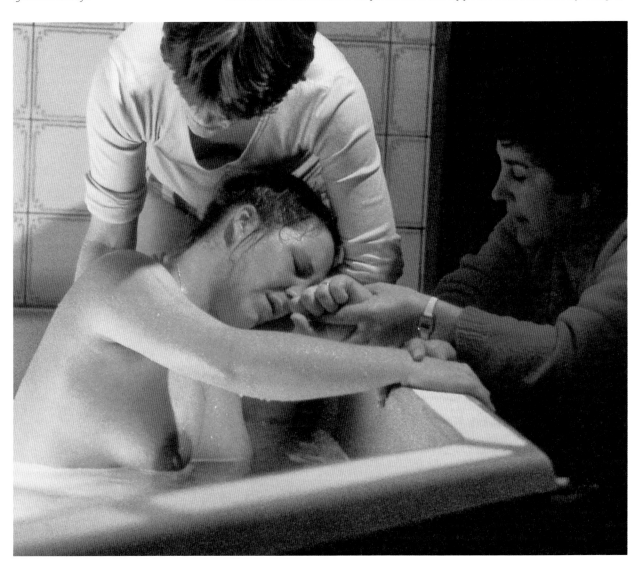

blanket over her shoulders; if hot, mop her brow. Try to encourage her to maintain an upright posture, rather than lying on her back, and offer physical support if necessary. Remind her to go to the toilet because this will keep her bladder and bowels empty, which in turn helps labour to progress.

Differing needs

A woman generally labours best when she is undisturbed and has privacy. Every woman is different and will have different needs and these will change at different stages of labour. Being able to provide the right amount of encouragement and physical support has been described as a difficult 'juggling act' requiring sensitivity, tact and insight.[○]

Don't worry if, as a birth partner, you feel redundant. Doing nothing can sometimes be the best thing you can do. Most women when asked, said they simply wanted their birth partner to 'be there'[○] – she'll probably tell you if she wants anything else. You may feel you're not doing anything but a labouring woman doesn't need the added pressure of making sure you're comfortable with the situation or finding things for you to do, so that you don't feel helpless.

Be reassured that birth is a normal process and try to stay as calm as possible, however distressed she becomes, as a calm presence conveys to a woman that her experience is normal. Your strength is what she needs now. Your quiet presence acknowledges that you accept her as she is and this will instil confidence and a feeling of psychological safety.

Act as go-between

Being a woman's advocate can also be considered part of a birth supporter's role. A woman can feel very vulnerable during labour and find it difficult (especially in hospital) to express what she wants, so a birth supporter can be helpful in this area and can liaise, if necessary, with medical staff. Being familiar with any particular wishes she might have is advisable as, if you are in hospital, staff may sometimes be too busy to remember her wishes, or there may not be enough time for staff to become familiar with her needs as birth is drawing near.

Supporting someone in labour can be intensive and take a long time. It is important for the birth supporters to take snacks and drinks for themselves and to wear loose, comfortable clothing. Some women find a couple of birth supporters useful as they can take breaks and cover for each other.

Giving birth can be seen as a journey and, as with all journeys, it takes courage and determination to keep going when it gets difficult. It follows that how a woman feels psychologically can have a tremendous effect on her labour. Support acts as a buffer against stress[○] and assists with coping strategies. With the right support, many midwives firmly believe most women can give birth naturally.

WHAT IS A DOULA?

A doula is a female caregiver who is not a midwife, but has had a basic training in labour and birth. Her job is to provide emotional support and a constant reassuring presence. She has basic skills in massage and is able to explain what is going on if medical intervention is needed. She can be around to support the mother during pregnancy and also after the birth to help with the care of the baby and general household duties. The constant, comforting support of a female caregiver has been shown to reduce the anxiety and the feeling of having had a difficult birth in mothers, and also to have a positive effect on the number of mothers who were still breastfeeding at six weeks after the birth.[○] Continuous support from caregivers such as doulas seems to have a number of benefits for the mother and baby and does not appear to have any harmful effects.[○] Organizations to contact to arrange a doula can be found on page 245.

see also

the role of your midwife	30–3
good positions	154–7
dealing with the pain	158–63

antenatal classes

Becoming a parent will change your life forever – so it can be helpful to meet up with others in your locality who are facing this big change too. Antenatal classes will give you the chance to meet other parents-to-be, to learn about what to expect, and will also help you make choices and decisions about your pregnancy and your baby's birth.

Many women who are pregnant for the first time can feel quite isolated. You are at the start of big changes and one useful way of working through these changes is to meet up with other women, other couples, who are facing the same new experiences. Sharing thoughts, comparing notes, putting your half-formed worries into words can really help.

So a good way of meeting other pregnant women, making new friends and gaining support, in addition to learning about pregnancy and birth, is to go to antenatal classes. These are usually offered in the last three months of pregnancy, though 'early bird' classes are available in months three or four in some areas.

Exercise classes, such as yoga or aquanatal, also provide the opportunity of meeting other pregnant women.

'The NCT friends I met during the antenatal classes were the greatest support. We continue to have contact four and a half years later.'

Why go to antenatal classes?

Going to antenatal classes is a good way of getting information about the later stages of pregnancy, labour and birth, and the early days with your new baby, but they offer lots more as well.

- Unlike other sources of information, such as books and magazines, classes give you the opportunity of asking questions about anything that you don't understand or would like to know more about, while learning from the ideas and experiences of other members of the group as well as from the class leader.
- Some classes will give you the chance to try out practical skills for labour and birth, such as labour positions, relaxation techniques and massage, as well as to practise some of the practical aspects of looking after your baby. This will help you to prepare and plan for your baby's arrival. It will also build your confidence.
- If you're feeling unsure about what to expect with regard to your pregnancy and the birth of your baby, what's normal, how to get what you want, what choices you have – or how to choose between them – sharing your concerns with other women and your class leader can help to clarify things for you so that you can firm up your ideas. It can also be helpful simply to talk to other women who are also pregnant about your

experiences and how you're feeling and to get support from them. Getting that kind of understanding can help to reassure you and make you feel more confident.

- Through classes, you may make friends who'll support you during your pregnancy as well as after your baby's born. Some lasting friendships are formed at antenatal classes.
- Some classes are for men as well as women, and these are a good way of helping your partner to feel actively involved in your pregnancy, and, if he's going to be your birth supporter, to learn about what to expect in labour and how he can best support you.

What classes are there?

NHS classes are free and are held either at a hospital clinic or at local health clinics or GPs' surgeries. They are usually run by midwives, though there may also be some input from others, such as physiotherapists and health visitors. The format of these classes varies from place to place. Ask your midwife how to book them.

NCT classes are led by trained NCT antenatal teachers and may be held either in the teacher's home or in a community centre. There is a charge and prices vary from one place in the UK to another, however, there is a reduced rate for those on a low income. The classes are small and informal, with the emphasis on the group learning together through discussion and practical activities. A standard course usually consists of eight two-hour evening sessions, but other formats are also offered in some areas. Contact the NCT to find out how to book classes in your area. It's advisable to book early.

All NCT antenatal teachers have had a thorough training with the NCT. In general, the following topics will be covered:

- coping with labour
- relaxation techniques
- pain management
- positions for labour and birth
- medical aspects of birth – such as induction, instrumental birth and caesareans
- recognising the signs of going into labour and what to do
- life with a new baby
- breastfeeding
- adjusting to parenthood
- needs and concerns of fathers.

Active Birth classes are run by teachers who have trained with the Active Birth Centre. There is a charge for these too. The classes are yoga-based and focus on preparing physically for labour, with an emphasis on using your own resources while you are in labour. Contact the Active Birth Centre (www.activebirthcentre.com) for booking information.

NCT POSTNATAL COURSES

After the birth of your baby, NCT Postnatal Courses are a really good way to meet other parents and make new friends in your area.

The groups are informal and enjoyable and provide an opportunity for you to get together regularly with other parents to share ideas and talk about the ups and downs of life with a new baby. They cover such issues as:

- the difference between the expectations and the reality of motherhood
- the pros and cons of returning to work – full time or part time
- balancing your time
- tips for settling a crying baby.

NCT Postnatal Courses provide you with somewhere to air your feelings and concerns and help you adjust to motherhood. Read more about the NCT on page 247.

see also

caring for your body   74–7

choosing where to have your baby

The decision of where to have your baby can be a difficult one to make, particularly when you are expecting your first baby and have no experience of labour and birth. It is worth taking time to investigate all the options available to you, so that you can choose the place that will be right for you.

In the UK, the place where you choose to give birth to your baby can have a profound affect on the birth itself. For this reason, it can be a good idea to think about what you really want and give yourself a lot of time before you make your decision. As long as yours is a normal pregnancy with no complications arising, you can leave the choice of where to have your baby until late on in your pregnancy, and even then you can change your mind up until the last minute.

Arranging your care

Your GP may be the first health professional you choose to see when you discover you are pregnant. However you don't have to see your GP in order to book your midwifery care, you can arrange it directly with local midwives.

If you do visit your GP, they are likely to ask you where you want to have your baby so that they can write a referral letter. Probably at this early stage of pregnancy you won't have decided, or may not know all your options. If you feel you want more time, let your GP know. If your GP refers you to a particular unit, and later in pregnancy you decide it is not where you want to give birth, you can change to another place.

Your choices

When making birth choices, there are two important factors to consider:
- the place where you will have your baby
- who will care for you during your pregnancy, the birth and afterwards.
These two factors are linked.

The place

In most areas of the UK, there will be:
- at least one hospital maternity unit staffed by midwives and hospital doctors (called a 'consultant unit')
- the opportunity to choose a home birth
- and there may also be a local midwifery-led unit or birth centre – either attached to a consultant unit (known as 'alongside') or in a separate place (which is called 'stand alone').

Who will care for you?

Wherever you choose to give birth, you will be looked after by midwives. If the midwives feel you or the baby need specialist care, then you will also been seen by a consultant obstetrician. Remember that for the vast majority of women, pregnancy and birth are normal, natural processes and your care should be given by midwives.

When choosing where to give birth, an important question to ask is 'Will I receive continuity of care?' Continuity of care means that the same midwife, or small team of midwives, will look after you during pregnancy, the birth and after you have had your baby. Research has shown that this kind of care is beneficial to women.[●] You are more likely to get continuity of care if you plan to give birth at home or in a midwifery-led unit. Some consultant units in hospital also arrange for this type of team midwifery and you can try to request it.

Think it over

These are very personal decisions. What choices you make will depend on many things: what is available in your area; the support you have from your partner, other family members and friends; and your own hopes for your birth.

Home birth

This choice should be available to everyone, regardless of age or whether it is a first baby. Your midwife will bring everything needed for the birth round to your house, including equipment for baby resuscitation. For pain relief, most women cope with 'gas and air', a TENS machine, warm water, self-help techniques and hands-on support from partners. Some women hire birth pools too. Pethidine is also available at a home birth.

Midwifery-led unit

Also called birth centres, these are informal 'home from homes' run by community midwives with the same medical facilities that you'd get at a home birth (and often with a birth pool installed). They are either attached to hospitals or in a separate locality. Should you need medical intervention, such as an epidural anaesthetic, you would have to leave the unit to transfer to hospital (just as with a home birth).

Hospital birth

Many women give birth in hospital simply because they don't realize they have other options. Others know that a hospital offers medical facilities and they specifically opt for these. There is quite a lot of difference between hospitals up and down the country regarding attitudes, facilities, intervention and infection rates. It's worth asking your midwife what the local statistics are before you make your choice.

IN YOUR AREA

For more information on your local options for giving birth, look at the www.birthchoiceuk.com website. This has been written by an NCT antenatal teacher who has compiled the available statistics from each maternity unit and can help guide you through the decision-making process. You could also contact a local NCT antenatal teacher to talk through your options.

If you are thinking about a home birth you could look at the www.homebirth.org.uk website or there may be a local home birth support group in your area. And if you are having problems finding the maternity care you want, you could contact Association for Improvements in the Maternity Services (see useful organizations page 245).

home birth

The UK's National Perinatal Epidemiology Unit found that 'There is no evidence to support the claim that the safest policy is for all women to give birth within hospital.'[⊙] There are enormous advantages to giving birth at home, in your own familiar space, surrounded only by people you have chosen to be with you and in the care of a midwife who will stay with you throughout the process.

'It was lovely to be at home, the pain didn't seem to get out of control and I never felt any need for anything other than gas and air.'

Giving birth at home is the best way of getting 'continuity of care', something that is known to make labour easier and shorter.[⊙] Many women feel more in control in their own home surroundings. They may also wish to use warm water for pain relief and know that the availability of a birth pool cannot be guaranteed in hospital.

Giving birth at home is the norm in the developing world and in some European countries, the Netherlands for example, it is a lot more common than it is here, where hospital births account for the vast majority of births.

However, home birth is becoming more popular in the UK and one midwifery practice in Peckham, London, based on a housing estate, has a home birth rate of about 40 per cent.

Am I a suitable candidate for a home birth?

Most home births occur after a normal, healthy pregnancy, with one baby who is lying in the head-down position. If you fall into a higher-risk category, home birth may still be an option, but seek specialist advice from your Supervisor of Midwives so that you can weigh up the pros and cons for your individual situation.

In certain situations, some professionals will advise you to give birth in hospital, while others may be willing to support you at home. In order to reach a decision, you will need to understand the risks and benefits of giving birth at home in your specific circumstances. For example, many women in the following groups have made an informed choice to give birth at home, despite encountering varying degrees of opposition:

- over 42 weeks' gestation (you may be offered the choice of induction of labour, and if you accept, this can only be done in hospital)
- moderately raised blood pressure
- anaemia (low iron count)
- previous difficult birth or heavy bleeding after the birth
- previous caesarean section
- fifth or subsequent baby.

Breech and twin births at home are rare, but they do happen – usually under the care of independent midwives who specialize in such cases.

NOT SUITABLE
A home birth is not possible if:
- you have a full placenta praevia (placenta covering the cervix)
- your baby is in a transverse lie (lying sideways across the womb).

How do you book a home birth?

You can book a home birth either directly through your local midwives or through your GP, although it's not necessary to involve your GP if you do not wish to. To book direct with midwives, write to the Supervisor of Midwives at your local hospital, stating that you are expecting a baby, you are planning to have a home birth, you would like her support and that you would like to book directly with midwives and not through a GP surgery.

If you would like some guidance on talking to your GP or midwives to help gain their support for your decision, contact your local NCT home birth support group. The NCT Enquiry Line (see page 247) will give you the relevant contact details for your area. You can also get in touch with the Association for Improvements in the Maternity Services (AIMS). You will find their details on page 245.

A private midwife

Independent midwives offer a private alternative for those who can afford their fees. They are fully qualified midwives who specialize in home births, and many women have found their support invaluable. They will accompany you to an NHS hospital if you need to transfer. Contact the Independent Midwives Association for more details (see page 245).

Is a home birth advisable with a first baby?

Some experts have said that the first labour is particularly suitable for a home birth because if anything goes wrong, it tends to do so very slowly, allowing plenty of time for transfer to hospital.[*]

In the UK, up to 40 per cent of first-time mothers who plan a home birth will eventually give birth in hospital.[*] Some will switch to hospital care in late pregnancy (usually in order to have labour induced, or because of concerns about blood pressure). Others will transfer to hospital in labour because of slow progress, or to have an epidural.[*]

If you decide during your labour at home that you want an epidural, you can transfer to hospital, if there is still time. Your midwife may phone ahead to try to arrange for this to be given soon after your arrival.

Pain relief options

An epidural anaesthetic is not available as pain relief in a home situation because it has to be administered by a qualified anaesthetist – and monitored carefully once it is in place. However, midwives will bring Entonox ('gas and air') and Pethidine to a home birth.

Women who give birth at home consistently rate the experience as less painful than a hospital birth, perhaps because they are more relaxed and are more likely to feel uninhibited.[*]

Other possible pain-relieving strategies at a home birth include massage,

'Luckily I was already fully dilated so not many hours later gave birth in front of the fire in our living room, with the day gradually lightening outside and the Christmas tree lights twinkling in the window… It was so nice to be in our own home afterwards.'

Home birth means your baby will arrive into a calm, loving environment without the bright lights and noise of hospital. Your midwife will guide her into your arms for your first cuddle, skin-to-skin.

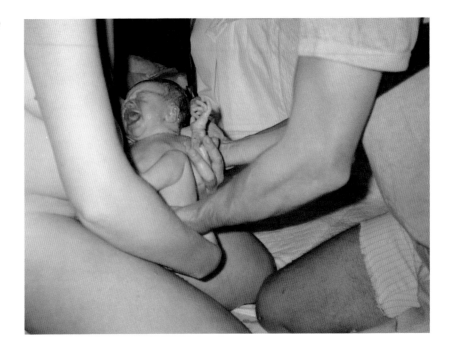

distraction techniques, moving around, 'visualization', hypnosis, breathing or singing/shouting through contractions. A TENS machine can be useful too, especially in the early stages.

Some women opt for self-help techniques alone, while others combine these with drugs supplied by their midwife. Many women find that a birth pool combined with lots of hands-on support from midwives and birth partners, plus 'gas and air' is adequate to deal with the pain.

Is a home birth safe?

Research over the last couple of decades has found that home birth is at least as safe as hospital birth for healthy women with normal pregnancies.⊙ Reviewing several studies, the *British Medical Journal* concluded that home birth was 'safe for normal, low-risk women, with adequate infrastructure and support'.⊙ The UK's National Perinatal Epidemiology Unit found that: 'There is no evidence to support the claim that the safest policy is for all women to give birth within hospital'.⊙

A recent study of nearly 6000 women who planned home births in the UK noted the benefits of home birth.⊙ Each woman was matched for risk level with a similar woman in the same area who planned a hospital birth. The study found that, compared to women planning a hospital birth, mothers in the home birth group had:

- roughly half the risk of having a caesarean section
- roughly half the risk of an instrumental delivery (forceps or ventouse)
- less risk of haemorrhage.

PAIN-RELIEF DRUGS:
- Entonox (nitrous oxide and oxygen or 'gas and air') which is inhaled through a mask or mouthpiece. Women often say that it 'takes the edge off the contractions'.
- Pethidine and other injected opiates – these relax your skeletal muscles and may make you feel sleepy, as if you were drunk, or confused. Some women love it, but others find it does not relieve their pain, and can make them feel nauseous and helpless.

Babies in the home birth group were:

- less likely to be in poor condition at birth
- less likely to have birth injuries
- less likely to need resuscitation.

Labours tend to progress well at home, where the mother is relaxed and free to move as she wishes. She will feel more comfortable and in control at home too and this can help to progress labour. She will also feel under less pressure to labour within the strict time limits that are set in some hospital consultant units. This means there is less need for intervention such as drugs to speed up labour, or delivery with forceps or ventouse. These interventions carry risks as well as potential benefits and are more likely to be suggested for a hospital birth. Finally, there is less risk of infection at home, for both mother and baby.

What if something goes wrong?

If there are complications with your labour, such as slow progress or concerns about your blood pressure or the baby's heart rate, you will usually be advised to transfer to hospital. You would travel either by car or by

'And I loved the idea of labouring and delivering my baby in my own home, bathing in my own bath, then getting into my own bed with the new baby...'

Giving birth at home means staying in your own familiar surroundings. Your baby will be gently introduced to the sights and sounds of your home.

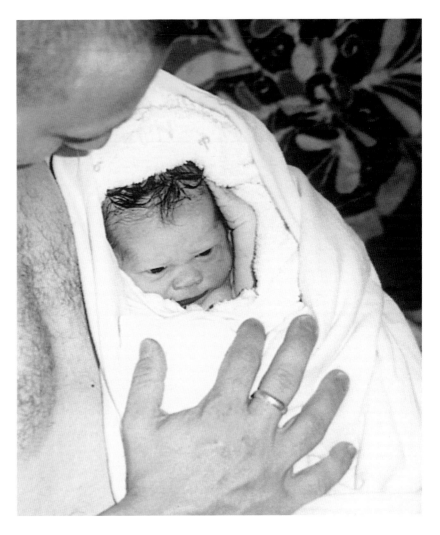

At a home birth, your partner can often feel more involved in what's going on. He will be able to hold and cuddle your baby while your needs are being cared for by your midwife.

ambulance, depending on how advanced your labour was, but very few of these transfers are due to real emergencies.[●]

Your midwife will monitor your baby's heart and your condition regularly through labour, and will advise that you transfer to hospital if she has any concerns about the health of either of you. The aim is to transfer well before the situation becomes an emergency.

It is always possible that you may need emergency treatment, and it may take longer to get if you have to transfer from home to hospital. However, it is extremely rare for an intervention such as a caesarean to suddenly become necessary with no earlier warning signs. If the midwife believes that you need an urgent caesarean then she will call ahead to have the operating theatre ready for your arrival. Even if you were labouring in hospital, there would normally be a wait of around 30 minutes while a surgical team was assembled. In a study of 29 midwifery practices in the United States, 8.3 per cent of women planning a home birth were transferred to hospital during labour and ten mothers (0.8 per cent) were transferred after delivery.[⊙] In an earlier UK study of 285 women who booked home births, 9.4 per cent were transferred to hospital during labour.[⊙] A large 1997 study showed a transfer rate of 16 per cent.[⊙] According to these statistics, transfer rates actually in labour average out at about 1 in 8 births.

Midwives are trained to provide emergency treatment if there are complications after the birth. They carry resuscitation equipment for babies who are slow to breathe and drugs to treat heavy bleeding after birth. Facilities vary between areas, so do discuss with your midwife what would happen in an emergency.

Occasionally, transfer to hospital occurs after the birth – perhaps because of problems with the delivery of the placenta, or because of concerns about the baby's breathing.

Although transferring from a planned home birth can be disappointing, most women who have transferred say that they were glad to have spent time labouring at home, and would plan a home birth for their next baby.

My partner is unsure about home birth

If your partner is worried about the safety of home birth, get him to talk to your midwife. Contact your local home birth support group to see if you can both talk to other couples about their experiences.

Many men who have been birth partners at home and in hospital say that they preferred the home birth, even if they had doubts initially. They are more likely to feel useful – that they have a definite role. You may be relying on your partner to provide practical support to a greater extent than in hospital – after all, he, and not the midwife, will know where you keep the towels, baby clothes, and so on! If he is nervous about this, you could invite a friend to help out as an additional birth partner.

Birth pool

Many people opting for a home birth also hire a birth pool for use at home. In this case, it helps if the partner can take responsibility for assembling the birth pool, and maintaining the water at the correct temperature. However, a pool is by no means essential for a home birth.

Is it messy?

Most home births produce little mess, which is easily contained with some forward planning. Midwives bring large absorbent, disposable pads to protect the surfaces you give birth on, and they take away all the mess when they leave. Floors or beds can be covered with waterproof sheeting, a large waterproof tablecloth or old sheets. Clearing up after a home birth is usually very straightforward.

'Afterwards, I asked Miles if it had stressed him out being at home, but he said that he much preferred it to being in hospital; he had a much more constructive role and felt more part of it all.'

water birth

Water has been shown to help many women manage the pain of contractions during labour.[o] Warm water can be relaxing, soothing and calming – and some women have found that being in a birth pool gave them a sense of freedom and privacy which enabled them to follow their instincts and trust their own body during labour.

> **BENEFITS FOR BABIES**
> In a UK observational study, fewer babies born in water were admitted to Special Care.[o]

'As soon as the pain became too much I got into the pool and it was like being wrapped in a cosy blanket and my whole body breathed a sigh of relief. The contractions didn't slow down, in fact the opposite: the more I could let my body relax in between contractions, the faster they came.'

Many women feel they have more control over their environment, even in a hospital setting, if they are in a birth pool. It means you can create your own space, which can give a welcome sense of privacy. It also means you can use the buoyancy of the water to support your body as you move around.

Advantages of water birth for you

There has not been a lot of in-depth comparative research, although common strands in studies show that labouring in water has these advantages over 'dry land' labour:

- Women feel more in control during their labour and are more satisfied with their birth experience.
- They feel more relaxed, contractions feel less painful and they use fewer pain-killing drugs.
- It is easier to move around and change positions between contractions.
- Labours are slightly shorter and less likely to be speeded up with a drip of oxytocin.
- There are fewer episiotomies and fewer serious tears with births in water.
- In a birth pool, you can create a quiet space around yourself. This helps you to feel private and keeps interventions to a minimum.
- If you are a wheelchair-user, or find movement on dry land difficult, a birth pool can really help you change positions in labour.
- Unlike most pain relief options, you can change your mind at any time about using water as a form of pain relief. If you do not like the sensation of labouring in water, you can get out. If you hadn't intended to use water (and haven't already had Pethidine or an epidural) and are able to gain access to a birth pool, you can just try it and see if it helps you.

Although some women find they don't like being in a birth pool, most women love the feeling of being in water during labour, and will stay in for the whole of their labour and the birth!

Possible disadvantages for you

- Getting into a pool may slow down your labour, so it can work well to wait until the contractions are regular and strong and getting difficult to cope with – then the soothing water can give relief but be prepared to get out for a while if your contractions slow down.

- If you are asked to get out of the pool, you may suddenly feel the contractions more intensely.

Advantages of water birth for your baby

- Your baby will be under less stress and will get a better oxygen supply if you are more relaxed and warm water can help you relax. In a recent study of births in water, babies were less stressed at birth.[⊙]

Possible disadvantages for your baby

- There is some suggestion that your baby may gasp for breath too soon if the water is too cold.
- In rare circumstances, a baby who is very stressed during labour may try to breathe under water.
- Your baby's heart rate may increase if the water is too hot. The Royal

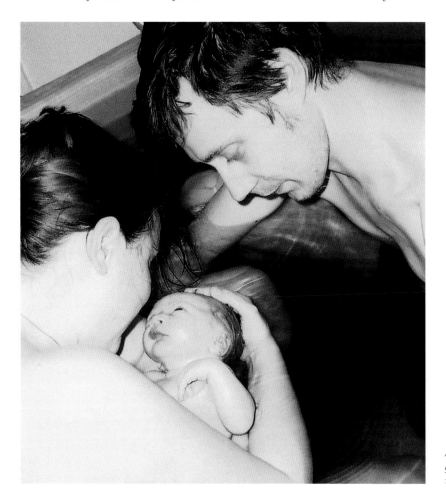

BENEFITS OF WATER

'Beneficial effects (of the use of immersion in water during labour) include maternal relaxation, less painful contractions, shorter labours, less need for augmentation, less need for pharmacological analgesics, more intact perinea, and fewer episiotomies.'[⊙]

At a water birth, babies must be brought gently to the surface of the pool, as soon as they are born.

College of Obstetricians and Gynaecologists says water must be kept at or below 37°C during the second stage of labour.[⊙]

If your midwife has any concerns about your baby's condition during labour, she will advise you to leave the pool.

Am I a suitable candidate?

The Royal College of Midwives has recommended that a pool is suitable for women who have:

- enough information to make an informed choice
- a normal pregnancy that has reached at least 37 weeks
- one baby lying head down (cephalic presentation)
- not been given any drugs which cause sedation (such as Pethidine)
- with intact waters – or whose waters broke spontaneously within the last 24 hours.

Discuss your options with your carers – different health service areas follow different criteria.

How can I book a water birth?

In hospital

Usually hospital pools cannot be booked; they're available on a 'first come, first served' basis. Discuss what will happen if another woman is using the pool when you go into labour.

It is possible to hire a pool yourself, bring it into hospital with you and set it up for your own use – but this would have to be agreed ahead of time with the midwives.

Many hospitals have birth pools and each hospital will have its own guidelines on pool use. Some require women to get out of the pool to actually give birth.

The staff should provide written information as well as discussion on using water in labour and birth.

At home

You can hire a pool to use in your own surroundings if you are planning to have your water birth at home. Ask to be looked after by a midwife with water birth experience. You may need to contact the Supervisor of Midwives at your local hospital for help in finding a midwife with suitable experience.

Practical considerations

Is your room big enough? Birth pools vary in size but are generally about 1.5m by 1.2m (5ft by 4ft). Smaller inflatable pools are also available from some hire companies.

- Is there room for the midwife to sit beside the pool and enough floor space in case you decide to leave the pool at any time?

- Is the floor strong enough? The large pools hold about 200 gallons of water, which weigh about 1 ton.
- Is there a convenient supply of water? How long will it take your own water system to fill the pool?
- Do you have a partner or friend who can set up the birth pool and keep the water warm for you?
- Is your hot-water system efficient enough to heat all that water? If you can afford it, would it be a better idea to hire a pool with its own thermo-statically controlled heating system?

Hiring a pool

Birth pools come in various shapes and sizes. Some are inflatable, others more permanent structures. Some have built-in heaters; others have to be filled with water from your own hot-water system. Do check that the pool is insured and meets the safety and hygiene requirements of the NHS. It's worth spending some time, looking into all the options. Most of the pool hire companies have websites or will be happy to give you lots of information by post or over the phone.

On the day

Whatever the stage of labour, you may find that when you get in the birth pool, you enjoy the sensation of the warm water and can find a comfortable position. Be guided by your own feelings and talk to your midwives, when the time comes. If you feel strongly that you want to get into the pool, you may well benefit. If you feel you want to leave the pool, you should do so.

If your labour is progressing slowly in the water, you might try moving into different positions or getting out and walking around for a while. Squatting, kneeling on all-fours or going up and down stairs can help move the baby into a good position for birth.

You know best the needs and comforts of your body while you are in labour. You may choose to stay in the pool to give birth, or find, as many women do, that dry land suits you better when the moment arrives.

Other ways of using water

If you are interested in the idea of using water but don't want to have a birth pool, relaxing in a bath or shower can provide some of the benefits.
- Blu-Tack™ blocking the overflow of the bath will give a greater depth of water, although you can't move around in the bath.
- You can use an upturned plastic bucket or a sturdy plastic chair to sit on under a shower.
- Warm water can be poured over you from a jug.
- A strong shower jet directed against the small of the back gives some women wonderful relief.

'Everybody expected the baby to be late, but my instinct told me to get a birthing pool for the due date. I remember coaxing my husband into assembling it the night before. The next morning, I started to feel the contractions.'

birth centre or midwifery unit

Although the majority of women in the UK go to a consultant unit in a hospital to have their baby, women who are hoping to have a straightforward birth with little or no intervention, can book into a midwifery-led unit.

Midwives who work in a midwifery-led unit rather than a hospital have the philosophy that pregnancy and childbirth are normal occurrences. For them, birth is not only seen as a physiological process, but one that involves psychological, social, cultural and spiritual aspects as well. Care is based on the needs of individual women rather than being dictated by hospital policies and protocols. This allows the midwives to be more flexible and encourages normal labour and birth.

In the past, as birth moved from home into hospitals, maternity services were provided by small cottage hospitals and units run by GPs. These were usually located within communities. Gradually maternity services became more centralized and became focused within district general hospitals. Women began to have their babies further out of their communities and except in a few rural areas, cottage hospitals and GP units closed down. The trend recently has been to amalgamate maternity services into larger and larger consultant units, and some of these big hospitals are now catering for more than 4000 births a year.

With the emergence of large consultant units, together with ever-increasing rates of medical intervention, and the lack of provision for home birth, there has been a realization that many women simply do not need to be cared for by doctors in labour. Midwifery-led care has been recognized as a valid alternative and many of the remaining GP units have now become midwifery-led units. In addition, new birth centres are opening up across the country and there are many more planned. At the same time, other midwifery-led units are under threat of closure, often for financial reasons.

Types of midwifery-led unit

Midwifery-led units – sometimes called 'birth centres' offer a useful option as a place to give birth for women with uncomplicated pregnancies. They may be totally separate and away from hospital (stand alone), or within the hospital grounds or simply in a separate part of a hospital building (alongside). They may be funded privately or by the NHS. They aim to provide as close to a home-like environment as possible. There are generally more facilities available to aid comfort such as birth pools, and the midwives

Birth pools and one-to-one care are more easily available at birth centres.

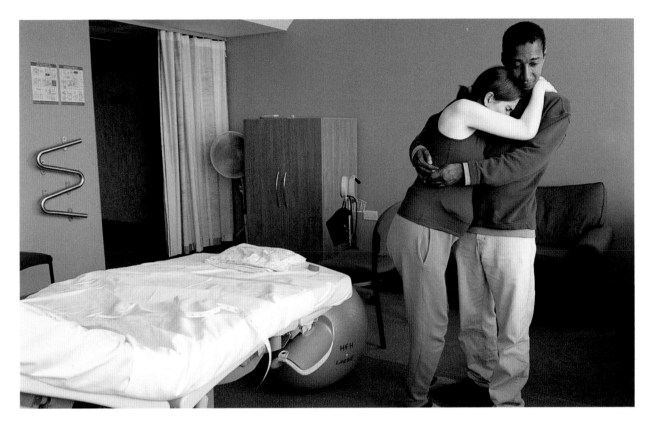

are experienced with water births. These units are usually small and family-centred and the women are more likely to get continuity of care.

Midwifery-led units are often much more 'like home' than hospital labour wards.

'Stand alone' midwifery-led units

Some 'stand alone' midwifery-led units are situated in rural areas and provide a place where women can give birth without having to travel a long way to a consultant unit during labour. However, if problems occur in pregnancy and labour, women may need access to the facilities of a consultant unit, so there may be a strict set of rules as to who is allowed to use the midwifery-led unit. In some remote areas, there may be facilities to carry out emergency operations. GPs may be available to assist with forceps deliveries, and in some units, midwives have been trained to do ventouse deliveries. When these facilities are available, it can mean that greater numbers of women are able to give birth in the unit without having to be transferred to a consultant unit.

Other 'stand alone' midwifery-led units have been set up near hospitals so that women can easily be transferred if necessary. Because there are usually no medical facilities available in the unit, these units are most suited to women with 'low risk' pregnancies who are likely to have a straight-forward birth. This includes first-time mothers.

'Alongside' midwifery-led units

'Alongside' units are set up on the same hospital site as a consultant maternity unit, and are often adjacent. It is hoped that women will experience the same type of 'low-tech' environment and care as they would get at home or in a birth centre, but with the added convenience of being right next to medical facilities if required.

Although there has been little research in this area, it has been suggested that where a midwifery-led unit is built alongside a consultant unit, it is much harder for the midwives within that unit to retain a philosophy of normal birth.

The benefits of a midwifery-led unit

One of the great benefits of choosing to give birth in a midwifery-led unit is that you are likely to receive continuity of care throughout pregnancy, labour and birth. This will be provided by a small team of midwives who are dedicated to helping women give birth without medical intervention, and whom you will get to know as your pregnancy progresses.

Research shows that women having continuity of care from a team of midwives are less likely to have drugs for pain relief in labour and less likely to be admitted to hospital and more likely to be pleased with their care than women who are not getting continuity of care. Further research shows that women who are supported throughout labour by an experienced female caregiver are less likely to need medical interventions.

This study was borne out in an evaluation of Edgware Birth Centre – a stand alone unit in North London – where it was found that there were significantly higher rates of normal vaginal births among women intending to have their baby at the birth centre when compared with a similar group of women planning to give birth in hospital. There were also lower rates of induction of labour, ventouse delivery, elective caesareans, episiotomy and fewer postnatal stays of more than three days.

A recent survey showed that women who had given birth at home, in a birth centre or a midwifery-led unit were more likely to believe they had been offered all the help, support and information they required, compared to women who had their babies in hospital.

Safety and birthing centres

Some birth centres have guidelines about who they can accept, although if you fall outside their specific criteria you may still be able to arrange care with them. Once booked with the birth centre, your care then rests in the hands of the midwives.

Having a baby at a midwifery-led unit is therefore generally equivalent to a birth at home as there are no doctors close to hand and limited drugs and technological equipment available. The midwives are experienced and competent to work in this type of environment, and have regular reviews of resuscitation and other emergency practices. There are usually excellent staffing levels and midwives can spend a lot of time with women, and have developed skills in supporting women who are labouring naturally. With this level of attention, potential emergencies can mostly be detected long before they occur and the woman in question transferred to the nearest hospital, where the staff will have been pre-warned and will be waiting for the woman's arrival.

What's different?

At a birth centre, the emphasis is on supportive care and creating a relaxing environment in which you will be able to labour naturally and instinctively. Because the main hormone responsible for stimulating contractions during labour – oxytocin – is produced when you feel protected and nurtured, labour progresses most easily if the surroundings are ones where you feel safe to let go and work with your body. Midwives experienced in normal birth will provide the environment you need and this works especially well where you have been able to build up a relationship of trust with your midwife during your pregnancy.

Also, because there is less access to medical pain relief at a birth centre, you are likely to be helped to cope with the pain of contractions in other ways. Many midwives at birth centres are experienced in water birth and often there are birth pools available for women who would like to use water for birth, or just for pain relief.

Other helpful methods include using upright positions and movement; the use of equipment such as birth balls, birth mats, beanbags or even bars and ropes to hold on to. You may also like to use TENS or Entonox (gas and air) or even aromatherapy and music. In the supportive environment, most women find that their labour progresses well and they can manage the pain.

You are also likely to be able to labour in a less rigid environment without reliance on strict rules, such as the need for vaginal examinations to assess the progress of labour, and the imposition of arbitrary time limits for labour. Monitoring the baby's heartbeat will also be carried out in a way which means you will not need to lie down strapped to a piece of machinery, and therefore does not interfere with your ability to move around and use positions that assist the natural process of labour.

Once your baby has been born you are more likely to have a natural third stage (delivery of the placenta) and there should also be the opportunity to have unhurried skin-to-skin contact with your baby.

For women who want a birth in a more relaxed environment where there will be less interference, and they can increase their chances of having a natural birth, a birth centre or midwifery-led unit is worth considering.

You can find out more about your local midwifery-led units at the website www.birthchoiceuk.com.

natural birth in hospital

It has been shown that you will recover from the birth more quickly, find it easier to bond with your baby, have a calmer, more settled baby and find it easier to breastfeed if you give birth without medical intervention when you are in hospital.

'I was lucky to have a corner bath in my room with a double bed in my hospital and sitting in it was great.'

A hospital maternity unit can be a difficult setting for birth. To keep birth safe and efficient in this environment, many rules and guidelines have been put in place for managing maternity care. Some women will need to have medical interventions for the safety of themselves or their baby, and in these situations everyone is grateful for the technological advances which have been made in recent years.

However, the management of labour in hospital can change its natural path, making other interventions more likely. This has been described as 'the cascade of intervention'.

Even so, you may feel that you would be more comfortable in hospital. You may feel that you are happy to have medical interventions when offered, or you want a natural birth but do not want (or are not able) to give birth at home or in a birth centre. Whatever decision you have made should be respected by those around you.

If you intend to have your baby in hospital and want a natural birth without intervention, you may come across difficulties especially if your labour doesn't fit into a standard model. Many hospital staff have little experience of labour without intervention and you may find you are working against the system.

If you are hoping to have a natural birth in hospital, there are certain things you can do to help yourself.

Preparation for labour

It is a good idea to prepare yourself as much as possible for the birth whilst you are pregnant. National Childbirth Trust (NCT) antenatal classes have a strong reputation for providing up-to-date evidence-based information on choices in maternity care. There is also lots of information available in books, the internet, and from other organizations campaigning for more awareness of natural birth (see useful organizations on page 245).

Taking good care of yourself on all levels is paramount (see Part Three) to ensure pregnancy progresses as trouble-free as possible.

As the birth draws near it is helpful to arrange to have with you one or two people you trust and feel comfortable with to be of support during

It's best not to lie back on a bed during labour: remaining upright and leaning forward helps labour to progress.

labour and pack everything you need to take to hospital well in advance of your due date so you aren't flustered doing this when things begin.

Be aware of your posture in pregnancy to help get your baby in the best position for birth.

Having your labour induced (started off artificially) needs careful thought, as this can start the 'cascade of intervention'.

When labour begins

Once you feel you might be in labour, it's wise to remain at home as long as you feel able to, to allow the hormones for labour to build. You are more likely to get into established labour if you are in an environment in which you feel familiar and at ease, and things will progress more quickly. If you are experiencing a false labour (one that fades away – very common when the body is preparing for birth) you may avoid going to hospital unnecessarily. Many women worry they won't be able to tell the difference between Braxton Hicks or 'practice' contractions and the real ones. It is quite rare for a woman to labour strongly without realizing, and the hospital midwives are always happy to give advice over the phone. If at any time while you are labouring at home, you feel worried or uncertain, trust your instincts and make sure you speak to a midwife.

While at home (and later in hospital), when the contractions are becoming more intense there are various things you can do to aid comfort and which act as natural forms of pain relief, such as a warm bath, a TENS machine, massage and complementary therapies.

Moving to the hospital

At some stage in labour a woman planning a hospital birth will decide the time is right to go to hospital.

When you arrive at the hospital, your midwife will check your notes for anything she needs to know about you and your pregnancy. She will find out when and how things started and what is happening now, length and frequency of contractions and whether the waters have broken or there has been a 'show' or any blood or fluid loss. She will also check your pulse and blood pressure and test your urine. The midwife will also feel your abdomen to establish how the baby is lying.

Your baby's heart rate will be measured. Many hospitals still have in place the procedure of a 'routine admission trace'. This is where the baby is monitored for about 20 minutes using belts around your abdomen. These are connected by wires to a machine which prints out a trace of the baby's heartbeat and your contractions. The latest national guidelines do not support the use of this admission trace and recommend that you are monitored using a small hand-held device instead.[©] This enables you to move around freely, changing positions as you choose. (For more on monitoring, see Part Four). If the hospital recommend a 'routine admission trace' find out why, and ask if you can have intermittent monitoring instead.

Keeping your birth natural

The hospital environment may not be an easy place to labour comfortably. Labour progresses best when a woman is feeling safe and relaxed, so it is worthwhile trying to turn the delivery room into your own space.

You may find that moving the bed out of the way, gives you more room to move about. Keeping in upright positions and being able to move freely, rather than lying on your back, is important to help your labour progress well. If you want to use the bed, try to make sure that it is in its lowest position and try to keep upright on it using beanbags or pillows. Many women feel more stable on the floor.

Remember that your baby will arrive in its own time and not to any agenda set by the health professionals around you. As long as you and the baby are coping well with labour there is no need to hurry it along to meet a fixed deadline. Two of the best ways to try and avoid unnecessary interventions are to trust that your body knows how to give birth, and to create the relaxing and safe environment in which it can do its job.

However, time can pass slowly when you are labouring in hospital and you can feel impatient for your baby to be born. If you feel you are not making good progress you may feel disheartened, and less able to cope with the pain of contractions.

It is at this time that the right support is crucial. Midwives vary in their experience of normal birth, and if they feel labour is not progressing well or that you are not coping with the pain, some may suggest various medical interventions. Other midwives may be more used to suggesting other ways of helping labour progress and helping you manage the pain. See Part Four of this book, which deals with the topic of medical interventions and how you can make decisions about them.

On the whole, if you can manage to avoid intervention, so much the better. The benefits of a birth without unnecessary intervention include:

- much less postnatal pain
- quicker physical recovery
- increased self-esteem
- enhanced bonding with the baby
- reduced risk of postnatal depression
- a calmer, more settled baby
- an easier breastfeeding experience.

There are times when medical assistance is necessary for the health of either you or your baby. If you need to accept help from medical staff, try to stay positive and know that you are doing it because you feel it is the best thing for either yourself or your baby. However, look at the alternatives shown in the table below. When medical assistance is being offered, it is not always possible to substitute a less-invasive procedure, but these alternatives are worth trying before going through the 'BRAIN' analysis outlined on page 125.

see also

the role of your midwife	30–3
other birth supporters	36–9
choosing where to have your baby	42–3
birth centre or midwifery unit	54–7
best baby positions for birth	114–17
going past your due date	118–19
induction and acceleration	126–7
going into labour	148–9
working with labour	152–3

Problem	Medical intervention	Alternative	
Going past your due date	Hospital induction	Book an ultrasound scan to check your baby's well-being and ask for your baby's heartbeat to be monitored twice a week	See page 126
Labour is not progressing	Acceleration with drugs	Avoid going into hospital too early in labour. Wait at home for as long as feels comfortable, moving around and staying upright	See page 127
Concern that your baby is finding labour stressful	Continuous electronic fetal monitoring with belt monitor and/or fetal scalp electrode	Ask to be monitored with a hand-held device every 15 minutes in first-stage labour and every five minutes in second stage	See page 128
You're finding labour difficult to cope with and more painful than you expected	Epidural anaesthetic	Move around; get more hands-on support from your midwife and birth partner; use gas and air and a birth pool; visualize holding your newborn baby and breathe through the next five contractions before re-considering	See pages 152–63
You are having trouble pushing the baby out on your own	Ventouse, forceps or caesarean help to be born	Move your body; getting onto all-fours or lying on your side can help; push only when your body tells you to; gas and air can help you push with less pain	See pages 164–5

a transverse-lie at 39 weeks birth story

A natural birth for a baby who can't make up his mind

'At 36 weeks, my baby is transverse, not too bothered as the girls were lying that way until about 34/35 weeks. I trawl the internet for ways to make babies turn. Among the suggestions are: crawling around on all-fours, wearing tight cycling shorts, doing handstands in a swimming pool.

'See consultant a week later, the baby is still transverse. I spend the week taking pulsatilla (homeopathic remedy), visiting osteopaths, and even doing handstands at the swimming pool! Have a scan at 38 weeks – baby is head-down at last. At 39 weeks I am examined and am shocked that the baby is now oblique (lying diagonally). The consultant says that he will do an external cephalic version (ECV) and induce me on Friday.

'At 39 weeks, the baby is in the right position. Decide to be induced in case the baby starts moving again. I am taken to delivery the next morning and have Prostin gel inserted. Spend the next five hours wandering around to no avail. More Prostin at 3.45pm and off to stalk the corridors again. Onto the monitor and have to sit still – very uncomfortable. An internal is carried out but I am still not officially 'in labour'. I'm kept in anyway because of the baby's 'unstable lie'. Caesarean looks inevitable.

'The baby is now breech, so spend morning on bed with bottom in the air. At lunchtime find that the baby is now transverse again.'

'39 weeks and 3 days – books read: 2½. Decide to have a 'day off' to see if labour starts naturally. Nothing happens. 39 weeks and 4 days – books read: 3. Have a show but sink into depression when the midwife tells me the baby is transverse again. 39 weeks and 5 days – books read: 3; miles walked round corridors: 4.3. The baby is now breech, so spend morning on bed with bottom in the air. At lunchtime find that the baby is now transverse again. People are saying *"Still here?"*. Doctor offers a caesarean! I ask if the consultant would be able to turn the baby using ECV and then induce me. Doctor returns to say they will try ECV tomorrow. I agree to stay in because of the danger of cord prolapse, should my waters break.

'39 weeks and 6 days – the consultant arrives and scans to see what baby is doing. The ECV is uncomfortable (feels like the baby was got by the scruff of his neck and his bottom and edged round to the right position). Spend the next eight hours standing up or on the birthing ball but the contractions are painless. When examined, I am 2cm dilated and have my waters broken. The contractions get painful and within an hour I'm on Entonox. At ten to midnight, I wanted to push. I was told that the baby had dark hair and within a few minutes Joseph Frederick arrives! I could not hold him as I was shaking – partly because I had had nothing to eat for 24 hours but also through exhilaration that I had "done it" without a caesarean! I stare at my son (who spends the next eight hours fast asleep and motionless, no doubt worn out by his acrobatics of the previous week!).'

a breech birth story

'When I started NCT classes, I became aware of my options and decided to give birth at the Edgware Birth Centre. However, my baby was breech and the centre only handles *low risk* births. They assured me that I could give birth there if the position changed, but if not – what then?

'At the Royal Free Hospital, doctors tried to convince me to have a caesarean. When I refused, wanting a vaginal birth, they said they were *"too dangerous"*. Without my antenatal teacher and yoga teacher at the Active Birth Centre, I would have given up.

'I encouraged the baby to turn using homeopathy, reflexology, acupuncture, and spending 20 minutes each day hanging head-down from the sofa – nothing worked. I went to St John's and Elizabeth's Birth Unit to try to turn the baby by external cephalic version (ECV); this was a failure, too.

'I asked St John's and Elizabeth's Hospital whether I could have a vaginal breech birth. They took time to think and then offered an elective caesarean!

'My husband searched for information on breech births and it emerged that they are something of a lost art. We found an article on the website of the Association for the Improvement of Maternity Services. It said a breech is best delivered by a non-interventionist approach. I cried with relief, there *was* hope! AIMS put me in touch with independent midwife Jane Evans who said she'd be delighted to deliver the baby. Jane shared my care with Brenda, another independent midwife. We agreed that, if necessary, I would transfer to the hospital and they would stay with me for a caesarean.

> 'I encouraged the baby to turn using homeopathy, reflexology, acupuncture and spending 20 minutes each day hanging head-down from the sofa – nothing worked.'

The midwives arrived

'I started to feel the contractions in the morning and pottered around totally relaxed. By lunchtime, the pressure in my pelvis meant that I could not sit and I called the midwives. Jane and Brenda arrived and helped me find comfortable positions while my husband filled the pool. I coped with contractions until they felt unbearable and then descended into the pool.

'In four hours I was 8cm dilated and then half an hour later, the urge to push became uncontrollable. I knelt in front of a bed and Jonas was born within 45 minutes. He was stuck at the perineum but after a few contractions his legs flopped out, followed by the arms and face. Brenda guided the back of his head – no medical intervention was needed. The fetal heartbeat was monitored so unobtrusively that I wasn't aware of it. It was better than I could have dreamt.

'The birth of my son was a rite of passage. I hope my account will encourage women also to trust their instincts and fight for the birth experience they want.'

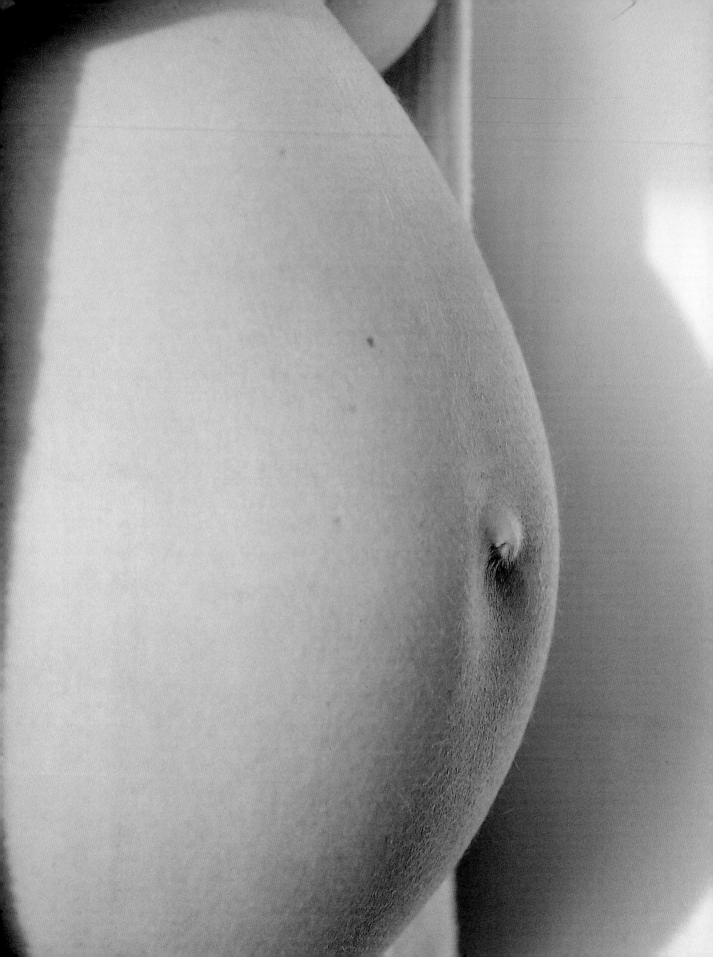

Self-care during pregnancy

changes in body and mind

Over the next nine months, more or less everything about your body – from the size of your breasts and your belly to the beating of your heart – is going to change as your baby grows.

Help your newly pregnant body by caring for it: protect it, feed it well, keep it fit, and give it plenty of time to relax and rest. This won't just be good for you, it will be good for your baby as well. By looking after your body, you are looking after your baby and helping him to grow healthy and strong.

Just as your body will be changing during your pregnancy, so your mind will be changing too. Your thoughts and your interests will alter as you focus on the life growing inside you. Your feelings will change as your baby becomes your new

the birth year

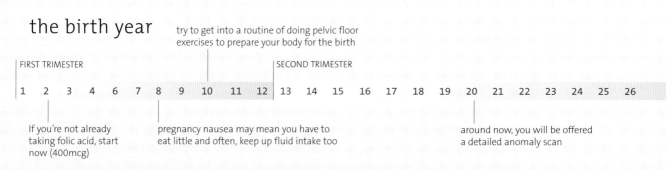

try to get into a routine of doing pelvic floor exercises to prepare your body for the birth

FIRST TRIMESTER | SECOND TRIMESTER

1   2   3   4   6   7   8   9   10   11   12   13   14   15   16   17   18   19   20   21   22   23   24   25   26

If you're not already taking folic acid, start now (400mcg)

pregnancy nausea may mean you have to eat little and often, keep up fluid intake too

around now, you will be offered a detailed anomaly scan

priority. If you have a job outside the home, you may find the world of work becomes less appealing. You will find that your priorities change significantly as you nurture your growing baby inside you.

These changes are all part of the process of adjusting and adapting to impending motherhood. As you adjust to the changes going on in your body and to feeling your baby growing inside you, so are you also adjusting to your new mental state, the new life that lies ahead of you, and the new person that you're becoming. For most women it is a time of ups and downs and emotional mood swings; a heady mixture of happiness and tears. Care for your mental well-being too, by sharing any concerns with the people closest to you.

Our frantic modern world often doesn't allow pregnant women the space or time to nurture themselves. Busy careers, demanding work schedules and increasing stress levels abound as we all struggle to balance home, work and family. So don't feel guilty at taking as much maternity leave as you can. Your body is doing the most important work possible: making a new human being. The following pages will give you lots of ideas on how to care for yourself and your growing baby. It's time to celebrate your new body and the new you.

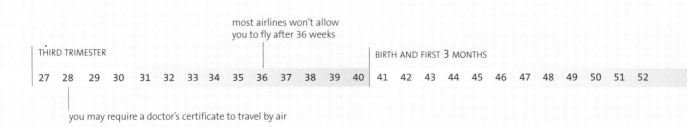

most airlines won't allow
you to fly after 36 weeks

THIRD TRIMESTER

BIRTH AND FIRST 3 MONTHS

27 28 29 30 31 32 33 34 35 36 37 38 39 40 41 42 43 44 45 46 47 48 49 50 51 52

you may require a doctor's certificate to travel by air

early signs

The beginning of your pregnancy is the beginning of a new life – not only your baby's, but yours as well. At this point, the birth probably seems a long way off, but that's good. You've got nine months to get used to the idea of becoming a mother.

PREGNANCY TESTS

Most women find out for sure that they're pregnant by doing a home pregnancy test. These test for the presence, in your urine, of the hormone, human chorionic gonadotrophin (HCG), which is only produced in pregnancy. Many of these tests will produce a positive result if you test on the first day of your missed period.

If your period is late but the test is not positive, you may have tested too soon, or your urine may have been too dilute at the time of the test (the tests work best on urine that has been in the bladder for at least four hours). You may get a different result if you test again in a few days on an early morning urine sample.

FINDING YOUR DUE DATE

Write down the first day of your last period (eg 3 July). Then, add nine months (which brings you to April) and seven days (which makes it 10 April). The average menstrual cycle is 28 days, but yours might normally be longer (or shorter) than that. If your average cycle is 33 days, then you need to add another five days to your due date (33 minus 28 equals 5). This will make your due date 15 April.

Becoming pregnant is the start of a big process of change, not just in your body, but in your heart and mind as well, as you adjust to new feelings and a different sense of what matters.

Some women have a strong sense of having conceived straight away but for most of us, the first obvious sign is a missed period.

Even before you realize you're 'late', there are other signs of pregnancy that you might notice. About a week before your period is due, your breasts might start to feel tender. You might also experience pains a bit like period pains or have some bleeding (these things happen when the cluster of cells that will develop into your baby is attaching to the wall of your uterus).

As you get to the time of your period being due, you may be starting to feel distinctly different. You may have a feeling of heaviness in your lower abdomen, and possibly some mild cramps that come and go. As time goes by, you may notice an odd, metallic taste in your mouth and go off things, like coffee or alcohol or fried foods. You'll probably find that you're unbelievably tired, almost as if you've been drugged, and you may start to feel – or be – sick. You may need to go to the loo more often too.

Doing the maths

Pregnancy is generally regarded as lasting for 40 weeks. The 40 weeks is counted from the first day of your last period, as this is usually easier to pinpoint than the day you conceived.

The formula that is usually used to work out your due date involves adding nine calendar months and seven days to the first day of your last period. This is based on your menstrual cycle being 28 days, though, so if it's longer or shorter than that, you need to add or subtract the difference (e.g if you have a 35-day cycle, add seven days to the total).

Sometimes your due date is calculated by counting forward 40 weeks from the first day of your last period. This will produce a slightly different result.

Ultrasound scans also provide estimates of due dates and you will probably be offered a scan at your first midwife appointment. These are considered to be accurate to within a few days if the scan is done in the first three months of pregnancy. This is because babies seem to grow at a similar

Exercising gently in the fresh air can help you stay both physically and mentally fit during pregnancy.

rate in the early months, so measuring your baby gives a good indication of how many weeks pregnant you are.

However, it's worth remembering that your due date is an estimate. A normal pregnancy can last anywhere between 37 and 42 weeks, and only about 5 per cent of babies are actually born on their due date. Although it can be hard to resist the idea of a due date, it might be more realistic to think in terms of a due fortnight and to think of your baby as being due, for example, 'in the middle of April' rather than on 15 April. You might find that this helps your peace of mind once you get towards the end of your pregnancy.

how pregnancy affects your body

Hormones have been called 'chemical messengers'. They are produced in one part of the body, pass into the bloodstream and are carried to distant organs or tissues to modify their structure or function. Pregnancy is a hormone-driven event, steered by your pituitary gland.

Changes in hormone levels during pregnancy have a profound effect on every part of your body.

Bones In the final 10 weeks of pregnancy your baby takes the equivalent of 80 per cent of your dietary calcium. However, if your calcium intake is adequate, this will not affect your bones.

Breasts An increased blood supply to the breasts makes them tingle and look marbled with veins. Your breasts will get larger and your nipples darken. From halfway through pregnancy, they may leak colostrum, the early milk your breasts produce.

Cervix Your cervix increases in width during pregnancy and the tissue becomes softer. Glands in the cervix secrete a thick mucus that forms a plug-like barrier protecting against bacteria until the start of labour.

Digestive system You may feel nauseous in the early months, and later, as the womb pushes upwards on your intestines and stomach. Your taste buds change in pregnancy and two-thirds of women have cravings (often for fruit and highly flavoured salty food) or aversions.

You may experience heartburn because progesterone affects the muscle closing off the stomach, which means stomach acid can be regurgitated. Also, food doesn't pass through the stomach so quickly and not as much gastric juice is secreted to digest it, which can result in nausea. Progesterone causes increased water absorption in the large intestine, which may lead to constipation, and as the womb enlarges and presses on the large intestine, increased flatulence.

Gums Oestrogen may cause your gums to become swollen and bleed easily.

Hearing and smell The nasal passages become congested, causing stuffiness and blocked ears. You may become very sensitive to smell and find particular smells nauseating.

SKIN

Melanocyte-stimulating hormone causes increased skin pigmentation, which is why your nipples darken. A dark line develops from the navel to the pubis in some women known as the *linea nigra*. A few also develop a 'butterfly mask' or chloasma, a mottled pigmentation in the shape of a butterfly around the eyes and forehead. Freckles and scars may darken and you tan more deeply in pregnancy.

Heart, circulation and blood clotting The volume of blood in your body increases by 30 to 50 per cent during pregnancy, more if you are expecting twins, and new vessels are formed to deal with this extra flow. However, blood pressure tends to fall before the volume of blood increases, which may explain why women feel faint in early pregnancy.

Later in pregnancy, lying flat on your back is uncomfortable and not advised, because the womb's pressure affects heart output. Swelling of the feet and ankles can be caused by relaxation of veins and the heavy womb impeding blood from returning to the heart. There also is an increased tendency to varicose veins and haemorrhoids. Bleeding time in pregnancy decreases by around one-third due to an increase in clotting factors in the blood, in preparation for labour when the placenta will separate from the womb.

Joints Hormones soften the connective tissue and ligaments in preparation for labour and the pelvis becomes wider. The weight of the womb and the combination of tissue-relaxing hormones cause the curve at the base of the back to curve inwards even more, with the shoulders thrown back to counterbalance the weight in front. Backache is common in late pregnancy and there are things you can do to help. Pressure from the womb on nerves and blood vessels may result in numbness and tingling in the legs. Symphysis pubis dysfunction (SPD) or pain in the pelvis can also be a problem.

Kidneys and bladder The kidneys increase excretion of waste products as more are now produced by you and your developing baby. The tubes from the kidney to the bladder elongate so they can take an increased volume of urine. This is, however, linked with increased risk of infection. The urge to urinate increases early in pregnancy as the growing womb puts pressure on the bladder. Later, the bladder is pushed upwards so you won't feel the need to empty it so often, but the lax walls of the bladder may mean you don't empty it completely, which also increases possible urinary infections.

Lungs Early in pregnancy the diaphragm shifts upwards and the chest broadens and ribs flare so there is more room for your lungs to expand and your diaphragm to rise. Progesterone also causes you to breathe more deeply and take in more oxygen.

Sight In the third trimester slight swelling of the cornea is common and this can distort light rays going into your eye, blurring vision.

Vagina Due to an increased blood supply caused by oestrogen, your vagina becomes softer and more stretchy, ready for the passage of the baby.

UTERUS/WOMB

The womb muscle is composed of involuntary muscle, which contracts slightly throughout pregnancy. This causes Braxton Hicks contractions, which are painless, irregular contractions measurable from the first trimester, although not all women can feel them. You may be aware of these contractions after orgasm, during sex. These contractions don't actually dilate the cervix but do help with blood circulation. Between two to three weeks before the birth, the baby may drop down into the pelvic brim as a result of the lower part of the womb softening. This means the top of the womb sinks away from the diaphragm, and eases your breathing.

relationship changes

Finding out you're pregnant for the first time starts a chain of events that will change your life forever. No wonder you feel a little uncertain about what you've taken on. Fortunately, you're not alone. You will find information, support and lots of friendly interest from other pregnant women.

PREGNANCY HORMONES

During your birth year, your feelings will go through changes, many of which are caused by increasing levels of the hormones progesterone and oestrogen. You will probably find your emotions fluctuate, especially at the beginning, but by the middle of pregnancy you may experience a sense of self-absorbed well-being. Towards the end, you may be looking forward to meeting your baby and may be anxious about what is to come. In the days before going into labour you'll probably be restless and feel energetic as you physically, and psychologically, prepare for the birth.

Discovering that you're pregnant can unleash a host of different feelings. You may be excited and thrilled, but will probably also be anxious and apprehensive – about miscarrying or whether the baby will be all right, about giving birth, or about whether you'll be a good enough mother. Pregnancy can also make you feel vulnerable and scared about the way you live and whether what you're doing, or eating or taking, or how you're feeling, might be affecting your baby.

Pregnancy involves huge changes in your body and your contours. Some women love their growing breasts and belly and feel proud of this new shape, but others are concerned about gaining weight and getting bigger. Some women enjoy the attention that their pregnancy receives from other people, while others feel embarrassed about their bodies being 'on show'.

Even if your pregnancy is much wanted, you may still have a feeling of 'Oh no, what have I done?' By becoming pregnant, you've shifted the focus of your life from yourself and you've set out on the journey to becoming someone's mum. This is exciting, but it can be alarming too, as you begin to realize what a big responsibility you're taking on. Some women feel trapped by this responsibility and worry about the impact the baby will have on their lives. Many women find that their priorities change significantly when they become pregnant – things that were once important to them now take second place to the baby they are nurturing inside. It has been said that a woman develops a fundamentally different mindset when she embarks on motherhood. Gradually, she begins to put the needs of her baby first.

Your moods

With so many mixed emotions and concerns going through your head, and such big physical changes going on in your body, to say nothing of the effects of pregnancy hormones, it's not surprising that many pregnant women find that their moods are up and down. Mood swings are quite normal, but if you feel persistently down or anxious, you may be suffering from antenatal depression (it's estimated that 10 per cent of women experience this). Talk through your concerns with your midwife or GP if you think this might be the case. They will be able to help.

You and your partner

Just as you are now having to adjust to a new life, so your partner is having to adjust too, and his feelings about the pregnancy may also be mixed. He may feel proud and excited, but also anxious about becoming a father. Some men feel particularly protective towards their pregnant partners – others feel shut out by their partner's involvement in her pregnancy. Make time to talk about how you're both feeling, share your worries, reassure each other of your love, and plan together for the arrival of your baby.

Sex during pregnancy

Some couples find that sex is more enjoyable than ever: they love the woman's new, fuller shape and their sex drive seems to increase. Others feel differently: they're tired and uncomfortable and are put off by the presence of the baby.

Some couples worry that making love will harm the baby. This is rarely the case (your midwife will advise you if there's any need to avoid sex in your particular circumstances). Some find it difficult to find comfortable positions, especially in later pregnancy. Some women may find their attitude to sex changes if there have been concerns about this pregnancy or the baby's health. A lot of screening tests, or frequent internal examinations at the beginning of pregnancy can interfere with a woman's libido. But if for whatever reason you don't want to have intercourse, don't forget that there are other enjoyable ways of being intimate.

Orgasm stimulates the production of the hormone oxytocin, which stimulates contractions. If you feel contractions in your uterus after making love, don't worry – these are just 'practice contractions' (see box page 71) and they will settle down again.

Telling people the news

The right time to break the news of your pregnancy is when it feels right for you. Some women want to tell the world straight away, while others prefer to wait until the risk of miscarriage has lessened (after around 12 weeks) before they let anyone know. There may be some people that it's hard to break the news to – someone you know who has recently lost a baby, for example, or who has been trying for a long time to conceive. Tell them with sensitivity – they will feel even worse if they find out the news from someone else.

If you are working, it's up to you to decide when you want to tell your employer about your pregnancy, as long as you notify them of your intention to take maternity leave at least 15 weeks before your expected week of childbirth (EWC). You will also need to show your MAT B1 form (proof of pregnancy which you get from your midwife or GP after 20 weeks). If your work involves anything that might put you or your baby at risk, then you may want to tell your employer as early as you feel ready. You will need to tell him or her in order to book time off for your antenatal appointments.

MATERNITY RIGHTS

Statutory maternity leave in the UK is now 26 weeks. The first six weeks are paid at 90 per cent of your salary and for the following 20 weeks you will be paid a flat rate of £100 a week. After that, an additional maximum of 26 weeks unpaid leave can be taken if you have been working for your employer for at least 26 weeks by the 15th week before the week when your baby is due. Fathers who have been working for the same stretch of time for their employer are also entitled to take two weeks paternity leave, paid at £100 a week, after the birth.

You are entitled to one year's maternity leave when you have a baby, and for half that time you will receive maternity pay. These figures show the basic minimum however; some employers offer more generous terms to their new mothers and fathers.

see also

the role of your midwife	30–3
choosing where to have your baby	42–3
what a new mother needs	198–9

caring for your body

Growing a baby makes big demands on your body: your blood supply can increase by as much as 50 per cent, your kidneys work harder and your need for oxygen increases. Look after yourself – you need to be fit and relaxed for labour and birth and your life as a new mother.

TAKE IT SLOWLY

If you're new to exercise, take things gently and build up slowly. Regardless of how experienced you are, though, there are a few precautions that it's wise to take:

- Avoid jerky movements or movements that put a strain on your joints.
- As your baby grows, and your belly gets bigger, your centre of gravity will change, which can affect balance, so move with care to avoid falls.
- Don't let yourself get too hot or out of breath. Take breaks every 15 minutes or so and drink plenty of water.
- Check your pulse regularly and slow down or stop if your heart rate goes above 140–150.
- In the second half of pregnancy, avoid exercising lying flat on your back.
- Consult your GP before exercising if you've had any bleeding, if you have high blood pressure, if your placenta is low-lying, if there are any problems with the growth of your baby, or if you're carrying more than one baby.
- If you've had two or more miscarriages, talk to your GP or midwife about whether exercise is safe in the early weeks.

If you go out to work every day, see if you can re-negotiate your hours for a while. If your journey is hard it may help to miss the rush hour and start later, leaving work earlier too. Go to bed early; have a warm (not hot) bath first and you'll sleep better.

Think, too, about following a gentle fitness programme to help strengthen your changing body.

Good forms of exercise to do in pregnancy are yoga and Pilates (as long as your teacher knows that you are pregnant), swimming and walking. Types of exercise that it's best to avoid include contact sports, competitive team sports, skiing, climbing, scuba diving, trampolining and gymnastics.

Yoga

Yoga is an ancient Indian philosophy and a discipline through *asana* (posture) and *pranayama* (regulation of breathing). The word means 'union', and the main principle of yoga is that it involves body and mind working together, the one influencing the other, to promote the well-being of both.

Certain yoga postures are ideal for pregnancy. Physically, the movements help to strengthen your body, and improve your flexibility and stamina. Mentally, they require you to breathe in a conscious way, and this helps to relax your mind, and to reduce tension and stress. Yoga helps you develop an awareness of your body and what's going on inside it, which in turn helps you to connect with your baby and to get to know him.

Many yoga positions are positions that are good to adopt in labour. The breathing techniques involved in yoga are helpful in labour too, as they help you to stay calm, and keep you and your baby well supplied with oxygen.

As well as helping you to prepare for labour, yoga can also help you to recover your muscle tone more quickly after your baby is born.

To find your nearest yoga teacher, contact the British Wheel of Yoga, or the Active Birth Centre (see page 245).

Pilates

Pilates is a form of exercise using controlled stretches and contracting and releasing muscles. It builds strength and improves your posture, flexibility

and stamina and by so doing, relaxes and releases tension in your body.

Pilates is based on several key principles, one of which is developing strength in your core postural muscles (your abdominal, back and pelvic floor muscles). This helps your body to support the growing weight of your baby and your abdomen, and protects your joints. To do Pilates exercises, you need to breathe deeply, and this reduces tension in your muscles as well as helping you to relax mentally. In addition, because the exercises require concentration, they also help to relieve stress.

You can find a teacher through the Pilates Foundation UK Ltd, The Pilates Institute, or the Body Control Pilates Association (see page 245).

Swimming is a wonderful way for pregnant women to exercise. The water bears your weight while also offering good resistance, ensuring that muscles are strengthened. It provides cardiovascular benefits and allows you to feel supported and weightless, despite your extra pounds.

Swimming and aquarobics

Swimming is an excellent form of exercise in pregnancy because the water supports your weight and there's little strain on your body. It's beneficial for your heart and lungs, strengthens your muscles, and helps to improve your stamina and flexibility. If you're suffering from pain in your pelvis, it's best to avoid breast-stroke leg actions when swimming though, as this stretches your front pelvic joint. Try not to hold your head up out of the water either, as this can put a strain on your back. Wear ear plugs and goggles and you won't have to hold your head up. If there's a jacuzzi at your pool, don't use it, as being in very hot water can lead to your baby becoming overheated.

Aquarobics or aquanatal classes are gentle aerobic exercise classes held in a swimming pool – often in the shallow end, so you don't have to be able to swim. The classes involve gentle stretches, as well as moving in the water, to tone your muscles. Many classes include a floating session (with floating aids) to allow you to relax. They are often run by midwives.

Ask your midwife about aquanatal classes in your area, or contact The Aquanatal Register (see page 245).

Walking

Walking helps to improve your strength and stamina, without putting much strain on your joints, and is good for your heart and lungs. Try to go out for a walk in the fresh air every day: it will help you to relax and give you the chance to think about and connect with your baby.

Relaxation

The more relaxed you are, the easier it is to cope with the demands of daily life. Relaxing your mind and body (rather than just slumping in front of the TV) has physical benefits too, as well as helping you to sleep better. It also ensures a good supply of oxygen to your baby.

Help yourself to relax by practising one or more of the following relaxation exercises for 10–30 minutes a day.

Ways of relaxing

It can help if you get someone to read out the following instructions to you.

Breathing deeply Sit in an upright dining chair, with a cushion behind you to support your lower back or sit with your back straight, cross-legged on the floor. Rest your hands loosely in your lap. Close your eyes. Breathe in, then breathe out slowly, dropping your shoulders and feeling your body relax as you breathe out. Keep breathing deeply and evenly, in through your nose and out through your mouth, concentrating on your out-breath. Part your lips as you breathe out. Rest your hands on your belly, feeling, thinking about and connecting with your baby. Because you'll be taking in lots of oxygen when you breathe in this way, your baby may well start to move.

Relaxing your body Lie on your left side with your right leg bent, and a cushion or pillow between your legs to support your bent knee. Rest your head on a cushion. Close your eyes and focus on your breathing and your body. With each out-breath, allow your body to become heavy and sink down into the surface you're lying on. Concentrate on each part of your body in turn, allowing it to relax more deeply. Relax your face and neck. Let your shoulders drop towards your feet. Let your arms, hands and fingers flop. Feel your chest and abdomen sinking down into the floor. Relax your hips and pelvis. Let your legs, feet and toes flop. Your whole body is now deeply relaxed.

Visualization You can practise this technique either sitting or lying down. Start by focusing on your breathing, concentrating on your out-breath, and letting your body relax. Then imagine that you're in a place you know where you feel particularly at peace. Everyone will have their own special place – it might be a cosy room, or a garden, or a beach, or a mountainside, or a warm bath. Think about what you can see in this place, what you can hear and smell and touch. Think about how you feel being there. If you find that other thoughts come into your mind, acknowledge them, and let them go. Just enjoy being calm and peaceful in your special place.

Complementary therapies Aromatherapy massage and reflexology are other good ways of relaxing. Always make sure your practitioner knows that you are pregnant.

TAKING CARE OF YOUR BACK

Back pain is a common pregnancy complaint, because pregnancy hormones soften all your ligaments, making the joints in your spine looser. Also, the weight of your abdomen tends to pull your lower spine forwards, putting a strain on your lower back.

To protect your back:

- Pay attention to your posture. Straighten your lower back and hold your bump in tight. Visualize your baby as being tucked into the pelvis, close to your centre of gravity. You may find that just thinking about your baby this way will help you stand more upright and hold a better posture. Open your shoulder blades to relieve upper back pain.
- Be careful about lifting any objects, particularly heavy things (avoid these if you can). Always bend your knees when you pick something up, especially something heavy.
- Wear flat or low-heeled shoes.
- Strengthen your back by doing Pilates or yoga or going swimming (but don't swim with your head up).

Here are some ideas for treating your back pain:

- Wear a maternity support belt.
- Ask your GP to refer you to a physiotherapist.
- Some women find reflexology or acupuncture helpful.
- See an osteopath or chiropractor.
- Ask your partner or a friend to give you a back massage.

---

see also

caring for your pelvic floor	78–9
early discomforts	96–9
later discomforts	100–3

caring for your pelvic floor

During pregnancy, the hormone 'relaxin' softens the supporting ligaments of your pelvic floor, allowing them to relax and become more elastic. However, these muscles need to support the extra weight of your growing baby and help you during the birth, so it's important to learn how to keep them toned and in good condition.

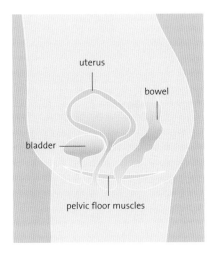

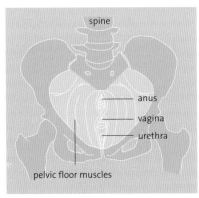

Your pelvic floor muscles support the weight of your internal organs. They need to be strengthened with specific, repeated exercises.

The pelvic floor is a hammock of muscle at the base of your pelvis. The deepest layer of muscle is attached to the pubic bone at the front of your pelvis, and to your tail bone or coccyx at the back. Another layer forms a swirling 'S' around the three female openings, the urinary outlet and the vagina at the front, and the back passage and anus at the back. The thick wedge of tissue between the back of the vagina and the back passage is called the perineum. This is also part of your pelvic floor.

To find out where your pelvic floor muscles are, imagine that you need to go to the toilet. The muscles that you hold tight to prevent passing urine or wind are your pelvic floor muscles.

The pelvic floor muscles need to be strengthened because they are there to support everything that is in your pelvis:

- the bladder and its outlet (urethra)
- your womb and your baby
- the vagina
- the back passage and the anus.

Towards the end of pregnancy, the weight of your baby is considerable. During labour, your pelvic floor muscles help your baby's head turn into the best position to be born. Damage to the pelvic floor is possible during childbirth when the muscles are stretched as your baby's head comes down the vagina. Exercising the muscles during pregnancy and especially afterwards helps keep them in good condition so that you don't leak urine when you cough or sneeze and you don't have problems with bowel control. Well-toned pelvic floor muscles also make sex more satisfying.

Exercising the pelvic floor muscles

There are two kinds of muscle fibre in your pelvic floor and you need to exercise both. There are the slow fibres which control the strength of the pelvic floor, and the fast fibres which help you tighten everything quickly when you cough or sneeze.

Exercise 1: Find a comfortable position, sitting down or lying with your knees a little apart. Tighten the muscles around your back passage, then around the front passage. Hold tight for a count of five. Make sure that you keep breathing while you are counting. Check by putting a hand on your abdomen. Now relax. Concentrate. Tighten the muscles from the back to the front again; hold for five; keep breathing. Relax. Try doing this five times and then, day by day, build up to 10 times.

Exercise 2: Imagine that your pelvic floor is like a drawbridge. Tighten the muscles around the back passage and then the front, just a little, and then a little bit more as if you're gradually raising the drawbridge. Now tighten them as hard as you can as if the drawbridge is closing. Keep breathing. Start to let the drawbridge down, relaxing the muscles a little, then a little more, and then let them relax fully.

Exercise 3: To exercise the fast twitch fibres, tighten your pelvic floor muscles as quickly and as tightly as you can. Relax them. Then immediately tighten them again, and relax them. Repeat five times. Finally – relax.

Do your pelvic floor muscle exercises when you're sitting on the toilet, *after* you've emptied your bladder. Do five drawbridge exercises and relax. Then 10 of the quick tightenings. Spend a few extra minutes in the toilet each time you go so that you can do your exercises.

Avoiding tears and cuts

There is some research to show that massaging your perineum from about six weeks before the birth can help prevent tearing.[⊙]

- Do perineal massage 3 to 4 times a week for 3 to 4 minutes (see box).
- Try to avoid having an epidural. Epidurals make it more likely that you will need forceps or ventouse to give birth and an episiotomy is essential if you have forceps and possible if you have a ventouse.
- Don't push too hard in the second stage of labour.
- When you're ready to give birth, go onto all-fours or into an upright kneeling position. Let your pelvic floor muscles bulge between your legs. Familiarize yourself with this sensation in pregnancy by pushing the muscles out as well as tightening them. Always return the muscles to their normal relaxed position.
- Consider a water birth. There's some evidence that being in water when your baby is born prevents tearing, and that the water helps make the tissues more soft and stretchy.[⊙]

The strategies listed above may help you avoid cuts or tears in the perineal area. And if you do have a tear or cut, pelvic floor exercises increase the flow of blood to your pelvis and will certainly help your perineum to heal more quickly. So start practising your pelvic floor exercises as soon as you can after the birth. Continue to do them for the rest of your life.

HOW TO DO PERINEAL MASSAGE

Do the massage after you've had a bath or shower, so that the tissues are soft and supple.

Use a little olive or grape seed oil to lubricate your thumb. Put your thumb about 5cm inside your vagina and sweep it gently from side to side, in a 180° arc. Press gently downwards at the same time. If you find this uncomfortable, take a deep breath in and then start massaging as you breathe out, letting all your muscles relax. Stop massaging, take another deep breath in, and then start to massage again while breathing out and letting go of any tension. Continue for about 3 minutes.

Then, with your thumb still inside your vagina, move two fingers gently down the perineum towards your back passage. If you feel a stinging sensation, massage as you breathe out. This sensation is very similar to what you will feel as your baby's head is about to be born.

antenatal testing

Although antenatal testing can identify problems with your pregnancy, assess the chance of your baby having particular conditions and diagnose specific abnormalities – this increased choice and knowledge can also lead to increased anxiety and confusion.

It may never have crossed your mind that there could be anything wrong with your baby, but as soon as you're offered a test to find out if he is OK, you start to worry. The decisions that you will need to make about whether to have a certain test and what to do if the result of that test is anything other than normal are complex and emotional. Before you say 'yes' or 'no' to any tests, do make sure that you fully understand:

- what the test involves
- what conditions it is testing for
- whether it is a screening or a diagnostic test (see below)
- how and when you will get the results
- what your options are when you get your results
- who you can talk to when you have received your results.

Talk to other women about their experience of having antenatal tests. And, most important of all, talk to your partner or the person you're closest to, about whether you want the information that tests give you, and what you would do if the results gave bad news.

Although for the majority of women they can give reassurance, antenatal tests can also raise strong feelings. Parents may find themselves making painful decisions including – for a small minority – whether to consider ending the pregnancy.

You may feel that your midwife or GP expects you to say 'yes' to ultrasound scans and routine screening tests, but it's up to you whether you choose to have some, all or none of them.

Not all tests are available everywhere, but you should be given clear information about any test you are offered.

Ultrasound scans from 8–12 weeks

Ultrasound used from 8–12 weeks can establish how many weeks pregnant you are and broadly how your baby is developing. It will also confirm whether you have a live baby and show how many babies you are carrying.

Before your early pregnancy scan, you will be asked to drink a lot of water so that your bladder pushes your uterus forward, making the image your baby clearer. The sonographer will spread a gel over your tummy and then roll a small 'transducer' over the gel to produce an image of your baby on a screen. Your partner or someone else of your choice should be allowed to sit with you during the scan. While it's exciting to see your baby on the screen, you may feel nervous about what will show up and it's good to have some support with you.

Screening tests

Antenatal tests fall into two categories: screening tests and diagnostic tests. A screening test is a non-invasive test offered to pregnant women. It can estimate your risk of having a baby with a serious chromosomal abnormality such as Down's syndrome, or a congenital abnormality such as spina bifida.

Screening tests are not diagnostic so cannot tell you for certain whether your baby has a particular condition. However, they can identify those women where the risk of their baby having, for example, Down's syndrome is greater than 1 in 250. They do not however, identify all women who have a baby with an abnormality.

A screening test for Down's syndrome (generally either a blood test, a nuchal fold test, or combination of the two – see below) will be considered 'positive' or 'high risk' if your risk is higher than 1 in 250. However, a risk of 1 in 100 is very different from a risk of 1 in 4, although both results would be described as 'screen positive'. A 1 in a 100 risk means that you have only a 1 per cent chance of having a baby with Down's and a 99 per cent chance that your baby will be perfectly normal. A 1 in 4 risk means that there is a

MATERNAL BLOOD TESTS

At your first midwife's appointment, your midwife will test your urine for sugar and protein (to check for diabetes, infections and signs of pre-eclampsia). She will also check your blood pressure. You will also be offered routine blood tests to show:

- your blood group
- your blood count (i.e. if you are anaemic or short of iron)
- your immune status for various infections – such as rubella (German measles)
- and an HIV test.

The Association of British Insurers has stated that having a negative HIV test, as part of routine antenatal care, is not a valid reason for refusing insurance or increasing payments.

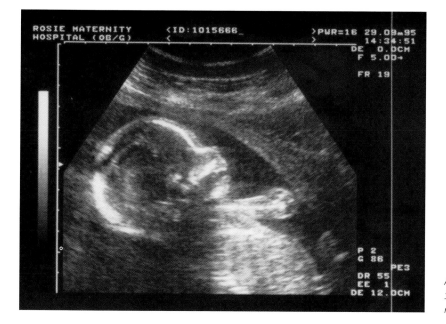

An anomaly scan will be offered between 16–22 weeks of pregnancy. You can accept or refuse the offer.

CHROMOSOMAL ABNORMALITIES

A chromosomal abnormality is due to a fault in the genetic information carried by the egg or the sperm which made your baby. It is built into a child's genetic make-up from the moment of conception and cannot be corrected. Down's syndrome is the most common chromosomal abnormality – babies have an extra chromosome. People with Down's syndrome have a very distinctive appearance and learning disabilities. Often they will also have more health problems, including heart defects.

CONGENITAL ABNORMALITIES

A congenital abnormality occurs when something goes wrong while the baby is developing in the womb. The congenital abnormalities looked for in screening tests are generally cardiac abnormalities or neural tube defects. There are two kinds of neural tube defects – spina bifida and anencephaly. Spina bifida is when the baby's spine has not formed completely and this can cause physical disabilities which can range in severity, from weakness to paralysis in the legs along with bowel and bladder problems. Anencephaly is when the brain has not formed and therefore, sadly, this is incompatible with life outside the womb.

25 per cent chance that your baby has Down's. If you receive a 'high risk' reading from a screening test you will be offered a diagnostic test to establish for certain whether your baby actually has the abnormality.

If your risk is less than 1 in 250, (e.g. 1 in 750) your result will be described as 'screen negative'. This does not mean that your baby definitely does not have Down's syndrome or some other abnormality, but that the risk is so low that it is unlikely.

There are several types of screening tests offered.

Serum screening

You may hear this screening test called many names, e.g the Triple Test, AFP Test, Quadruple Test, etc.

Your hospital may offer you this test between 16–18 weeks of pregnancy. A sample of your blood is taken to measure various, naturally occurring substances, which have crossed into your blood from your baby. The concentration of these substances, together with your age will be used to estimate the risk of your baby having either Down's syndrome or spina bifida. These substances are called markers and the number measured will vary according to hospital policy.

The marker that you are most likely to hear referred to by name is AFP – alpha-feto-protein. Low levels of this substance can be a sign of Down's and high levels can be a sign of neural tube defects (e.g spina bifida). The blood test is not absolutely reliable. It can be affected by the following factors:

- your ethnicity
- whether you are diabetic
- early pregnancy bleeding
- whether your due date has been correctly calculated
- how many babies you are carrying.

If you do get a 'screen positive' result, remember that this screening test is only an estimate of risk – you will be offered a further test to establish whether your baby does have a particular problem.

Only about 1 in 60 women whose blood tests suggest there might be a problem actually have an affected pregnancy.

Nuchal Fold/ Translucency Test

In some areas, women are offered a nuchal translucency test at 11–13 weeks, which is sometimes combined with an early pregnancy scan. If it is not offered at your hospital it is often possible to have this test done privately.

This test is an ultrasound scan, which carefully measures the pocket of fluid at the back of the baby's neck, known as the nuchal translucency. An increased amount of fluid may mean that the baby has Down's syndrome.

The measurement of fluid is combined with your age to give an estimate of the chance of your baby having Down's syndrome. If the test shows a 'high risk' (1 in 250 or more) then you will be offered a diagnostic test such as chorionic villus sampling (CVS).

Combined Test

This test, which is not available everywhere, is done between 11–13 weeks of pregnancy. It is a combination of the nuchal fold test, a blood sample from the mother (to measure the concentration of the substance PAPP-A) and the mother's age, used to estimate the chance of having a baby with Down's.

Serial testing (the integrated test)

This is a test in two stages, but is not available everywhere. In the first stage, at about 12 weeks, you will have a nuchal scan and a blood test to measure the concentration of PAPP-A. In the second stage, at around 15–16 weeks, you will have a blood test to measure the concentration of four naturally occurring substances that have crossed into your blood from your baby. These four markers along with the results of the nuchal scan and first blood test are combined with your age to estimate the chance of your baby having a neural tube defect or Down's syndrome. If you have a risk greater than 1 in 100 you will be offered an amniocentesis which is a diagnostic test.

These screening tests are useful for many parents as they are not invasive and do not involve an increased risk of miscarriage.

What if I get a 'high risk' result?

If you are given a 'high risk' or 'screen positive' result for a blood test or scan, you will face more decisions. Remember, the majority of women with this result go on to have a healthy baby.

- Ask for counselling from medical staff straight away.
- Explore what you can learn from further tests such as a more detailed ultrasound scan, CVS or amniocentesis.
- Take time to talk things over with a friend or partner and don't allow yourself to be pressurized into taking a hasty decision.
- Telephone the NCT Enquiry Line (0870 440 8707) or Antenatal Results and Choices (020 7631 0285) for further information and guidance.

Diagnostic tests

Unlike screening tests, diagnostic tests can find out for sure whether your baby has an abnormality and can give you a yes/no answer, but these are invasive tests and do carry a risk of miscarriage.

Chorionic villus sampling (CVS)

(From 11 weeks)

CVS involves taking a tiny tissue sample from the developing placenta to check the baby's chromosomes and test for Down's syndrome and certain

INHERITED GENETIC CONDITIONS

When both partners are carriers of a specific gene but neither have the disease, there is a 1 in 4 chance of the condition being passed to their baby. If you think you may be affected by any of these or any other inherited conditions, you can ask for counselling before you get pregnant or whilst you are pregnant.

- Sickle cell disease: 1 in 10 black people in the UK carries the sickle cell gene. Sickle cell anaemia is a life-threatening disease which cannot be cured. However, people with sickle cell anaemia can get treatment for tiredness, headaches, shortness of breath and jaundice.

- Thalassaemia: This condition affects families who come from the Mediterranean, Middle East and South East Asia. Thalassaemia affects the red blood cells and cannot be cured. However, treatment is given to reduce the risk of serious illness which can include jaundice, diabetes and disease of the spleen, liver and heart.

- Cystic fibrosis: This is the most common inherited disease among white people. It causes serious, life-threatening lung infections, which are treated with antibiotics and physiotherapy.

inherited disorders. However, gene defects are not looked for routinely. Using ultrasound as a guide, the tissue sample is taken either through the cervix or through the abdomen. (This test cannot diagnose spina bifida, which is most often diagnosed using ultrasound.)

You may feel some discomfort afterwards, similar to period pain and you may have a little bleeding. Preliminary results are usually ready in a week, which will give a definite answer for Down's syndrome. A full set of results, after checking all the baby's chromosomes, will normally be available in about three weeks. The rate of miscarriage caused by CVS is 1–2 per cent, slightly higher than amniocentesis, but an advantage for some parents is that it allows an earlier diagnosis.

Amniocentesis

(From 15 weeks)

A tiny sample of the amniotic fluid that surrounds the baby in the womb is taken using a needle guided by ultrasound. There is a 0.5–1 per cent risk of miscarriage as a result of the test. The results usually take about three weeks or more because cells from the sample have to be cultured so that all the baby's chromosomes can be checked.

Some hospitals now offer amnio-QPCR or amnio-FISH. These are special molecular tests (so the cells don't have to be grown) that look at the sample from the amniocentesis and check for the three most common chromosome abnormalities: Down's, Edwards' and Patau's syndromes. The results are usually available within 72 hours but you will probably have to pay to have these special tests. You would still get the full set of results after three weeks, if you do not have the special tests.

Cordocentesis/Fetal blood sampling

In very rare cases, you may be offered this test between 18–20 weeks. A sample of the baby's blood is taken from the umbilical cord or vein. It is only offered in specialist centres. Results take 3 to 4 days. It carries a risk of miscarriage of 1–2 per cent.

Anomaly scan 16–22 weeks

Most hospitals offer a detailed ultrasound scan at between 16 and 22 weeks. This scan will check the structure of your baby and look carefully at his organs, including brain, spine, heart and kidneys and take measurements. It is not 100 per cent guaranteed to spot anything that's wrong with your baby, and some hospitals have better scanning equipment than others. The Royal College of Obstetricians and Gynaecologists (RCOG) is currently setting minimum standards for the anomaly scan and if a hospital cannot meet these, then it will not be allowed to offer the scan.

What next?

It's very common to feel unsure about which tests to accept or ask for. You may find it helpful to talk it through with other parents, your midwife or a counsellor. Think about the advantages and disadvantages, your personal circumstances and how you and your partner feel about possible outcomes.

If a screening test suggests that there is a high risk of your baby having a problem, will you go on to have a diagnostic test and run the small risk that it will cause a miscarriage and then confirm that nothing was wrong?

If a diagnostic test definitely shows that your baby has a problem, would you terminate your pregnancy? Or would you go ahead and have the baby? How would you feel? How would your partner feel?

You should be given time to think through your options. Go home and talk to the important people in your life. Don't be hurried into any decision. A few days will not make any difference. Remember you can always call the NCT (see page 247) or Antenatal Results and Choices (ARC – see page 245).

see also

pregnancy sickness	94–5
early discomforts	96–9
going past your due date	118–19

Test	Advantages	Disadvantages
Blood test	These tests may help you to decide whether to have a diagnostic test.	If you get a high-risk result you will feel anxious. The tests do not identify all affected babies.
Nuchal translucency scan	You find out early about your chance of having a baby with Down's syndrome.	Not widely available. If you get a high-risk result you will feel anxious. The tests do not identify all affected babies.
Ultrasound scan	You don't have to wait for information. Detailed scans by experts give fairly accurate results. Ultrasound is not painful. There is no increased risk of miscarriage. Scans can show if you have more than one baby.	Sometimes ultrasound identifies conditions that are worrying but not significant such as a 'low' placenta or cysts in the baby's brain. However, there are limitations to scans and many malformations will not be detected. There is a risk of false positive findings which could lead to unnecessary anxiety and interventions.
Chorionic villus sampling and amniocentesis	These tests give accurate results about whether the baby is affected by a particular condition. Chorionic villus sampling gives accurate information earlier in pregnancy than amniocentesis. Ending a pregnancy before about 16 weeks does not involve an induced labour.	The procedure can be worrying. You may find it painful. There is an increased risk of miscarriage – about 1 per cent for amniocentesis and 2 per cent for chorionic villus sampling. You may find out that the baby is fine and you still miscarry.

travel in pregnancy

Being pregnant doesn't mean that you need to avoid travelling, unless your midwife or doctor advises you otherwise, though there are some precautions that it's best to take to protect yourself and your baby, whether you are travelling abroad or in the UK.

DON'T FORGET YOUR NOTES!
Wherever you're travelling to, whether it's in the UK or overseas, don't forget to take your maternity notes with you.

For most women, the middle three months of pregnancy are when they feel best, so this may be the best time for travelling if you have a choice, but this doesn't mean that you can't travel at other stages if you want or have to.

Travelling by car

To make sure that both you and your baby are as safe as possible when you're in a car, position your seatbelt so that the lap belt goes under your bump, across your pelvis, and the shoulder belt over the top of your bump, between your breasts (see picture). Don't wear it across your bump. If you are passenger, have your seat as far back as possible. It's OK to drive, or be a passenger in, a car with airbags, but if you're driving, sit so that your breastbone is at least 25cm (10in) away from the centre of the steering wheel.

If you're making a long car journey, stop every hour or two to get out and stretch your legs. If you're not driving, do foot and ankle exercises in your seat – point your toes up and down, circle your ankles and wiggle your toes. This can help stop your feet and ankles swelling. Make sure you drink plenty of water too. This can also help prevent swelling.

Three-point seat belts should be worn whenever you are in a car, with the lap strap placed as low as possible beneath your bump, across your thighs, and the diagonal shoulder strap above the bump, lying between your breasts. The belt should be adjusted to fit as snugly as possible.

Travelling by air

Commercial air travel is generally regarded as being safe in pregnancy, but if you have any complications such as high blood pressure, diabetes or severe anaemia, or have had problems with bleeding, check with your midwife or family doctor before you make your trip.[○] If you're planning to fly (or fly back) after 28 weeks, find out from your airline what their policy is on carrying pregnant passengers. Some airlines require a note from your doctor certifying that you are fit to fly after 28 weeks and most will not carry you after 36 weeks (32 weeks if you're pregnant with more than one baby).

Pregnancy puts you at an increased risk of deep vein thrombosis (DVT), so during your flight, get up and move around the cabin every hour or so, and do foot and ankle exercises while you're seated. If you are seated in an aisle or bulkhead seat, you'll be able to stretch your legs. Drink plenty of water and avoid coffee or alcohol. You'll be more comfortable wearing loose clothing, and, if possible, slip-on shoes. If you're travelling long-haul (a flight of more than three hours), wear flight socks[○] (put them on as soon as you get up on the day you're travelling and keep them on till you go to bed). If there's any history of DVT or other clotting problems in your family, see your midwife or doctor before making a long-haul flight. You might be able to get a prescription for free compression stockings from your midwife. Ask your health professionals about taking a paediatric aspirin (75mg) before any flight.

As in a car, wear your seatbelt under your bump, not across it.

Overseas travel tips

- If you're travelling abroad, check your travel insurance to see what cover it provides for pregnancy-related incidents. If you're going to a country within the EU, an E111 form will entitle you to the same level of medical care that is given to citizens of the country you're visiting.

- Follow the usual precautions about food and drink. Drink bottled water if you're unsure about the quality of the tap water in the area you're visiting and avoid ice in your drinks. Make sure you drink lots of water if you're going somewhere hot.

- Check if any vaccinations are required for the area you're going to. Not all vaccinations can be given during pregnancy. The practice nurse at your GP's surgery will be able to give you information about this. It's best to avoid going to an area where malaria is a problem, as pregnant women are especially vulnerable to malaria and catching this disease in pregnancy can have serious consequences. If you are travelling to somewhere where there is malaria, check with the practice nurse which prophylaxis tablets are advised for that area and whether they are safe to take whilst pregnant – as not all can be taken during pregnancy.

- Take a first aid kit with you – remembering to include any remedies you're taking for any pregnancy complaints.

healthy eating

With fresh food plentiful all year round, eating well has never been easier. This is good because it's one of the best things you can do for the future health of your baby and yourself. A nutritious, balanced diet is vitally important during pregnancy.

IRON LEVELS

Iron is needed by you and your baby, who builds up a supply in the liver to last until after birth. Iron is contained in haemoglobin, which carries oxygen round your body in red blood cells. During pregnancy, fluid levels increase which 'dilutes' the red blood cells. In the past, this was seen as iron deficiency. However, research shows that the increase in red blood cells does meet the mother and baby's increased need for oxygen. There is therefore no need for routine iron supplements in pregnancy if you have (and have had) a good intake of iron-rich foods such as red meat, sardines, wholemeal bread, baked beans and green, leafy vegetables (see chart).

Think carefully about what you eat during your pregnancy, because all the nutrients in your diet pass to your baby via the placenta. A healthy diet is made up of starchy carbohydrates, fruit and vegetables, protein foods, dairy foods, and (small amounts of) fats and sugar.

Starchy carbohydrates are things like cereals, bread, potatoes, pasta, rice. They give you energy, as well as containing vitamins, minerals, protein and fibre. They're also filling and not expensive. Aim for five or six servings of carbohydrates a day (a serving would be a bowl of cereal, two slices of bread, a couple of potatoes, or three tablespoonsful of cooked rice or pasta).

All of us, pregnant or not, should eat five portions of fruit and vegetables a day, but this is particularly important in pregnancy. Fruit and vegetables contain essential vitamins and minerals, as well as carbohydrates and fibre.

Protein is needed to maintain our bodies and for the growth of new cells. Your baby needs protein in order to grow and develop. Protein is found in meat, fish, pulses (dried beans, lentils, chickpeas), eggs, nuts and seeds. These foods also contain certain vitamins and minerals. During pregnancy, you need two or three servings of protein foods a day (a serving would be a couple of slices of lean meat or a small chop, a piece of fish, two eggs, or three or four tablespoonsful of beans).

Dairy foods (milk, cheese, yoghurt) are another source of protein and are high in calcium. Calcium is needed for the growth of your baby's bones and teeth. Dairy foods also contain vitamins. Aim to have two or three servings of dairy foods a day (e.g a glass of milk, a small yoghurt). Low-fat dairy foods provide just as much calcium and protein as higher-fat versions. (See page 92 for dairy products to avoid.)

Fats occur in a lot of foods, such as meat, oily fish, dairy foods, nuts and vegetable oils, and they contain important nutrients. However, it's best not to eat too much fat. You can reduce the amount of fat in your diet by cutting the fat off meat and the skin off poultry, grilling rather than frying, making sandwiches without butter or margarine, and cutting down on foods like pies, sausages, cakes and biscuits, and crisps.

Sugar is a source of energy, but unlike other energy sources, such as starchy food or fruit, it doesn't provide any vitamins or minerals, so it has

Vitamins and minerals

Vitamins and minerals are needed for your own health as well as for your baby's healthy growth and development.

Which vitamin/mineral	What it's needed for	What it's found in
Folic acid	The development of your baby's nervous system; and for healthy blood.	Green leafy vegetables, other vegetables (green beans, cauliflower, potatoes), fortified breakfast cereals and bread, pulses, baked beans, citrus fruits. Folic acid is destroyed by cooking, so cook vegetables lightly.
Calcium	The development of your baby's bones and teeth.	Dairy products (but not butter), tinned salmon and sardines, fortified soya products, spinach and spring greens, chick peas and kidney beans, sesame seeds, almonds and brazil nuts, white flour products.
Iron	Healthy blood for you and your baby, and your baby's growth and development.	Red meat, sardines, breakfast cereals, wholemeal bread, green leafy vegetables, pulses, dried fruit, nuts. Vitamin C helps your body to absorb iron. Drinking tea or coffee with, or immediately after, meals impairs iron absorption.
Vitamin C	Helps your body to absorb iron and keeps your immune system healthy.	Most fruits and vegetables, especially citrus fruits, kiwi fruit and blackcurrants. Prolonged cooking and storing destroys vitamin C, so eat fruit and vegetables raw or lightly cooked and as fresh as possible.
Vitamin B12	For cell growth, especially blood cells, and nervous system.	Meat, fish, eggs, milk, fortified breakfast cereals and yeast extracts.
Vitamin D	Helps your body to absorb calcium for strong bones and teeth.	Sunshine. Oily fish, fish oil, fortified margarine, milk, eggs, fortified cereals.
Omega-3 essential fatty acids	For the development of your baby's brain and nervous system.	Oily fish, fish oil, flaxseed, walnuts, eggs.

Your fluid needs are increased during pregnancy, so you should try and drink at least 2 litres of fluid a day. Water is best. You can also drink fruit juice – though remember that this contains sugar – but it's best to limit the amount of cola drinks you have, especially if these contain caffeine.

little nutritional value (and can lead to tooth decay and weight gain). This doesn't mean that you need to avoid all sweet foods, but it's best not to be eating them frequently or in large amounts. Processed foods (e.g canned and packet foods) tend to be high in sugar, so it's best to eat fresh food whenever you can.

A healthy diet is also a varied diet. By eating different combinations of foods each day, you'll ensure that you get all the nutrients you and your developing baby need.

Taking supplements

The only vitamin supplements that it's officially recommended that you take are folic acid and, for some women, vitamin D. Women are advised to take 400 mcg of folic acid a day while trying to conceive and for the first 12 weeks of pregnancy. Folic acid is important for the development of your baby's nervous system, and taking a supplement in this way has been shown to protect against neural tube defects.

A balanced diet, as described above, will meet all of your nutritional needs and your baby's. However, while this is the ideal, sometimes it's not possible to eat as healthily as you would like – if you're suffering from nausea or heartburn, for example, or are otherwise unwell, or you simply don't like certain types of foods that contain important nutrients. In this case, taking a special pregnancy multivitamin might be helpful. If you're concerned that your diet might not be adequate, speak to your midwife or GP about whether some kind of supplement would be a good idea for you.

Eating safely

While you're pregnant, your immune system functions at a slightly lower level, which means that you may be more vulnerable to food-borne infections, which can affect you or your baby. There are also certain foods that can be harmful to your baby in other ways.

Infection risks from food

The two main food-borne infections that pose a risk in pregnancy are listeriosis and toxoplasmosis. Listeriosis, caused by the listeria bacteria, causes a mild flu-like illness in the mother, but can lead to miscarriage or stillbirth, or to the baby being severely ill at birth. Toxoplasmosis is caused by the toxoplasma parasite. It can also cause mild flu-like symptoms in the mother, though it may cause no symptoms at all, but can cause serious problems for the baby, especially if the mother develops it during the first six months of pregnancy. Both listeriosis and toxoplasmosis are very rare, however. See table overleaf on how to avoid them.

Another infection that you may be vulnerable to during pregnancy is salmonella, which causes food poisoning. This doesn't affect the baby, but can make you quite unwell.

Eating a lot of fresh fruit and vegetables is important because these foods are full of vitamins and minerals as well as antioxidants – chemicals that protect our bodies against heart disease, cancer and the effects of pollution.

Other food-related risks

High intakes of the animal form of vitamin A (retinol) have been found to be associated with birth defects in the baby. It's therefore best to avoid foods containing large amounts of this, particularly liver and liver products. There are no risks associated with eating the plant form of vitamin A (betacarotene), which is found in carrots and other orange or red vegetables and fruit.

Taking in high levels of mercury can affect the development of the baby's nervous system. High levels of mercury are found in certain fish, and it's advised that you avoid these during pregnancy (see table overleaf).

Harmful substances

If drinking and smoking were part of your lifestyle before you were pregnant, you should reconsider these now. Both alcohol and nicotine cross the placenta, and may affect your baby.

There are differences of opinion amongst experts on how much, if any alcohol, it's 'safe' to drink during pregnancy. The broad consensus among medical professional organizations is that you shouldn't drink more than one

PEANUTS

If you or your partner's family has a history of asthma, eczema, hayfever or other allergies, then you are advised to avoid eating peanuts or peanut products during pregnancy (and while breastfeeding). It's thought that this may help to reduce the risk of your baby developing allergies. This advice doesn't extend to other types of nuts.

What you can eat and what to avoid

It's OK to eat	It's best to avoid	Why
Hard cheeses, such as cheddar, parmesan, mozzarella, Gruyere (even if these are made from unpasteurized milk), and soft processed cheeses, like cottage cheese, cream cheese and cheese spread	Ripened soft cheeses, such as Brie and Camembert, and blue-veined cheeses (even if they're made with pasteurized milk). They can be eaten if they've been thoroughly cooked, though. Avoid cheese from unpasteurized sheep or goat's milk.	Risk of listeria
Yoghurt, fromage frais (including bio products)		
Pasteurized, sterilized and UHT milk	'Green top' milk and unpasteurized sheep and goat's milk, unless it's been boiled for at least two minutes.	Risk of listeria or contamination with toxoplasma parasite
Ice cream in cartons	Home-made ice cream or soft whipped ice cream from machines.	Risk of listeria
Meat and poultry that have been thoroughly cooked all the way through	Raw or undercooked meat. Ready-cooked poultry unless thoroughly reheated.	Risk of toxoplasmosis or salmonella Risk of listeria
Cooked ham	Raw cured meat (e.g Parma ham, salami).	Risk of toxoplasmosis

or two units once or twice a week.⊙ A 'unit' is half a pint of ordinary strength beer or cider, a pub measure of spirits or a small glass of wine. However, there have not been enough in-depth studies to be conclusive about the effects of alcohol. Because it is a poison, and does cross the placenta, some women choose to avoid alcohol altogether, as the only way of being 100 per cent certain that their baby is safe from its effects. The risks associated with alcohol are increased if you smoke, or if your diet is poor. And if you're small, a unit of alcohol is likely to have more effect on you and your baby than it does on larger women.

Smoking is known to be potentially harmful to unborn babies. It can affect their growth, make their heart beat faster, and put them at risk of being premature or affected by cot death after they're born. If you're a smoker, stopping is one of the best things you can do for your baby's health,

What you can eat and what to avoid

It's OK to eat	It's best to avoid	Why
	Paté (meat, fish or vegetable) unless it's tinned or marked pasteurized.	Risk of listeria – plus high levels of vitamin A
	Liver and liver products.	High levels of vitamin A
White fish, such as cod, plaice, haddock Oily fish like salmon and mackerel	Shark, swordfish and marlin. Limit your consumption of tuna to one fresh steak or two cans a week.	High levels of mercury
Cooked shellfish	Raw or undercooked shellfish.	Risk of bacteria that can cause food poisoning
Eggs cooked so that the white and yolk are solid. Commercially prepared mayonnaise and salad cream	Raw or runny eggs. Mousses made with raw egg. Mayonnaise made with raw egg.	Risk of salmonella
Washed salads	Packaged salads unless you wash them first. Ready-prepared dressed salads like coleslaw or potato salad.	Risk of toxoplasmosis Risk of listeria
Cooked-chilled foods that have been thoroughly heated through	Unheated cooked-chilled foods.	Risk of listeria

as well as your own. If you're finding it difficult to stop, speak to your midwife or GP about the support available to help you give up.

Another harmful substance that can affect your baby is caffeine. Too much may be associated with an increased risk of miscarriage, as well as of the baby not growing properly. The government advises that you limit intake to not more than 300mg a day.[⊙] A cup of instant coffee contains 75mg, a cup of brewed coffee 100mg, a cup of tea 50mg, a can of cola 40mg, a can of 'energy' drink up to 80mg and a 50g bar of chocolate up to 50mg.

Babies can also be affected if their mums use recreational drugs, such as cannabis, cocaine or heroin, during pregnancy. If you're a user of these drugs, you may find it hard to stop and also hard to talk about, but your midwife won't be judgemental, so do tell her. She'll be able to put you in touch with specialist help to give up.

pregnancy sickness

One of the earliest signs of pregnancy can be an odd, metallic taste in the mouth and sometimes a sudden aversion to tea and coffee. Nausea and, perhaps, vomiting tend to start in the second month, but most women feel a lot better after about 12 weeks.

'First time around I was nauseous and very sensitive to smells, and ginger worked like a charm. Second-time around I was sick until 28 weeks and couldn't stand the sight of ginger – nothing worked.'

As many as 70 to 80 per cent of women experience sickness of some kind, ranging from feeling slightly nauseous to vomiting several times a day, in the early weeks of pregnancy. Sickness can start even before you miss a period, though it's more common for it to begin in the second month. It usually passes after around three months, but for some women it lasts into the fourth and fifth month, and for an unfortunate few it persists throughout pregnancy. Some women find that it passes after the first three months only to return towards the end of pregnancy. Pregnancy sickness is often referred to as 'morning sickness', but it can occur at any time of the day.

What causes it?

What causes pregnancy sickness isn't yet fully understood. It may be due to a combination of factors. In part, it may be a reaction to the hormone human chorionic gonadotrophin (HCG) circulating in your body. Levels of this hormone start to tail off at around 12 weeks, which may be why nausea often improves after then. Sickness may also be a reaction to increasing levels of another hormone, oestrogen, which continue to rise throughout pregnancy. Tiredness, which is very common in pregnancy, especially in the early weeks, may contribute to sickness too, as may low blood sugar and low blood pressure. Some experts think that sickness may also be associated with stress and/or anxiety.

Although it's unpleasant, there's a theory that nausea is a way of protecting your baby from harmful substances, and some research has also suggested that it's linked to a lower risk of miscarriage.[⊙] In fact there is an association between nausea and vomiting in early pregnancy and favourable birth outcome. The research also shows a link with increased placental weight to support this theory.[⊙]

Not all women experience sickness, though, and if you don't, it's unlikely to mean that there's any problem with your pregnancy. It's also possible for sickness to fluctuate, being worse some days than others.

The main thing to remember is that normal pregnancy sickness will not harm your baby. Even if you are eating very little, drinking only water and vomiting several times a day, your baby will continue to develop and grow.

What might help

There are various strategies different women have found to help with pregnancy sickness. There have been few in-depth studies however, so the research evidence on their effectiveness is limited.

- Eating frequent small snacks (every two or three hours).
- Avoiding rich, fatty or spicy foods.
- Eating bland foods, like crackers, bread, cereals, home-made popcorn.
- Eating fruit.
- Eating or drinking things made from ginger, such as ginger biscuits, crystallized ginger, ginger ale.
- Sucking or sniffing a cut lemon.
- Sucking peppermints.
- Drinking plenty of water or fruit juice.
- Drinking herbal tea, such as lemon and ginger or peppermint.
- If you feel sick first thing in the morning, try having a dry biscuit or cracker, and a cup of tea, before you get up.
- Taking a vitamin B6 supplement. Ask your midwife or GP about this. Foods that contain vitamin B6 include bananas, potatoes, avocados, brown rice, wholegrains, nuts, fish, lean meat and poultry.
- Wearing sea sickness bands.
- Listening to a special audio tape which is said to interrupt the signals between the gut and the brain that lead to sickness (this is available from NCT Maternity Sales – see page 247).
- Resting as much as possible.
- Acupuncture or acupressure helps some women.
- Reflexologists offer treatment for sickness.
- There are various homeopathic remedies for sickness. Consult a homeopath to find out which would be the most suitable for you.
- Herbal remedies, such as slippery elm, help some women, but it's best to consult a herbalist about these.
- Some women find hypnotherapy helpful.

If you're feeling sick, it can sometimes be difficult to eat even small amounts. Or it may be that the only thing you can stomach is something that's not 'healthy'. Some women worry that if they're not eating well, this will be harmful for their baby. However, while it's always best to eat a good, balanced diet during pregnancy, if you can't do this in the early weeks because of sickness, don't worry. Babies are very good at ensuring that their needs are met and your body will have stores of nutrients that your baby can draw on.

If you're being so sick that you're finding it impossible to keep anything down, though, do see your GP. Severe sickness (or *hyperemesis gravidarum*) affects about 1 per cent of women, and if not treated can lead to dehydration and malnourishment. Contact the Hyperemesis Gravidarum Support Group for support and information on this condition (see page 245).

Experiment with herbal teas – anise, fennel, meadowsweet, spearmint or peppermint have all been recommended for sickness.

early discomforts

Growing a baby involves your whole body and it's hardly surprising that the changes that occur in early pregnancy can result in a range of minor physical discomforts. But there are things that you can do to help ease them and reduce their effects.

When you are pregnant, all the systems in your body are working harder than usual to meet you and your baby's needs. The hormones that you produce during pregnancy circulate all over your body and affect how it works as a whole. This can lead to various minor discomforts and ailments. They're minor in the sense that they don't – mostly – put you or your baby at any risk, though they may not feel minor in terms of how uncomfortable they can make you feel.

Breast tenderness

Breast tenderness can be one of the first symptoms of pregnancy, especially if you're pregnant for the first time, and can occur even before you've missed a period. Your breasts become enlarged and may throb and feel painful. This is due to the hormones oestrogen and progesterone preparing them for breastfeeding – blood flow to them is increasing and milk-producing cells are growing.

Wearing a good supporting bra should help to make you feel more comfortable. Make sure that your bras fit you properly and aren't too tight. Your bra size may go up several times. If your breasts feel hot, put a cold flannel on them. Massaging your breasts gently can also help. Some women find that avoiding caffeine (found in coffee, tea, cola, 'energy' drinks) helps too.

Tiredness

Tiredness is a very common experience in early pregnancy. It's thought to be partly due to the sedative effects of pregnancy hormones, but it also occurs because your body is working very hard to support your developing baby. There isn't a great deal that you can do about tiredness, other than resting as much as possible, which isn't always easy. Eating frequent small meals may help to keep your energy levels up. Extreme tiredness does usually pass after the first three months.

Constipation and bloating

One of the effects of pregnancy hormones is to soften your muscles, including those of your bowels. This can make your bowels sluggish, leading to constipation, bloating and wind. If you're prescribed an iron supplement at any point in your pregnancy, this can cause constipation too.

To help with constipation, eat lots of fibre, fruit and vegetables – though note that cabbage-type vegetables, as well as beans, lentils and eggs, sometimes make bloating and wind worse. Try sprinkling linseed, available from health food shops, on your breakfast cereal or drink a teaspoon of olive oil. Drink plenty of water, fruit juice (especially orange or prune juice) or herbal tea (normal tea sometimes makes constipation worse). Take regular exercise (e.g walking, swimming). Some yoga positions can also help with constipation. Get someone to massage your tummy in a clockwise direction from your belly button. And when you are opening your bowels, relax and avoid straining.

Headaches

Headaches can be caused by a widening of the blood vessels in your brain, under the influence of pregnancy hormones, and by the extra blood that you have in your circulation putting pressure on blood vessels. Other possible causes are your blood sugar levels being low, not drinking enough fluids, and swelling in your sinuses. Anxiety and tension can lead to headaches too.

You may be able to help prevent headaches by drinking lots of water and avoiding caffeine, and by not going too long without having something to eat. Try and make time to relax each day too. If you have a headache, massaging your scalp with your fingers (as if you were washing your hair), or getting someone to massage your shoulders, might help. Getting some fresh air can help too.

Bleeding gums

The softening effects of pregnancy hormones and the increased amount of blood that you have can combine to make your gums soft and spongy, and prone to bleeding. Because of this sponginess, bits of food may get trapped in your gums, which can cause infection. Severe gum infection may cause problems with your pregnancy as the infection can travel around your body and may affect your baby. Brush your teeth gently twice a day with a soft toothbrush, paying particular attention to your gum-line, and floss every day. Eat plenty of fruit and vegetables (for their vitamin C content) and avoid sugary foods. Make sure you visit your dentist if you are worried about your teeth or gums. You qualify for free dental care on the NHS during pregnancy and for the first year after birth.

Stuffy or bleeding nose

The softening effects of pregnancy hormones and your increased blood volume can also make the lining of your nose and your sinuses soft and spongy. This can make your nose feel blocked up, or cause nosebleeds. The

THE ROLE OF HORMONES

The initial classic signs of pregnancy such as a missed period and sensitive breasts are caused by alterations in hormone secretion. One hormone involved is human chorionic gonadotrophin (HCG) which may be partly responsible for the nausea and vomiting many women experience in the first few months because it affects appetite and the laying down of fat. It also affects thirst and promotes the growth of the muscle layer of the womb. In addition, it suppresses your immune system so that your body will not reject the baby. Human chorionic gonadotrophin reaches a maximum level by around 12 weeks of pregnancy and then drops for the rest of pregnancy, which may be why many women feel less sick after this time.

increased blood supply to your nose can also lead to you producing more mucus, which can make your nose run.

Be gentle with your nose, and don't blow it too hard. If your nose is stuffy, try steam inhalation. Don't take any decongestants without medical advice. If you have a nosebleed, pinch the sides of your nose gently and lean forward slightly.

Dizziness

It's quite common to have dizzy spells in pregnancy. There are two main causes of this. One is your blood pressure being low. This happens because pregnancy hormones make your blood vessels dilate, which can slow the flow of blood to your brain. This can occur particularly if you stand for too long or get up too quickly. The other cause of feeling faint, especially if it comes on more gradually, is due to your blood sugar levels getting too low.

To try and prevent dizziness, avoid standing for long periods of time, and get up slowly from sitting or lying down. Eat small regular snacks to keep your blood sugar up. If you feel faint, sit down with your head between your knees, and breathe deeply.

Thrush

Thrush is a thick white vaginal discharge, which often causes redness and itching around the vagina. It's caused by a fungus, which normally lives in the vagina without producing any symptoms. During pregnancy, however, the acid–alkali balance of the vagina changes, creating conditions that make it possible for the fungus to overgrow, leading to thrush.

Thrush likes sugar, so avoiding sugary foods might help to prevent it or to get rid of it. Eating live yoghurt can also help as this contains organisms that destroy thrush. Because thrush flourishes in a warm, moist environment, wear loose cotton knickers and avoid wearing anything that's tight around your crotch. Use a clean towel every day and wash your genital area with your hand rather than a flannel, to prevent thrush from spreading. Contact your GP if symptoms persist and your doctor may prescribe an antifungal pessary for you and a cream for your partner.

Urinary complaints

Needing to urinate frequently is a common symptom in the first three months of pregnancy. This is due to pressure on your bladder as your womb starts to enlarge. Also, the increased blood supply to your pelvic area can make your bladder feel full so that you need to empty it more frequently. It also makes you produce more urine.

Another urinary complaint that pregnant women are susceptible to is cystitis (a urine infection). Pregnancy hormones make your bladder softer, so it may not empty so efficiently, and if the bladder isn't emptied properly, bacteria in the urine that's left behind can multiply, causing infection. Symptoms of cystitis include wanting to pass urine frequently, but only producing a small amount, and burning or stinging when you urinate. Drinking lots of water and cranberry juice can help to flush bacteria out of your system, but if your symptoms persist, contact your GP.

For information on bleeding and abdominal pain in early pregnancy, see pregnancy at risk pages 104–7.

Allergies

If you suffer from allergic reactions, you may find that they get worse while you're pregnant. Some women even find that they develop allergies for the first time during pregnancy. This is because your body's immune system has to get weaker so that it doesn't reject your baby – since half the baby's genetic make up is the father's, not yours. If you're already taking medication for an allergy, check with your midwife or doctor that it's safe to use in pregnancy. Eating healthily can help reduce the risk of allergies making your life a misery.

Cravings

The desire to eat certain foods can strike early on in pregnancy. In fact, strong dislikes or cravings for specific tastes may be the first clue that you are pregnant. You can probably expect to go off drinks containing caffeine. If weight is a problem, try to fight that longing for ice cream or chips. 'Pica' – strong cravings for unlikely things like soap or coal – could probably be mentioned to your midwife, but they are rarely a problem.

Weight gain

Weight gain in pregnancy varies from woman to woman. It averages around 10kg to 12kg (22lb to 26lb), but women having perfectly normal pregnancies can put on a lot more or a lot less than this. Many midwives and doctors feel that there isn't anything to be gained from routinely weighing women at their antenatal appointments.

In the early weeks of pregnancy, the baby weighs very little, but you may put on weight as your body starts to lay down fat, your breasts get bigger, your blood supply increases and you retain fluid (after the birth, the most rapid weight loss occurs in the first few days as the extra 2 to 8 litres of water that you're carrying by the end of pregnancy is passed out in the urine). As your pregnancy progresses, the placenta and amniotic fluid also contribute to weight gain.

On the other hand, you may find that in the first three months you actually lose some weight – perhaps due to sickness, perhaps because you've started eating more healthily and are consuming fewer 'empty' calories, or perhaps because your metabolism has speeded up. If this happens, it won't harm your baby – he'll still be getting what he needs from you.

COMPLEMENTARY THERAPIES

If you want to try complementary therapies to help with pregnancy discomforts, it's always best to consult a qualified practitioner.

- Acupuncturists offer treatment for constipation, headaches and cystitis.
- There are homeopathic remedies for constipation, headaches, bleeding gums, thrush, cystitis.
- Herbal remedies exist for constipation, headaches, thrush and cystitis.
- Aromatherapists use essential oils to treat constipation, headaches, stuffy nose, thrush and cystitis although some advise against using them in the first three months of pregnancy.
- Reflexologists treat constipation, headaches, stuffy nose and cystitis. Some reflexologists will not offer treatment in the first 12 weeks of pregnancy, however, especially if you've had a previous miscarriage.
- Osteopathy provides treatment that may help constipation and headaches and back pain.

later discomforts

By the time you reach the second trimester, some – though not all – of the complaints you may have had in the early months will probably have disappeared. However, from the second half of pregnancy, as your body continues to change to meet your baby's needs, you may develop some new discomforts.

After the first three months of pregnancy, your uterus will rise up out of your pelvis into your abdomen where, as it gets bigger, it will take up space that was previously occupied by other organs. As your baby grows and your body grows to accommodate him, so you may develop other discomforts. By the time your due date approaches, you may well be feeling cumbersome and uncomfortable – and more than ready for your baby to arrive.

Heartburn

The symptoms of heartburn are a burning feeling in your chest and throat, sometimes accompanied by nausea. It happens because pregnancy hormones relax the muscle at the entrance to your stomach, allowing stomach juices to back up into your gullet. During the last 10 weeks or so, pressure on your stomach from your growing uterus contributes to it too. Heartburn tends to be worst when you're sitting or lying down.

Eating little and often, and avoiding rich, spicy or greasy foods, can help relieve heartburn. Some women find drinking milk, fizzy water or peppermint or fennel tea helps too. Allow at least two hours after eating before you go to bed and sleep slightly propped up. Some yoga positions may help alleviate heartburn.

Varicose veins

Pregnancy hormones soften the walls and valves of your veins, which can result in blood pooling in your legs. This can lead to swollen, itchy and painful varicose veins in your legs.

Help keep your circulation going by avoiding standing for long periods, and try to exercise regularly (yoga is good for your circulation and may help with varicose veins). Don't cross your legs when you're sitting down. Put your feet up whenever you can. Raising the foot of your bed by 10cm or so might also help. Don't wear clothing that's tight round your knees or crotch. Wearing compression stockings helps to prevent your blood from pooling (you may be able to get a prescription for these).

Using a shower attachment to spray your legs alternately with hot and cold water, or putting your feet alternately into buckets of hot and cold

Some women find that drinking fizzy water can help to relieve heartburn. It's always a good idea to drink water because its important to keep your body hydrated.

water, might help to relieve the discomfort of varicose veins. The symptoms should disappear once you've had your baby.

Piles

Piles are varicose veins in your back passage that tend to get worse as pregnancy progresses. Their symptoms include itching, soreness, pain when you open your bowels and sometimes a small amount of red bleeding afterwards.

Doing pelvic floor exercises can help to keep blood flowing through the area. Putting a cold compress or a sanitary towel soaked in witch hazel against your back passage may help to shrink the piles. You can also buy gel-filled pads that you cool in the fridge to use in the same way (these are available from NCT Maternity Sales – see page 247). Avoid constipation by eating plenty of fibre and drinking lots of water.

Itchy skin

Hormonal changes and your skin stretching can lead to your skin being itchy, especially on your belly. Wearing loose cotton clothing can help to reduce itching. Moisturizing your skin or applying calamine cream or lotion may help too. You can also try putting a cupful of bicarbonate of soda in your bath, or tying a handful of oatmeal in a muslin square and letting the water run through it as you fill the bath, or washing yourself with it.

See page 107 for circumstances in which itching may be a sign of something more serious.

Cramp

Many women experience painful cramps in their legs in the last 10 weeks of pregnancy, especially at night. What causes this isn't really known, although there are various theories about it. They haven't been shown to be connected with any deficiencies. Doing foot and leg exercises for 10 minutes or so before you go to bed (rotate your ankles and legs, and point your toes upwards) may help to prevent cramps occurring.

If you get cramp, flex your foot upwards, or lean forewards against a wall with the cramped leg stretched out behind you and your foot flat on the floor. Relaxing may help the cramp to pass more quickly.

The pain associated with cramp usually passes in a few minutes. If you have longer lasting pain in either of your calves, especially if there's also any redness or swelling, see your doctor as soon as you can. Leg pain can be associated with a blood clot having developed in one of your veins.

Swelling

Your body retains extra fluid during pregnancy to soften your joints so that they can make space for your baby. Some of this fluid may collect in your feet and hands, causing swelling. This tends to be worse if you've been standing for a long time, or if the weather is hot.

Avoid standing for long periods, especially when it's hot and rest with your feet up as much as you can. Don't wear clothes that are tight around your ankles or wrists. Wearing support tights or stockings can help reduce swelling. If your feet are swollen, massage your legs firmly upwards from your ankles, using both hands, or apply dark green cabbage leaves, cooled in the fridge, to your feet. Spraying your legs alternately with hot and cold water, or putting your feet alternately into buckets of hot and cold water, might help reduce swelling too. Drink plenty of fluids (some women find nettle tea helpful). There are also some yoga positions that can help with swelling.

See pregnancy at risk pages 104–7 for circumstances in which swelling may be a cause for concern.

Carpal tunnel syndrome

If fluid collects in your hands, this can put pressure on the median nerve that passes through the carpal tunnel in your wrist, causing 'carpal tunnel syndrome'. The symptoms of this are numbness, tingling and pain in your hands and fingers, and occasionally your arm, sometimes making it difficult even to do simple things like holding a pen. Tell your midwife who should be able to get you a special wrist support. Or you can try the following exercises. Hold your fingers stretched out, then relax them. Make a fist, then straighten out your fingers. Move your hands up and down, from side to side and round and round (you can do this in cold water). Flick your wrists. Press your hands down on a flat surface, then turn them over so that the backs of your hands are pressing down. You can also try putting your hands alternately in bowls of cold and warm water. Keep your hands raised as much as possible – put them up on a pillow when you're resting.

Symphysis pubis dysfunction (SPD)

SPD is a loosening of the joints of the pelvis – the pubic symphysis joint which is low down at the front and the two sacro-iliac joints which are at the back, where the pelvis joins the spine. It causes, sometimes severe, pain in your pelvis, particularly at the front. If you are experiencing pain in the pelvis, tell your midwife. Pain from SPD tends to be worse when you do anything that involves the two sides of your pelvis moving against each other, such as going up and down stairs or getting in and out of bed. In severe cases, it can seriously affect your mobility, and crutches, or even a wheelchair, might be needed.

Minimize pain from SPD by keeping your knees as close together as possible. Walk with small steps, go up stairs one at a time, and when you get into bed, a car or the bath, sit with your knees together and swing your legs round. Avoid standing still for too long and rest as much as possible. Place a cold pack (wrapped in a towel) on your pubic joint. Make an appointment to see your midwife or doctor: wearing a special pelvic support often helps and your midwife or GP can provide you with one.

Anaemia

Your baby's need for iron increase in later pregnancy, and this can lead to you becoming anaemic. Symptoms of anaemia are looking pale, feeling tired, and sometimes feeling dizzy and breathless. You can boost your iron intake through your diet (sources of iron include red meat, dark chicken or turkey meat, fortified breakfast cereals, sardines, wholemeal bread, pulses, egg yolks, green leafy vegetables, cashews or dried apricots) or by taking a liquid iron supplement, available at health food shops. If your symptoms persist, though, inform your midwife or GP.

Stress incontinence

Stress incontinence is the technical term for the leaking of urine that can happen when you do something like cough or sneeze or lift something. It happens as a result of pressure on your pelvic floor from the weight of your baby and your enlarged uterus. The best way of preventing – or reducing – it is by doing pelvic floor exercises. Emptying your bladder frequently so that there's less to leak out can help, too.

COMPLEMENTARY THERAPIES

If you want to try complementary therapies to help with pregnancy discomforts, it's always best to consult a qualified practitioner.

- Acupuncturists offer treatment for heartburn, varicose veins, piles, swelling, carpal tunnel syndrome, SPD and anaemia.
- There are homeopathic remedies for heartburn, varicose veins, piles, cramp, fluid retention and anaemia.
- Herbal remedies exist for heartburn, varicose veins, piles and anaemia.
- Aromatherapists use essential oils to treat heartburn, varicose veins, piles and swelling.
- Reflexologists treat heartburn, varicose veins, piles and swelling
- Osteopaths and chiropractors manipulate your joints to help ease SPD. Osteopaths also treat heartburn, swelling and carpal tunnel syndrome.

---

see also

caring for your pelvic floor	78–9
pregnancy at risk	104–7
best baby positions for birth	114–17

pregnancy at risk

The vast majority of pregnancies are completely straightforward. Yet many women will find that something happens during the nine months that causes them anxiety. While it's really important to enjoy your pregnancy as much as you can, it's also a good idea to know the warning signs that mean you need to consult your midwife or doctor.

BEFORE 20 WEEKS

Symptom Watch: Bleeding

- a small amount: probably OK
- a heavy loss: could mean a miscarriage (see right)
- passing clots: also likely to mean a miscarriage
- dark brown, watery bleeding: may mean an ectopic pregnancy (see below).

AFTER 20 WEEKS

Symptom Watch: Bleeding

- slight bleeding at the end of pregnancy may indicate that labour is starting

otherwise

- any bleeding should be reported to your midwife.

Miscarriage

It's quite common to lose some stale brown blood or even a little bright red blood in the first 14 weeks of pregnancy. You can consult your midwife or GP about it, but provided you have no other symptoms, you will probably be reassured that, in all likelihood, the bleeding will stop quickly and there will be no more.

A heavy loss of blood, particularly if you are passing clots and have low backache, could mean a miscarriage. Sadly, about a quarter of confirmed pregnancies end this way. Often the miscarriage is because there is something wrong with the baby. Some women want to consult their midwife if they think they are having a miscarriage, and others prefer to cope on their own.

Occasionally, the baby dies in the womb, but isn't expelled from the body. You may feel that 'something isn't right' and 'less pregnant' than you did before. This is called a 'missed miscarriage' and can only be confirmed on a scan. You may prefer to wait for the miscarriage to complete itself naturally, or you may choose to have a minor operation (called a D&C – dilation and curretage) to empty your womb.

Following a miscarriage, your body will probably return to normal in four to six weeks, but your emotions may take much longer to heal. Some women seem to take miscarriage in their stride while for others, it is a bereavement that stays with them for a long time.

If you are having difficulty dealing with your loss, find someone to talk to who will understand, perhaps a friend who has experienced miscarriage. Or you could contact the NCT or the Miscarriage Association and they will put you in touch with someone who will listen sympathetically to you.

Ectopic pregnancy

An ectopic pregnancy is when the fertilized egg implants somewhere other than in the womb – most commonly in the Fallopian tube, but occasionally in the ovary or on the outside of the womb.

If the egg implants in the Fallopian tube, the tube will be stretched as the embryo grows. This can cause severe pain on one side of the abdomen and shoulder pain is also common. Serious internal bleeding takes place if the tube bursts and the situation then becomes a medical emergency.

If you think you have signs of an ectopic pregnancy, you should consult your midwife or GP straight away. Don't hesitate. The pregnancy will need to be removed surgically and possibly the Fallopian tube, although this isn't always necessary.

An ectopic pregnancy is very frightening, and you may worry about your chances of having another baby, especially if you have lost a tube. Get as much information as you can from the hospital, and find someone to support you. The Ectopic Pregnancy Trust and the Miscarriage Association help women who have had ectopic pregnancies, and your local NCT teacher may know of someone in your area who has been through the experience and will be very happy to talk to you.

Placenta praevia

This is the medical term for a placenta which has implanted low down in the uterus so that it partly or completely covers the cervix. In the first half of pregnancy, before the womb has become very large, it is quite usual for the placenta to be close to or over the cervix. However, by about 32 weeks of pregnancy, 99 per cent of placentas have moved well away from the cervix as the womb has stretched and only one per cent still cause a problem.

A minor degree of placenta praevia, when the placenta is just at the edge of the cervix, is unlikely to cause any problems either during pregnancy or at the birth. However, you will be offered regular checks and scans to ensure that all is well.

If the placenta covers the cervix, this can lead to serious bleeding during pregnancy and it is impossible for your baby to be born vaginally. The bleeding associated with placenta praevia is bright red and painless, and can be very heavy. It generally stops and then starts again, perhaps heavier than before. If you have a bleed, you might be admitted to hospital for the rest of your pregnancy, or you might be able to go home if you are not too far away from the hospital. You will have to take it very easy and avoid sex until your baby is born by caesarean section.

Pre-eclampsia

It is thought that this disease starts right at the very beginning of pregnancy when the placenta is in the early stages of development. However, it's un- usual for signs to appear before 30 weeks. The main symptom is high blood pressure, accompanied by protein in the urine and sometimes, swelling of the face, hands, or feet. About five per cent of women having their first babies develop pre-eclampsia. It sometimes runs in families.

Having very high blood pressure can cause difficulties for both you and your baby. The circulation of blood through the placenta may be affected so

SYMPTOM WATCH: PAIN
- period-like: quite common in early pregnancy
- cramps: also common, generally due to wind or constipation
- however, both period-like pain and cramps might indicate a miscarriage
- severe pain in the abdomen and especially if it radiates to your shoulder, should ALWAYS BE REPORTED AS SOON AS POSSIBLE to your midwife or doctor. This kind of pain could mean that you have an ectopic pregnancy.

GESTATIONAL DIABETES

The way in which your body produces insulin changes during pregnancy, and in some women this can lead to the development of gestational diabetes.

The condition doesn't usually produce any symptoms, though it may be suspected if high levels of sugar are found in your urine or blood, or if you have an unusually large bump. Gestational diabetes is diagnosed by a blood test (a glucose tolerance test). Following diagnosis, it can usually be controlled through diet, though occasionally insulin needs to be given. Gestational diabetes needs to be well controlled because if not, it can lead to the baby becoming big, which can cause complications with the birth, and/or to him having low blood sugar after birth.

After the baby is born, the condition disappears though women who have had it are at increased risk of subsequently developing Type 2 diabetes (non-insulin-dependent diabetes).

that your baby does not grow properly, and, in extreme cases, you may have problems with blood clots, and even have fits. This is why your midwife checks your blood pressure every time you go for an antenatal appointment. Because antenatal care in the UK is so good, it is very unusual for pre-eclampsia to become life-threatening.

The kidneys do not normally allow protein to pass into the urine. However, if your blood pressure is too high, protein will be squeezed out, and this is why having protein in the urine is another sign of pre-eclampsia. The amount of protein in the urine is shown as +, ++, +++, ++++.

If your blood pressure creeps up from week to week, and there is an increasing amount of protein in your urine, your doctor may advise you to have an induction at around 37 weeks of pregnancy, as soon as your baby's lungs are mature.

Sometimes, pre-eclampsia develops very suddenly. Your blood pressure may have been fine at your last clinic visit, but, out of the blue, you may become very swollen, you may have bad headaches and your vision may be blurred. Act on these signs immediately and contact your midwife or doctor. Your baby may need to be born quickly.

You will be offered regular checks if you have any symptoms of pre-eclampsia. You can help yourself by trying to make your pregnancy as healthy as possible:

- Avoid too much stress (bad for blood pressure)
- Take some gentle exercise three times a week
- Learn some relaxation techniques – an NCT teacher will help you
- Perhaps consult an aromatherapist to find out which relaxing oils are appropriate for pregnancy.

Placental abruption

Occasionally, the placenta starts to peel away from the wall of the uterus during pregnancy. It's a very uncommon occurrence, except in cases of severe placenta praevia. A placental abruption could be brought on by a serious car accident or a blow to your abdomen, or by very high blood pressure (see pre-eclampsia), or perhaps by smoking or taking street drugs such as cocaine.

If the placenta only separates a little from the wall of the womb, there will be some bleeding and pain, but things should settle down again, although you may be offered regular scans for the rest of your pregnancy.

In the case of a serious abruption, the symptoms are heavy dark bleeding and severe abdominal pain. Your tummy feels rigid and your womb may start to contract strongly. This is a medical emergency and you and your baby need immediate attention. You will probably be offered a caesarean section.

If your baby is born as an emergency following a serious bleed, he may need to go to the Special Care Baby Unit for a while. And you will need a blood transfusion and specialist nursing.

A birth like this can leave you feeling emotionally battered. Before you leave the hospital, make sure that you understand exactly what happened and what treatment you and your baby received. Find out if there are any long-term implications and whether the same thing is likely to happen in another pregnancy.

Obstetric cholestasis (OC)

This condition, sometimes called 'cholestasis of pregnancy' or obstetric cholestasis, is caused by a problem with the liver. Bile is produced in the liver and normally travels down the bile ducts into the intestines where it helps in the digestion of food. For some reason that no one quite understands, the flow of bile can be obstructed in pregnancy and this results in large amounts of bile salts accumulating in the mother's blood. The main symptom is unbearable itching all over the body, generally starting from about 30 weeks of pregnancy. The itching is worst on the palms of the hands and the soles of the feet, and at night-time.

The percentage of women who have obstetric cholestasis varies from country to country. For some reason, Chile has the highest rate in the world; in Europe, it's only about 1 per cent of women. You're more likely to get obstetric cholestasis if someone else in your family has had it or if you're expecting twins.

Bile is needed for the absorption of vitamin K from the gut. If no bile is reaching the gut, vitamin K can't be absorbed from the food. Vitamin K is one of the factors that makes the blood clot. Women affected by obstetric cholestasis can have problems with bleeding during or after the birth. And, for some reason not yet understood, their babies are at increased risk of being stillborn between 36 and 40 weeks of pregnancy.

If you have obstetric cholestasis, you may be given weekly vitamin K injections during pregnancy to help your blood clot, and your doctor may advise inducing labour at around 37 weeks. Some women may be advised to take a specific drug. After the birth, your baby will need an injection of vitamin K, but otherwise he shouldn't have any problems. Your liver will return to normal. However, you need to bear in mind that you are very likely to get obstetric cholestasis again if you decide to have another pregnancy.

To cope with the itching, try calamine lotion and creams containing chamomile. Have a look at your diet. Make sure that it includes plenty of wholegrain cereals, rice, raw vegetables and fruit. Avoid dairy products, fatty foods, wheat and alcohol. Try and distract yourself from the itching by keeping as busy as you can. It's worth contacting the Obstetric Cholestasis Support Group (see page 245) who will have more ideas on how to manage your condition and will certainly listen very sympathetically to you.

BABY 'SMALL FOR DATES'

An ultrasound scan might show that your baby is not growing well in the womb, usually as a result of not enough blood flowing to and from the placenta (placental insufficiency). This can lead to the baby not growing properly (intrauterine growth retardation) or him not getting enough oxygen.

There are various things that can cause placental insufficiency, including problems with the development of the placenta or its blood supply, high blood pressure, smoking, certain medical conditions, and certain infections.

Signs of placental insufficiency include the baby being small, or having a slow heartbeat, or his movements being reduced. It's generally diagnosed through a doppler ultrasound scan, which measures blood flow through the placenta. If the condition is found, the baby is usually then carefully monitored. It may be necessary for him to be born early.

premature birth

The UK has the highest rate of low birthweight babies in Western Europe and the proportion of premature and low-weight babies being born and surviving is increasing every year.[⊙] Twenty years ago, approximately 20 per cent of babies weighing less than 1000g at birth survived; nowadays, about 80 per cent survive.

NEONATAL CARE

Figures show that 10 per cent of UK babies spend at least a few days in a neonatal unit, which is an average of 70,000 babies a year.[⊙] Not all of these babies are pre-term. Some are 'term' babies who are unwell and need intensive care, but the proportion of premature and low-birthweight babies being born and surviving is increasing every year. Over the last 15 years, there has been an increase by 40 per cent in live births of babies weighing less than 1500g (3lb 5oz) and for babies weighing less than 1000g (2lb 4oz), an increase of 60 per cent. One in a hundred babies born each year weighs less than 1500g.

DEFINITIONS

Term baby	38 to 42 weeks
Premature	born before 37 completed weeks
Very premature	29 to 34 weeks
Extremely premature	24 to 28 weeks

These days, a significant number of babies born prematurely at less than 24 weeks will survive.

There's still a lot we don't know about why some babies are born spontaneously very early. About a third of premature births occur for no apparent reason.

Reasons we do know include:

- infection – although whether the infection causes the premature birth, or the other way round, is still open to debate
- congenital abnormalities may be associated with a premature birth
- a multiple pregnancy: twins are often pre-term
- a premature birth can be associated with heavy smoking
- the mother might have an 'incompetent cervix' (see page 234)
- occasionally, mothers who have already had one premature birth, may have another.

In some cases, the mother's waters break early (premature rupture of membranes or PROM), starting labour. If labour starts while your baby is less than 35 weeks, you may be given two sets of drugs. One is to delay the labour for a day or two, while the other is to help the baby's lungs to mature quickly so that they will function better after delivery.

Induced or caesarean birth

Sometimes a baby needs to be born early to avoid risks to the baby's or mother's life – as with pre-eclampsia (see page 105). This dangerous disorder occurs in about 1 in 14 pregnancies and causes around a third of all premature births. The main symptoms are headaches and swollen feet which are associated with high blood pressure. Although bed rest can help, the only way to stop pre-eclampsia is to give birth to your baby early: either an induced birth or a caesarean section.

In a few cases, an ultrasound scan might show that a baby is not growing well in the womb (intrauterine growth retardation) – usually as a result of not enough blood flowing to and from the placenta. If you have been told that your baby is 'small for dates' (see page 107) it can be worrying, but rest assured that he will be carefully monitored. It may be that your baby would be safer outside the womb and in this case, a caesarean birth would be recommended because it puts less strain on the baby.

Hospital care

Whether born spontaneously, or with a planned induction or caesarean, it can be hard at first to take in the fact that things have not gone according to plan. A baby born very early may be too small to be held, may need to stay in hospital for a few weeks or even months, and at times the level of hospital involvement may be so high that your baby may not feel like yours.

Premature babies will have to spend their early weeks in neonatal care.

Neonatal units are divided into different levels of care, according to the baby's needs:

- intensive care – for the very tiny or sick baby. Babies will be in an incubator and mechanical ventilation may be necessary
- high dependency – includes breathing support and intravenous nutrition
- special care baby units – continuous monitoring of respiration or heart rate; may involve tube-feeding, extra oxygen support or phototherapy (light therapy). 'Transitional' care refers to out-of-incubator care. Babies will be tube-fed and may have phototherapy but are able to be nursed in air. It may be possible for mothers to have babies by their beds.

If a baby needs to be transferred between hospitals, specialist teams will assist with full intensive care support throughout the journey.

Feeding

At first your baby may need to be fed using a naso-gastric tube. This is a tube that goes through the baby's nose and into his stomach and is left in place, with sticking plaster over his nose, between feeds. Sometimes the milk is given as a continuous feed with the help of a small electric pump, which makes it possible for your baby to get his food without expending energy.

When he is ready, he can progress to feeding from a cup or bottle, but even while he is still at the tube-feeding stage you can cuddle him close to give him comfort and stimulation.

Expressing for premature babies

If your baby is very small, or unwell, he may not have strong sucking or swallowing reflexes yet, so to give the benefits of breastmilk, you'll need to express your milk by hand or with a pump.

The most common method of expressing milk for a pre-term baby is with an electric breast pump. If you can start pumping as soon as possible after the birth, you will be able to give your baby more of your valuable colostrum, although you may not be in a fit state to even think about it.

It's best to express your milk frequently and regularly – little and often is more productive. You could aim for six to eight times over 24 hours, including a session at night. If you find that expressing is slow, most electric breast pumps allow dual pumping. Expressing from both breasts at the same time is more efficient and gives your breasts maximum stimulation. Don't

BENEFITS OF BREASTMILK

Expressing your milk is not a lot of fun; it's hard work and you'll need all the support and encouragement you can get – but it's worth it. Many mothers find it really comforting to provide breastmilk for their pre-term baby because it's the one thing they alone can do.

Breastmilk is especially suited to pre-term babies because of their immature digestive systems. It contains factors that protect from infection and allergy and research has even shown that the milk from mothers of premature babies is higher in protein than the breastmilk of mothers of full-term babies. Breastmilk also protects babies from the very dangerous bowel disease, necrotizing enterocolitis.

forget that every drop of milk that your baby receives is a bonus, so try not to worry if the volume seems small.

When your baby is ready to try breastfeeding properly, you can put him to your breast with the tube still in place. If your baby is not strong enough to get all his nutritional requirements at the breast, he can be supplemented later, or at the same time, through the tube.

Getting to know him

Although it might seem as though the hospital staff know more about how to care for your baby than you do, there are many things that you alone can do for him. Let the staff keep an eye on the equipment while you and your partner spend time talking to and touching your baby. 'Positive' touch (meaning loving touch that does not involve a medical procedure) will be very important to him. However, at the early stages stroking or patting can over-stimulate a premature baby. Instead, what's called 'containment holding' can help. Place one hand firmly but gently on your baby's head while he lies in the incubator, and the other hand on his middle. If your baby is small enough, allow your hands to come together on his middle. This containment holding can help a baby feel secure, relaxed and loved.

Kangaroo care

When your baby is strong enough, 'Kangaroo care' is the name of an effective way of keeping him warm outside an incubator and it helps him feel secure at the same time. This involves skin-to-skin contact with your baby, who is placed naked against his mother's or father's bare chest and both of you are then covered up. It has been shown that parents' own skin temperature adapts to rises and falls in the baby's body heat. Babies who are given even small amounts of kangaroo care put on weight more rapidly (and are allowed home earlier) than those in standard special care.[◎] Kangaroo care can also improve a mother's milk production. Babies who have kangaroo care tend to cry less and sleep more deeply.

Going home

Planning to take your baby home can cause great anxiety as well as relief. Over the weeks or months that you and your baby have been in neonatal care, you may have grown used to the high level of support – always having people around to answer questions and help you. At home, you will be much more on your own, although a health visitor should be able to give you support along with your local GP and many pharmacists can also help with issues that may crop up from time to time.

Some areas also have specialized neonatal outreach teams, or possibly community-based paediatric homecare teams who can also provide support. Make sure you know about services available before you leave the hospital.

Home oxygen

A number of babies who need extra help with breathing will go home 'on oxygen'. This means that the baby needs to have a supply of oxygen to support his breathing, and the need may continue for several months or longer. Your paediatrician will tell you which level of oxygen your baby needs and you will be shown what to watch out for and how to tell if your baby needs more oxygen.

The staff looking after your baby will arrange a meeting with you before your baby goes home so that you can discuss the future and ask any questions. If there's a community outreach worker attached to the neonatal unit, it's likely they will co-ordinate the discharge and provide you with all the information you need about preparing your home, and other practicalities.

You should not be expected to do anything at home that has not been explained and shown to you by a health professional on the neonatal unit.

Planning to leave

Plan your move carefully. Once your baby is stable enough not to need the specialist help in the neonatal unit, staff will start to make sure that you can provide all aspects of your baby's care. Staff should give you training in how to perform basic resuscitation and give guidance on 'safe sleeping'. Resuscitation skills will be useful to have because they enable you to save anyone's life as well as equipping you to handle emergencies with your baby.

Some neonatal units have facilities where you can 'room in' for one or two nights and practise caring for your baby independently, but within easy access of staff if you have any questions. This can help build confidence.

INFORMATION AND SUPPORT
You can find more information and support at Bliss, the charity for the parents of premature babies. They produce a lot of excellent literature, including a *Parent Information Guide*. Contact details on page 245.

Once at home a premature baby can feel especially demanding and it can be difficult to feel able to join in postnatal groups. The NCT can help to put you in touch with other parents who have been through the experience of prematurity, as well as providing an understanding environment in which to take part in postnatal activities. The NCT also has an online support group for parents of pre-term babies: http://groups.yahoo.com/group/nct-preterm/

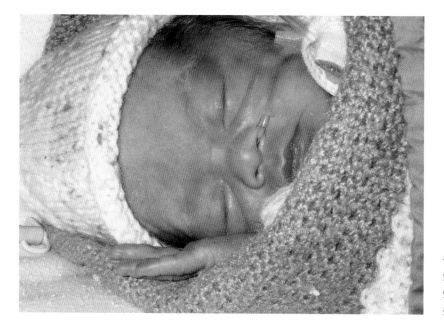

By the time he comes home, your baby should be able to maintain his body temperature as well as any full-term baby.

getting ready

You may be feeling a mixture of anxiety, elation, perhaps even sadness that your pregnancy will soon be over, but most of all, you'll be impatient to see your baby at last, so these last few weeks are the time for final preparations and making sure you have everything you need.

As your baby will be mature enough to be born from 37 weeks, it's a good idea to have everything you need for his birth organized by then.

Having your baby at home

If you're having a home birth, your midwife will probably visit you at around 37 weeks to drop off a pack containing the things she will need for the birth. You might also like to have the following to hand:

- some plastic sheeting, a plastic shower curtain or some old newspapers to protect your floor and furniture
- protective covering for your bed, if you plan to use it
- birthing ball (available through NCT Maternity Sales, see page 247)
- Plasticine or Blu-Tack™ to block the overflow if you want to use your bath
- snacks for you to eat – and drinks with bendy straws
- food and drink for your midwives that your partner or birth supporter can leave out
- large towel to put round you and your baby after he's born
- bowl or bucket to put the placenta in
- bin liners for clearing up
- emergency bag in case you need to transfer to hospital (see below).

Water birth

If you're having a water birth, there are different pools that you can hire, with differing costs. Things to consider when choosing a pool include your height, whether you want your birth partner to be in the pool with you, the size of the room in which you'll be using the pool and the strength of the floor, how quickly the pool can be filled, whether the hose supplied is long enough to reach your taps, and whether the hose adaptor will fit your taps. Check with the pool hire company too about things like what the hire period is and what happens if you go over it, and what the fee covers.

Extra things that you might need for a water birth include:

- some plastic sheeting to put under the pool
- water thermometer (this may be supplied by the pool hire company)
- inflatable pillow for your head and/or swimming floats to rest your arms on

- piece of sponge or a folded towel for you to kneel on
- something similar for your midwife to kneel on, on the floor
- plastic sieve or fish net and bucket
- lots of towels and a thick, warm dressing gown
- small stool or chair to sit on or use to get in and out of the pool
- T-shirt to wear in the pool if you want
- swimming trunks for partner, if he's going to join you in the pool.

If you're hoping to have a hospital water birth, ask your midwife at one of your antenatal appointments what you will need to bring with you on the day.

Having your baby in hospital

Different women find different things useful during labour and for a hospital stay after the birth.

For labour:

- your maternity notes and your birth plan
- big old T-shirt or long shirt
- warm socks
- water spray, baby wipes or flannel, to freshen your face
- new natural sponge, to freshen your face or dip in cold water to suck
- hair ties or clips to keep your hair off your face
- toothbrush and toothpaste or mouthwash
- lipsalve
- talcum powder or oil or wooden roller for massage
- hot water bottle, or ice pack in case of backache
- ice cubes in a thermos (to suck or put in drinks)
- fruit drinks, with bendy straws
- music and player (and batteries)
- notebook and pen for recording your labour
- mirror (so that you can see your baby's head when he's born)
- food and drink for your birth partner
- change of clothes for your birth partner
- camera and film (and battery)
- change for the phone, or phonecard
- toiletries and towel
- maternity sanitary towels
- clothes and a few nappies for your baby
- you might like to bring a pillow from home.

In the final days, it can be a good idea to get your hair cut into a fuss-free style, fill the freezer with meals you've prepared earlier and buy two of everything when you go shopping for basics. Visit a friend with a new baby, if you can, and ask her advice on what to organize ahead of time.

IF YOU'RE STAYING IN HOSPITAL

- nightie or pyjamas, light dressing gown and slip-on slippers
- old (or cheap new), paper or mesh knickers (mesh knickers are available from NCT Maternity Sales, see contact details on page 247)
- day clothes
- nursing bra and breast pads
- maternity sanitary towels
- toiletries and towel
- nappies and cotton wool
- clothes for your baby
- towel for your baby
- ear plugs and/or sleep mask
- change for the phone, or phonecard
- birth announcement cards, address book, pen, stamps
- books/magazines.

Don't forget that if you're going home by car, you'll need a car seat for your baby.

best baby positions for birth

The way in which your baby lies in your pelvis is important: it can affect how smoothly your labour progresses. In the last few weeks of your pregnancy, it's a good idea to stand and sit as much as possible in ways that will encourage your baby into the best position, prior to birth.

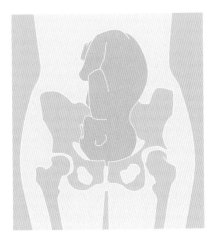

ABOVE *When your baby lies 'left occiput anterior' with spine facing outwards, his head will press neatly on your cervix, helping it to open up.*
BELOW *If your baby lies the other way round 'right occiput posterior' – this can slow down the first stage of labour.*

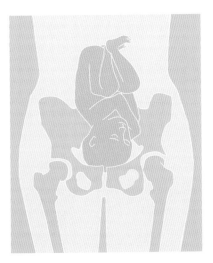

The best position for your baby to be in for birth is head down, with his back against your belly, facing your back. This way, he can fit through your pelvis as easily as possible, and 'flex' his head (ie tuck his chin into his chest) so that the narrowest part is pressing on your cervix.

This position is known as 'occiput anterior' (OA), meaning that the back of the baby's head, or 'occiput', is at the front, or 'anterior'. It is the most usual position and may be written in your notes as LOA ('left occiput anterior') if the baby is lying to your left or, less commonly, ROA ('right occiput anterior') if the baby is lying to your right.

Some babies, however, lie with their back against their mother's back, which is known as an 'occiput posterior' (OP) position. Labour tends to take longer if the baby is in this position because he can't tuck in his chin very well and getting through the pelvis is more awkward. If a baby is lying OP, this often causes backache during labour.

Certain aspects of our modern lives, such as lounging on sofas and sitting in cars, may make babies more likely to lie in a posterior position. Because the back of your baby's body is heavier than the front, his back will tend to roll towards the direction you're leaning in. So if you're leaning backwards or reclining (as on a sofa), his back may roll towards your back – ie he will be in a posterior position.

If you're leaning forwards, however, his back may roll towards your front – an anterior position. Leaning forwards is therefore better than leaning backwards. Also, if you're in a position in which your knees are below your hips, this creates more space for the baby's head to lie in the front of your pelvis. Some babies, however, will not shift their position.

Back or front?

It's not always easy for you to tell which way round your baby is lying, but your midwife should be able to tell you.

There are also some signs that you can look for. If your baby is lying OP or 'back to back', your bump may feel squashy and you may feel (and see) kicks in the middle of your belly. Another particular tell-tale sign of the baby facing forwards is a dip around your belly button.

Helping your baby into a good position

To help your baby to get into a good position before birth, spend as much time as you can in positions in which you can lean forwards and where your hips are above your knees particularly from 34 weeks if this is your first baby, or 37 weeks if it isn't. For example:

- Sit the wrong way round on an upright chair and lean over the back.
- Sit on an upright chair and lean forwards with your elbows resting on a table.
- Sit on the edge of a chair or sofa with your feet apart and lean forwards so that your belly hangs between your knees.
- Sit on a birthing ball.
- If you sit a lot at work, take regular breaks to stand up and move around. If necessary, sit on a couple of cushions to keep your hips raised up above your knees.
- Kneel forwards over a pile of pillows, or a beanbag, or a birthing ball, with your knees apart and your bottom down. Try to get used to watching TV in this position.
- Get onto all-fours.
- Put a cushion under your bottom if you're travelling by car.
- Lie on your left side, with your right leg over and in front of your left leg (with a cushion or pillow between your knees).
- Swim or float on your front (avoid breast-stroke leg actions if you have any pelvic pain).

Positions to avoid

- Sitting leaning back on a squashy sofa or chair.
- Sitting with your legs crossed.
- Squatting deeply.

Descent through the birth canal is easiest if your baby has his chin tucked into his chest. The back of his head will fit the cervical area neatly and help the cervix dilate. The flexible joints in the baby's skull allow it to change shape and negotiate the birth canal during birth. The majority of babies lie in this anterior position before birth, with head down and back lying against your abdominal wall. Ideally, arms and legs will be folded in front too. A baby in this position has only a short distance to turn to get through the vagina. Evidence that 're-positioning' your baby works, however, is mainly anecdotal.[©]

Breech babies

Although most babies turn head-down towards the end of pregnancy, about 3–4 per cent of babies will be breech at full term. This means the head stays uppermost in the womb with bottom or feet positioned to come out first. It's perfectly possible for a baby in a breech position to be born naturally, but a head-first position makes birth easier.

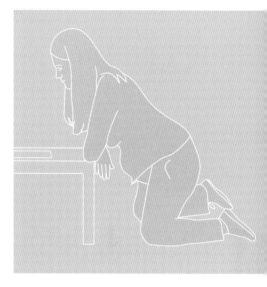

ABOVE *Towards the end of pregnancy, it can be good to spend some time each day in upright, forward-leaning positions.*
BELOW *Leaning over the back of a chair is another good forward-leaning position that will encourage your baby to settle 'occiput anterior'.*

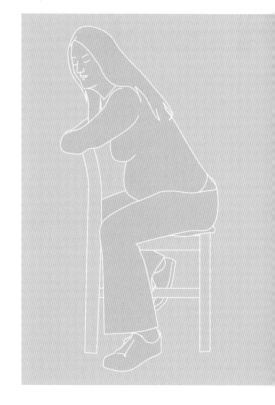

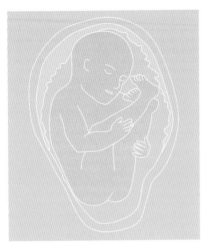

Extended, or frank, breech.

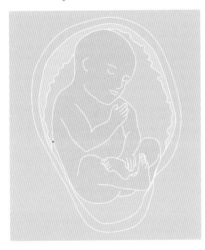

Complete breech.

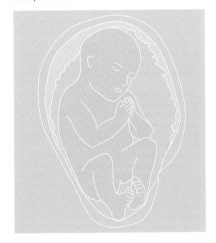

Footling breech.

Turning a breech baby

If your baby is breech (bottom down) before 34 weeks, it's quite likely that he will turn by himself.

If he's still breech after 34 weeks, you can try to encourage him to turn by using 'bottom-in-the-air' positions. Either kneel with your forearms on the floor, your head down, and your bottom up, or lie on your back with your feet on the floor, your knees bent up and three or four pillows under your bottom, for 10–15 minutes two or three times a day. There is currently insufficient research evidence to say how effective these positions are.

Complementary therapies offer ways of turning a breech baby. The acupuncture technique of moxibustion, which involves burning a small stick of the herb, mugwort, on your little toe, has been found to have a success rate of as high as 70 per cent in a small study.[*] Reflexologists also have techniques for trying to turn breech babies, and there is a homeopathic remedy for this too. Consult a qualified homeopath.

External cephalic version

If he won't move by himself, an experienced midwife or obstetrician may be able to turn your baby manually – a process known as external cephalic version (ECV). If this is carried out after 37 weeks of pregnancy, research has shown a 58 per cent success rate, with a 48 per cent reduction in the risk of a caesarean.[*]

Breech presentation

- Extended or frank is the most common breech presentation in first babies: the baby's legs are straight with toes by ears.
- Complete is the next most common breech presentation where the baby's knees are bent.
- Footling breeches, where a foot is coming first, and 'knee breeches' are very rare and more complicated. With a smaller presenting part (such as a foot or knees rather than a bottom) there is a greater risk of the cord coming down and getting squashed, cutting off the baby's oxygen supply.

Why are some babies breech?

Most babies are breech for no obvious reason. Premature babies are often breech and in about 40 per cent of twin pregnancies, one baby is in the breech position. Other possible causes include:

- a uterus which has a divider or 'septum' running down the middle
- a tumour or fibroid low in the pelvis
- placenta praevia (placenta in the lower half of the uterus, instead of the upper)
- too much amniotic fluid.

All these conditions make it difficult for the baby to settle head down.

Breech birth

Results of an international trial of over 2000 women around the world giving birth to babies in the frank or complete breech position, were published recently.[*] Conclusions drawn in the study were that it's best for a breech baby to be born by caesarean as the risk to the baby was higher with a vaginal birth. There are many experienced midwives who would challenge this view and mothers who plan to give birth vaginally to their breech baby will need to make sure they receive care from a midwife experienced in natural breech births. The Association for Improvements in the Maternity Services (AIMS) can help you find a midwife with experience in breech birth, or contact the Independent Midwives organization. You will find their details on page 245.

Nobody knows what influences a baby to move into the best position for birth, or why some babies are more contrary than others, but when a baby is lying awkwardly the natural process of labour cannot work so efficiently. About one in 200 babies lies 'transverse' and about one baby in 75 can lie 'oblique'.

Transverse and oblique positions

Transverse means the baby lies across the womb. If he stays that way, a caesarean will be necessary. Oblique means that baby is lying diagonally across the womb and will usually straighten up before birth.

Twin presentations

Twins may be both head down (also known as 'cephalic' or 'vertex') – the presentation likely to be the easiest, or both may be breech (feet or bottom down) or one head down and one breech. Sometimes, when the first twin has been born, the second twin turns around spontaneously, as a result of the sudden extra space.

Twin birth

Your twins are slightly more likely to be born by caesarean compared to a vaginal birth, but you should discuss this carefully with your midwife and doctor. Your own preferences for the birth should be taken into account in any decision you make – just as with one baby.

In some instances, there's a clear cut case for a caesarean section – pre-term or otherwise vulnerable twins may need to be born swiftly and be unable to risk a prolonged or difficult vaginal birth. The birth of the second twin can be delayed, and he may be showing signs of fetal distress, in which case you might then be advised to have a caesarean. Some doctors may suggest a caesarean because one or more of your twins is breech, and there is a growing trend for all breech babies to be born this way. However, a vaginal birth means you will almost certainly be fitter sooner, and more able to cope with the demands of two new babies.

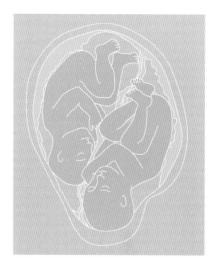

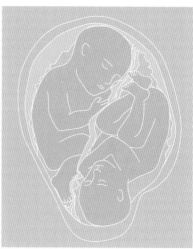

FACING PAGE *Diagrams show the most common breech positions adopted by babies in the womb.*

ABOVE *Twins are usually (though not always) either both head down or one head up, one head down.*

going past your due date

Most people tend to think of babies as being 'due' on a specific date, and of pregnancy as lasting 40 weeks, but exactly what triggers labour is still not known. Only a small percentage of babies – about five per cent – are born on their 'due' date.

YOUR DUE DATE

Calculating your due date is not an exact process because it depends on factors that it's difficult to be certain about. The first of these is when your baby was conceived. The formulas used for calculating due dates on the basis of your last period make certain assumptions, while estimates based on a scan always have a margin of error.

The second area of uncertainty is how long the average pregnancy actually lasts. In the UK, it's calculated at 40 weeks, but there's debate about this, backed up by research evidence. In France for example, it's regarded as lasting 41 weeks.

It can be disappointing and frustrating to sit through your 'expected day of delivery' with no baby yet in your arms to show for it. Most babies (around 80 per cent) are born at 'term', which means between 38 and 42 weeks. Babies who are born before 37 completed weeks are therefore considered to be 'pre-term', while those born after 42 weeks are 'post-term'.

Why are some babies late?

In most cases, it isn't known why babies arrive when they do. However, one thing that may affect the start of labour is the baby's position. It is also possible that the mother's emotional state might influence when her baby is born, and that if she's anxious, her body may 'hang on' to the baby.

Self-starting labour

If you're feeling fed up and uncomfortable, and are desperate to meet your baby, or if you want to avoid a medical induction, you might be tempted to try and start labour off yourself. There are many different ways that women have used over the years to do this, including sex, or arousal, and nipple stimulation, drinking castor oil or eating curry. But there are few, if any, studies of these measures, so how effective they are hasn't been established. Although some women will find that they will go into labour after trying one of them, this could be just coincidence.

Acupuncture, reflexology, homeopathy, herbalism and aromatherapy all offer methods of encouraging labour to start, but again, the effectiveness of these has not been established by research.

Your body produces labour hormones more readily if you're relaxed, and one way of helping labour to start might be to try some relaxation exercises, and perhaps to spend time thinking about your baby, picturing him in those tiny clothes, and imagining holding him close to you.

Avoiding induction

Once you've gone a certain number of days past your due date (usually between seven and 14), the issue of induction (starting labour artificially) will probably be raised by your carers. An induction has various potential

GUIDELINES ON INDUCTION

Clinical guidelines have been drawn up to help guide decision making in situations such as this one where choices need to be made. When induction of labour is being considered, your obstetrician should fully discuss your options with you before any decision is reached.

Even if you have had a healthy, trouble-free pregnancy, you should be offered induction of labour after 41 weeks because from this stage the risk of your baby developing health problems increases.⊙

Relaxing baths can be enjoyed throughout pregnancy, but make sure the water's not too hot – around blood heat (37°C) is fine. Your body produces labour hormones more readily if you are relaxed.

implications in terms of labour and if all is well with you and your baby and you would prefer your labour not to be induced, you can decline the offer. If you do, you'll be advised to have frequent checks on your baby while you're waiting for labour to start.

If you've gone past your due date, your midwife may offer to 'sweep' your membranes. This involves her inserting a finger gently into your cervix and running it between the top of the cervix and the bag of waters. Sweeping the membranes has been shown to increase the likelihood of labour starting in the next few days, and to decrease the need for induction, but it isn't always effective.

when labour leads to an unplanned caesarean

A fortunate outcome from a frightening situation

'When the registrar said we would reconsider the options, she meant we were running out of options fast!'

'The day after my due date, I started having contractions that continued all day without increasing in intensity or frequency. I went to bed, but was awake at 1.30am since the contractions started to become more intense. By 10am the contractions were five to six minutes apart. I phoned the hospital and they asked me to come in. After being examined I was told I was 1cm dilated. We were admitted and I was told to walk around. At about 4pm, Michael went home to have some sleep to conserve energy for what was ahead. At this point, my contractions were every five minutes and the pain was manageable, so I was given some sleeping tablets and painkillers and left to sleep. The following morning the contractions had decreased to every 15 minutes so I was allowed to go home.

'By 5pm the contractions had started increasing again, so I was back on the TENS machine, and by 7pm, they were quite intense. I needed something more, so we went to the hospital, having phoned our friend Rachel, who we had invited to be present at the birth. After being monitored at the hospital, I was given gas and air.

'The midwife examined me and pronounced me 5cm dilated, so the baby was on its way, but the initial period of monitoring indicated that the baby's heartbeat was fast. The midwife called the registrar who decided that I needed to be monitored for longer. At 11.30pm the registrar examined me to find I was still 5cm dilated. She broke my waters, which were stained with meconium. The midwife was worried about the baby's oxygen supply so in between contractions I was given an oxygen mask to wear.

Caesarean suggested

'The registrar decided to put in a drip to speed up the contractions and asked whether I wanted an epidural. This was put in, and the drip was started. Although Rachel was reassuring me her face looked scared. The baby's heartbeat was dropping and was now half its previous rate. When the registrar said we would reconsider the options, she meant we were running out of options fast! This is when a caesarean was advised.

'I was whisked down the corridor to the theatre and the epidural was topped up to make me free from pain, though aware of movement. Michael was brought in wearing hospital greens. The operation was very quick. The anaesthetist checked the epidural and minutes later we heard the first cry, with the doctor pronouncing "What a whopper!" Michael and the baby were taken off so that the baby could be weighed and after half an hour I was wheeled through to the recovery room. I held my baby Matthew for a proper cuddle and after 20 minutes he had his first feed.'

a second-time-round home water birth

'When I realized I was pregnant again, one of my first thoughts was, "Oh no! That means I've got to give birth!". I spent the first few months planning to use all the drugs this time and make it easy on myself – no heroics.

'My partner encouraged this; he really didn't want to see me in that sort of pain again. But something about this made me feel uneasy. What did I really want this birth to be like? In my heart of hearts, what I really wanted was to be at home with no drugs, in a birthing pool. But this seemed to me the kind of thing that other women did: Mother Earth-types, yoga fanatics, stronger women than me.

'As the baby grew inside me, I felt a powerful urge to own the whole experience. I didn't want to put it all in someone else's hands at the end of nine months. I wanted to be that stronger woman who just did it.

'The possibility thrilled me and I decided to go for it. I ordered the pool, asked my mum if I could borrow her back room (nice view of the garden) and planned my joyful birth experience. To put my mind at rest (and the minds of those who love me) I asked for the hospital notes of my last labour and discussed with a consultant if there was any reason why I shouldn't have the baby at home. There are many scaremongers around this issue but basically the odds are that it will be fine. You just have to trust your instincts. My midwife gave me all the support I needed.

Like a true pro

'When the day came and my labour began, I did not for one second regret my choice. It was just as I had hoped it would be. No drugs; feeling the pain but controlling it; breathing through the contractions. I was doing it like a true pro! When it was all over and I sat there with my new baby, I was struck by the enormity and the simplicity of what had just happened. Women do have babies all the time and you do have to literally *push* them out – simple. But isn't it just the most full-on amazing thing? And I had done it! To have had a bad birth experience, but then to trust myself to do it right the second time, and succeed, was liberating.

'I had exorcized the horrors of the first time and become that strong woman I had dreamed of being. Does that sound over the top? Try it and see for yourself!'

After a first bad experience, a joyous home birth helps to heal the wounds

'In my heart of hearts, what I really wanted was to be at home with no drugs, in a birthing pool!'

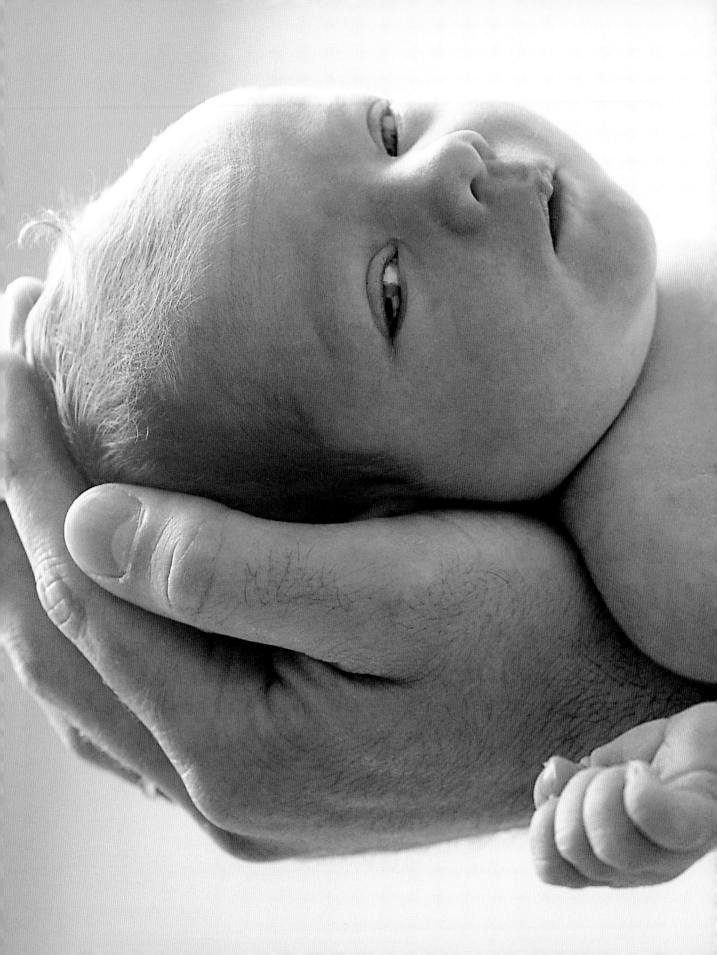

Medical intervention

when extra help is needed

induction and acceleration

electronic fetal monitoring

epidural anaesthesia

instrumental delivery

caesarean birth

birth stories

when extra help is needed

Birth is a natural process, and women's bodies are designed to have babies naturally. Sometimes, however, things don't go according to plan and medical assistance may be necessary for the health of either baby or mother.

In England less than 45 per cent of women give birth without some form of medical intervention, such as induction, epidural, forceps, ventouse or a caesarean.[○] It's a fact that simply having your baby in hospital increases your risk of intervention – one study showed that women without complications or high-risk factors who planned to have their baby at home were half as likely as women planning to give birth in hospital, to have a caesarean section or an instrumental delivery (and their babies were just as healthy as those born in hospital).[○]

If you were hoping to have a natural birth, accepting medical help can be a disappointment. If you are having your baby at home or in a birth centre, and

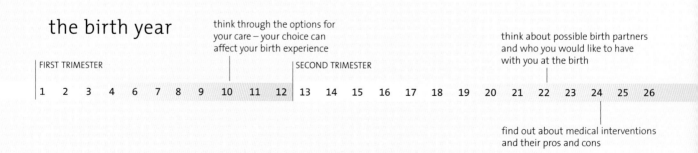

the birth year

think through the options for your care – your choice can affect your birth experience

think about possible birth partners and who you would like to have with you at the birth

FIRST TRIMESTER												SECOND TRIMESTER													
1	2	3	4	6	7	8	9	10	11	12		13	14	15	16	17	18	19	20	21	22	23	24	25	26

find out about medical interventions and their pros and cons require medical help, you will almost certainly need to transfer to hospital. Even if you are already in hospital, intervention can change the atmosphere from one of intimacy with your birth partner and midwife, to that of a medical event. On the other hand, it may come as a relief to you that 'something is happening' – particularly if you are finding labour a lot more difficult than you imagined.

As all the interventions have some unwanted side-effects, it is helpful to have a strategy for making decisions when medical help is offered. Try thinking through the '**BRAIN**' analysis:

- What are the **B**enefits of the intervention?
- What are the **R**isks, both to the baby and me?
- What **A**lternatives are available?
- What do my **I**nstincts tell me?
- What if we do **N**othing?

Asking these questions and thinking through the answers will help you make decisions that are right for you, which in turn will help you to feel satisfied with your birth experience.

The following pages will give you some basic information about common interventions: why and how they are done, and what you can do to reduce your chances of needing them.

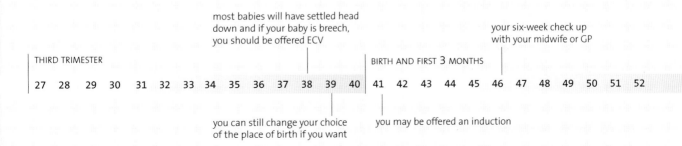

most babies will have settled head down and if your baby is breech, you should be offered ECV

your six-week check up with your midwife or GP

THIRD TRIMESTER | BIRTH AND FIRST 3 MONTHS

27 28 29 30 31 32 33 34 35 36 37 38 39 40 | 41 42 43 44 45 46 47 48 49 50 51 52

you can still change your choice of the place of birth if you want

you may be offered an induction

induction and acceleration

Induction means starting labour off by artificial means. A 'post-term' pregnancy is usually considered to be one that has lasted for longer than 42 weeks and, although most babies born after this point are fine, a small number seem less able to deal with normal labour and birth – which is why doctors and midwives may strongly recommend induction at this point.

HOW LABOUR CAN BE INDUCED

- Sweeping the membranes – done as a vaginal examination where the membranes are separated from the uterus around the cervix. This procedure, which can be done at an antenatal appointment, can trigger contractions. *If labour does not start within a few days, then the following would be offered:*
- Cervical ripening – using prostaglandin pessaries. This is usually done in hospital and can be enough to start labour.
- Breaking the waters (amniotomy) – the membranes are ruptured using a plastic hook. It can only be done if the cervix has started dilating.
- Synthetic oxytocin (syntocinon) – this is given via a drip into a vein in your arm. Electronic fetal monitoring is always recommended to ensure that the baby is coping well. The syntocinon makes the uterus contract.

GROUP B STREPTOCOCCUS

If your waters break spontaneously before you go into labour, the risk of infection to your baby is increased. For more about Group B Streptococcal infection, see page 151.

Rather than waiting until you go into labour naturally, induction is usually offered where:

- there is a problem with you or the baby and an early birth is advisable
- your baby is 'overdue' (41-plus weeks)
- your waters have broken but labour has not started.

If you are being offered induction, make sure you fully understand the reasons why this has been thought beneficial. You can choose whether or not to accept the offer – induction of labour is a major intervention and is best used only when medically indicated.° A common reason why women with an otherwise normal pregnancy are offered induction is 'going overdue'. A lot of doctors are unwilling to let a woman carry on beyond 10 days after their due date, while others are happy for the baby to stay inside for up to 21 days after 40 weeks. If your waters have broken and you are more than 37 weeks pregnant, but you have not gone into labour after, at most, four days, induction is strongly recommended due to the risk of infection.°

What are the disadvantages of being induced?

Induction by sweeping the membranes increases the chance of labour starting naturally within 48 hours but there is a risk that the waters could be accidentally broken. Once this has happened, there is no turning back, and because of the worries about infection, there is a need to get labour going and for the baby to be born within the next few days.

Very occasionally women react to prostaglandin pessaries by having very strong painful contractions, which can be difficult to cope with and which can affect the baby's heartbeat.

Breaking the waters can cause discomfort, and the contractions following it tend to be stronger and more painful.

A syntocinon drip can increase the strength, length and frequency of contractions. For this reason, women who are induced in this way are more likely to have an epidural to cope with the pain and will also need electronic fetal monitoring. This means, in turn, that there is a greater risk of the labour ending in a ventouse or forceps delivery, or even a caesarean section. This is an example of what's known as the 'cascade of intervention'.

What if I am intending to have a home birth?

Apart from sweeping the membranes, all the methods of induction will be carried out in hospital. Therefore accepting an offer of induction will mean putting aside your plans for a home birth.

What are the alternatives to induction?

If, after 42 weeks gestation, an induction has been suggested, you should also be offered, as an alternative, monitoring of your baby's heartbeat twice a week, and an ultrasound test to check the depth of amniotic fluid surrounding your baby.⊙

You can also try other methods of induction following your due date (see box). The evidence for these methods is largely anecdotal.

What will happen if I am not induced?

In an uncomplicated pregnancy, there is small but definite increased risk of your baby developing health problems after 42 weeks.⊙

In situations where the waters have broken but labour has not started at term, 91 per cent of women go into labour naturally within 48 hours, and induction is strongly recommended after four days.⊙

Speeding up labour

Acceleration of labour (sometimes called augmentation) is a process designed to strengthen contractions and speed up the dilation of the cervix. It is achieved in similar ways to induction – by amniotomy and using a synthetic oxytocin (syntocinon) drip. If you do choose to accelerate your labour, remember that the benefits of a faster labour in terms of not getting so tired and seeing your baby sooner, have to be weighed against the risks of acceleration which are the same as those for induction.

What are the disadvantages of acceleration?

These are similar to the disadvantages of induction – sudden, painful contractions that can be difficult to cope with and may require an epidural. In addition you are also likely to be continuously monitored. All these factors will reduce your ability to move around and adopt comfortable positions.

What alternatives are there to acceleration?

Alternatives to acceleration usually focus on helping the body to produce its own oxytocin so that it does not need an artificial supplement. Oxytocin is produced in the absence of stress, when you feel safe, nurtured and relaxed (see box on right). Natural stimulation of oxytocin can take some time, so you may need to request being left in private for a while.

If you do accept syntocinon and are finding the contractions too hard to cope with, ask for the drip to be turned down.

ALTERNATIVES TO INDUCTION

- Sex – semen is rich in prostaglandins; kissing, nipple-stimulation and orgasm all increase oxytocin
- Eating spicy food or fresh pineapple
- Acupuncture
- Homeopathy
- Reflexology
- Aromatherapy
- Gentle exercise
- Going for a vigorous walk.

WAYS TO AVOID ACCELERATION

- Get yourself into a comfortable, upright position
- Move around between contractions – even pace the room if you feel like it
- Improve the environment – make it dark and cosy
- Use relaxation techniques
- Request privacy – ask extra people in the room to leave
- Ask your birth partner for lots of positive support: 'You can do it!' 'You're doing great!'
- Focus on your baby
- Keep your energy and fluid levels up
- Kissing and nipple stimulation encourage the release of oxytocin
- Don't worry if labour is slow as long as you and baby are coping well.

electronic fetal monitoring

During labour, your baby's heartbeat will be checked to make sure that she is getting enough oxygen. This checking can be done with a hand-held Pinard (ear trumpet) or a hand-held doppler (Sonicaid ultrasound machine) or by electronic fetal monitoring with an abdominal transducer. This last method involves you being strapped to a monitor and does restrict your movements.

WAYS OF CHECKING THE BABY'S HEARTBEAT

- Using an ear trumpet (Pinard stethoscope). This is a tube that allows the midwife to hear the heartbeat just with her ear.
- Using a hand-held ultrasound machine (doppler or Sonicaid).
- Using an electronic fetal monitor (EFM). This has two receivers held in place by belts around your waist and hips. The patterns of the baby's heartbeat and your contractions are printed out on a piece of paper (the 'trace').
- Using a sensor fastened to the baby's head by a small hook (fetal scalp electrode). The sensor is on the end of a wire that is put inside your vagina. Once in place it stays there until your baby is born.

The way you are monitored can have a profound effect on the progress of your labour. If you and your birth partner are familiar with each type of monitoring it can help with decision-making.

Which type of monitoring is best?

If you are healthy and have had a trouble-free pregnancy, the recommended way of being monitored is at least every 15 minutes using either the hand-held doppler/Sonicaid or the Pinard. This is increased to every five minutes in the second stage of labour.⊙

The advantage of this is that you are free to get off the bed and can move around, or use a birth pool. Research shows that this kind of intermittent monitoring is as effective as other forms of monitoring.

When are the other types of monitoring used?

Electronic fetal monitoring (EFM) involves a belt monitor (see box on left) and is used when the midwife or doctor wants to follow the pattern of your baby's heartbeat more closely. You could be attached to it for 20 or 30 minutes at a time, or it can be used all the way through labour. There are several situations when this might be recommended (see box on right). Sometimes a fetal scalp electrode is used for EFM – attached to your baby's head using a metal clip that breaks the skin. The wire from the electrode

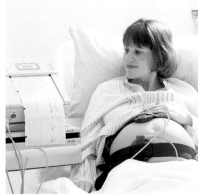

New national guidelines no longer support an 'admission trace' but if electronic fetal monitoring is required, it helps to stay as upright as possible.

passes down your vagina, across your thigh to the monitor. It can only be used if your waters have broken.

Are there any disadvantages to EFM?

Because the usual position for EFM is lying down, being monitored continuously can slow labour and can make the contractions more painful than if you were able to move around and change positions easily. This can make it more likely that your labour will then need to be accelerated with the use of drugs or that you will want an epidural to cope with the pain.

This is especially true of the 'admission trace', which is often done when you first arrive at hospital. If you are offered one, ask why. If it's done purely as a routine, you could ask instead for the hand-held Sonicaid to be used.

Another disadvantage of EFM is that being able to read and understand the trace depends on the skills of medical staff. Evidence shows that false readings do occur, which causes an increased incidence of caesarean, forceps and ventouse births, with no health benefit to mother or baby.

Is it safer for my baby to have EFM?

Where there are no complications, intermittent forms of monitoring are recommended as being the best method of monitoring. There is no evidence to support the use of EFM routinely on arrival at hospital or during labour for low-risk women.

Where there is a higher risk of fetal distress, there is some evidence that supports the use of EFM.[⊙] You may find that continuous monitoring is reassuring for you in these circumstances. It is, of course, your choice whether you accept EFM or not and your decision will depend on your particular situation.

What happens if my baby is suffering from fetal distress?

If your baby is not getting enough oxygen, she will need to be born quickly. You may be offered a test called 'fetal blood sampling' to confirm the situation. A sample of blood can be taken from the baby's head and tested for oxygen levels. It is an invasive test, and may require that your waters be broken. However, it makes it much less likely that a caesarean section would be performed unnecessarily.

Sometimes, the pattern of the baby's heartbeat shows unequivocally that the baby is in distress. In these circumstances a caesarean would be strongly advised immediately. Babies who are having problems can be delivered very quickly by caesarean. There is no doubt that caesareans have saved many lives but studies also show that EFM itself increases the caesarean rate.[⊙]

Remember, most babies come through labour without any problems at all, and you can help to make it easier by 'listening to your body' – moving around and changing your position when you feel that you want to.

EFM MAY BE OFFERED:
- on arrival at hospital (the 'admission trace')
- routinely during labour when there is concern that your baby is not getting enough oxygen
- if you have a particular health problem such as diabetes or pre-eclampsia
- if you are having another intervention such as induction or an epidural
- you are having twins, a breech or premature baby, or have had a previous caesarean.

HOW TO MANAGE EFM
- Be sure that you agree that there is a need for EFM, and if you are not sure, you could choose to be monitored intermittently instead.
- If you decide to have EFM, you can try to stay upright at the same time. You could either stand or sit, or try sitting backwards on an upright chair, supported by a cushion over the back of the chair.
- If you decide to accept EFM, you could ask for the belt monitor to be left on for no more than 30 minutes at a time.
- Lying on your left side is preferable to lying on your back if very tired.

epidural anaesthesia

An epidural means an injection of local anaesthetic into the lower part of your spine to relieve the pain of labour. It can only be administered in hospital. Although this is a very effective form of pain relief, the benefit needs to be weighed against the increased risk of a longer labour and a greater likelihood of needing instrumental help to birth your baby.

An epidural is given by an anaesthetist. A hollow needle is placed in the spine, close to the nerves which transmit the pain of labour and a fine tube is threaded into the needle. The needle is then taken out and an anaesthetic is fed down the tube, which remains in place for as long as you have the epidural. The anaesthetic drugs can be given in a single dose (which can be topped up), continuously, or by a pump that you control yourself.

The drugs used vary between hospitals and can be a local anaesthetic alone or mixed with an opiate. When the opiate is given as well, the amount of local anaesthetic used can be smaller: this is called a 'low-dose' epidural. An epidural usually starts working within 10 to 20 minutes.

How effective is the pain relief?

Because the local anaesthetic numbs the nerves that transmit the pain of labour, it gives very effective pain relief to most women when it is set up.

What are the disadvantages?

There are a number of disadvantages with epidurals that have to be weighed against the benefit of effective pain relief.

An epidural can make labour longer, and make it more likely that labour will need to be accelerated using syntocinon. It is also more likely that you will need an assisted delivery.[©]

Epidurals block the nerves involved in movement and cause you to lose the feeling in your legs. This means that after a conventional epidural you will need to stay lying on the bed for the rest of your labour (or until the epidural has worn off). As a result, you lose the advantages of being able to adopt upright positions and move around, which helps labour to progress.

With low-dose epidurals, the mixture of drugs means that you retain some mobility and may even be able to walk with help. However research has shown that the increased risk of an assisted birth remains.

Other side effects of epidurals are low blood pressure, a raised temperature and the need for a catheter to be used to empty the bladder.

After labour, approximately 1 per cent of women who had an epidural experience a 'dural tap' headache. In over half of these women it will be a

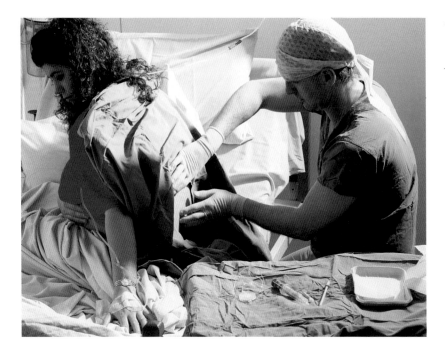

An epidural has to be administered by an anaesthetist in hospital. It usually starts working within 20 minutes but it increases your risk of having an assisted delivery.

severe headache. Very rarely a woman has a serious complication as a result of having an epidural. Medical staff on the labour ward are trained to deal with this type of situation.

Is an epidural available at a home birth?

An epidural has to be administered in hospital. If you are labouring at home, or in a midwifery-led unit (birth centre), and decide you would like to have an epidural, you will have to transfer to hospital. Some hospitals offer a 24-hour epidural service, but in others it depends on the availability of an anaesthetist. If you are hoping to have an epidural, ask your midwife how readily available they are in your local hospital.

How can I help myself if I want to avoid having an epidural?

In advance of labour, you can try to ensure that your baby is in the best position for an uncomplicated birth.[⊙] You can also try to arrange your maternity care so that you know the midwife who will be with you in labour,[⊙] and to make sure that you are well supported in labour.[⊙]

Only you will know if you need an epidural. If you had hoped to labour without one, you could try to manage for, say, one more hour, or five more contractions without one and then reassess the situation.

Don't feel guilty, or that you've 'failed', if you find you need an epidural to deal with your labour pain. Everyone's experience of labour is different – what really matters is that you get the support to make the choice that's right for you on the day.

instrumental delivery

The second stage of labour begins when your cervix is fully dilated and it ends with the birth of your baby. This, the 'pushing' stage, is the most stressful part of labour for your baby, and if you have had epidural pain relief, you may find it harder to 'feel to push'. For this reason, you might be offered help to give birth to your baby with either ventouse (vacuum extraction) or forceps.

Sometimes when the second stage of labour is very long and a woman is having problems pushing the baby out herself, the process can be helped with the use of either ventouse (vacuum extraction) or forceps. This is also called an assisted delivery.

A vacuum extractor or ventouse, is a silicone cap which fits on your baby's head with suction and helps you push your baby out. As a method of instrumental delivery, ventouse is generally used in preference to forceps (lower picture).

Ventouse

A ventouse is a silicone cap attached to a suction pump. The cap is fitted on the baby's head while it is in the birth canal and is kept in place using suction. The ventouse is then pulled at the same time as the woman pushes, to help the baby be born. An episiotomy (a cut in the back wall of the vagina) is not always necessary with ventouse.

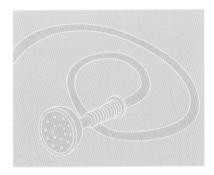

Forceps

Forceps come in two halves which look a bit like metal salad servers. These fit together to form a surgical instrument that can help your baby to be born. Each half of the forceps is carefully put round the baby's head while it is in the birth canal and the two handles fit together. The doctor then pulls as for the ventouse delivery. With forceps, it is usual to have an episiotomy or cut in the back wall of the vagina to help the baby out. You would be given an anaesthetic first to numb the area.

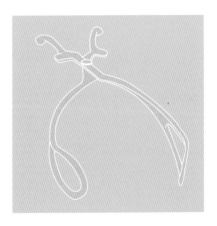

When would an instrumental birth be suggested?

An instrumental delivery can usually only be carried out in the second stage of labour when the cervix is fully dilated and the waters have broken.

This procedure might be suggested if you were getting very tired and finding it difficult to push the baby out. It could also be done if the baby were having a problem moving down through your pelvis. This can happen particularly if your baby started labour in a difficult position, such as the 'occiput posterior' position where your baby is lying with her back against your back.

An assisted birth can also be recommended if either you or your baby is having problems coping with this stage of labour. Unfortunately, epidural anaesthesia can increase your chance of needing help to get your baby born.

What choices can I make?

As with all interventions, it is your choice whether to accept help during the second stage of labour or not.

If you decide after discussion that you would like to have an assisted birth, you may be able to choose whether to have forceps or ventouse, although this will depend on your particular circumstances. The doctor involved may also have a preference.

Which is best, forceps or ventouse?

Research shows that for most instrumental deliveries, ventouse should be used rather than forceps.[⊙] This is because ventouse is much gentler for the woman than forceps, and an episiotomy may not be necessary. Women who have had a ventouse delivery also have less postnatal pain than those who have forceps.[⊙] When ventouse is used first, fewer caesareans are performed because forceps are the next likely option if ventouse doesn't work (see below).

What is the effect on the baby?

Both the use of forceps and ventouse can have short-term effects on the baby. Forceps can cause bruising or facial injuries, and ventouse can temporarily affect the shape of the baby's head and cause bruising. There is not enough research to be able to say which is preferable in the long term.

Some women find that their babies are more unsettled following an assisted delivery. If this is the case, babies may benefit from visiting a cranial osteopath.

Can my birth partner stay with me?

Yes, if they wish. If you decide to have an assisted delivery, you will be asked to lie on your back and put your feet up in stirrups. After the forceps or ventouse are applied, the doctor will have to pull quite firmly during the contraction to help the baby be born. Your birth partner may find this distressing to watch so he or she may prefer to sit near you at the other end of the bed and concentrate on supporting you.

Will I need extra pain relief?

If the baby is still quite high up, you will need to have an epidural in place, or a one-off injection called a 'spinal'. This will give good pain relief to the whole area. If the baby is very low and just needs lifting out, either with a ventouse or forceps, then an injection of local anaesthetic around the perineum will be sufficient.

What if it doesn't work?

If a ventouse delivery is not successful, forceps may used, or a caesarean. If forceps are not successful, you would be offered a caesarean operation.

AVOIDING AN ASSISTED BIRTH

- Opt for non-epidural methods of pain relief.
- Try not to lie on your back during the second stage of labour.
- Relax your pelvic floor.
- Conserve your energy by listening to your body and pushing only when your body is telling you to, rather than being directed when to push by someone else.
- Breathe as your body tells you during a contraction, rather than holding your breath and pushing as hard as you can.
- A syntocinon drip can sometimes be used to strengthen second stage contractions.

caesarean birth

Birth by caesarean section is now far more common than it was a few years ago. In some parts of the UK, as many as 30 per cent of births are caesareans, so it is unwise to assume that 'it won't happen to me' or ignore the possibility that your baby could be born this way.

CLEAR EVIDENCE FOR A CAESAREAN

- placenta praevia: when the placenta lies across the cervix or opening into the vagina
- placental abruption: when the placenta comes away from the wall of the uterus
- pre-eclampsia: which can develop into a serious medical condition of pregnancy
- medical conditions of the baby.

INDICATIONS WHERE THE EVIDENCE IS LESS CLEAR

- breech presentation: when the baby lies bottom down
- failure to progress: when the progress of labour is considered to be too slow
- fetal distress: when the baby is believed to be in difficulty
- previous caesarean deliveries
- twins or more.

For some women the suggestion of a caesarean, or the decision to carry out the operation, will come as a welcome relief. The circumstances of their situation and the information they have been given will combine to reassure them that a caesarean birth is right for *this* woman and *this* baby at *this* time.

For other women the prospect of a caesarean can be disappointing or distressing. If she has not been given enough information, or she is not convinced of the need for or the 'rightness' of a caesarean, then a woman can feel she has no option but to agree, despite her misgivings. Under these circumstances a caesarean can, sadly, be experienced as traumatic.

If you do not feel you have been given sufficient information, or you do not understand your circumstances as well as you would like to, do ask for more information. You have a right to a second opinion, and if there is time you can seek further information from elsewhere such as caesarean support organizations or the internet.

When would a caesarean be recommended?

A caesarean may be recommended at any time during pregnancy or labour. A caesarean planned in advance is termed an 'elective' caesarean, whereas one agreed at short notice, especially during labour, is termed an 'emergency' caesarean.

In some cases, there is clear evidence that a caesarean is needed to save life or safeguard the health of mother or baby. However in many cases the best option is not so clear. Obstetricians can read the same evidence in different ways and hold differing opinions on the need for a caesarean.

Parents may have different priorities when making decisions. There are occasions when the choice is left to parents – who may feel they have insufficient information on which to base an informed decision.

Can I choose not to have a caesarean?

As with all interventions, you have to give your consent before you can have a caesarean. However, if you are uncertain about the need for a caesarean it can be very difficult to disagree with your medical professionals, particularly if you are in labour.

Not all 'emergency' caesareans are dire emergencies. The urgency of a caesarean (elective or emergency) has been graded into four categories:[○]

- An immediate threat to the life of the mother or baby.
- Mother or baby are in difficulty but it is not immediately life threatening.
- Mother should be delivered shortly but neither mother nor baby are in difficulty.
- Delivery timed to suit the mother and the staff.

Unless the circumstances of your caesarean fall into the first two categories there should be time for you to seek more information to help you to understand your situation and come to your own decisions. Turn to page 125 for more about using a 'BRAIN' analysis to work out what would be right for you and your baby.

How can I avoid a caesarean?

There are ways to make a caesarean less likely:

- If your baby is breech, you should be offered ECV (external cephalic version) to try to turn the baby round. You could also consult a homeopath, acupuncturist or reflexologist.
- In the later part of pregnancy you could try to get your baby into a good position for labour.
- During labour you can encourage things to progress by keeping mobile and trying different positions. Intermittent monitoring of the baby's heartbeat with a Pinard or Sonicaid, rather than EFM, also reduces the likelihood of a caesarean.
- Mothers who book a home birth are less likely to need a caesarean.

What are the main risks and side-effects of having a caesarean?

Although a caesarean is generally considered to be 'safe' it is major abdominal surgery and there are some risks to both you and your baby.

- Vaginal birth is about four times safer for the woman than having a caesarean[○] but in both cases the risk is very small. An elective caesarean is thought to be safer than an emergency caesarean.[○]
- The mother is at risk of haemorrhage, wound infection or small blood clots (thrombosis). Recovery can take longer and varies considerably from woman to woman.
- One of the long-term effects of the operation is having a scar on your uterus which may affect future fertility, pregnancies and births, and complicate any later gynaeocological surgery, if required. A few caesarean mothers have been known to suffer long-term pain.
- The major risk to babies born by caesarean is the higher risk of having breathing difficulties which may continue for a while after the birth. The

'We were kept informed of what was happening and the anaesthetist was brilliant. Phillippa was checked over within our sight and then handed to us and tucked up beside me.'

If monitoring during labour shows that your baby is 'in distress' and not getting enough oxygen, a caesarean is sometimes offered. There is no doubt that caesareans have saved many lives, but studies also show that electronic fetal monitoring itself increases the caesarean rate without safeguarding the health of all babies.[⊙]

When fetal distress is suspected, fetal blood sampling reduces unnecessary caesareans.

birth process itself helps the baby to breathe once she is born. Babies born by caesarean – particularly elective – have not had this benefit. These babies may be more likely to need care in the special care baby unit after birth.

- Breathing difficulties due to prematurity can be reduced by waiting until at least 39 weeks of pregnancy to have a caesarean.[⊙]

Can I choose to have a caesarean for non-medical reasons?

If you want a caesarean birth discuss this with your obstetrician. Some consultants believe that any unnecessary operation should be avoided, whereas others believe it should be available as a choice for women who are fully informed of the risks. If your obstetrician is not comfortable with your reasons for wanting a caesarean, you can be referred for a second opinion. Some women with a severe fear of childbirth have found that with the right support and counselling they have been able to cope with vaginal birth even when they thought they would never be able to do so. Others have been given a caesarean on psychological grounds, which *is* a medical reason.

What sort of anaesthetic will I have for my caesarean?

If you know you will be having a caesarean you should be given the opportunity to meet the anaesthetist to discuss your anaesthetic options.

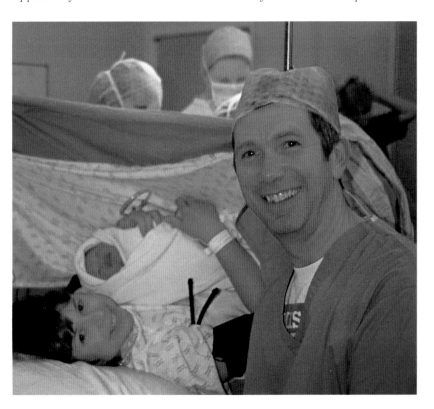

Your baby will be born very quickly, during the first five minutes. Stitching up, after the birth, will take around half an hour.

These days, the considerable majority of caesareans use spinal anaesthesia. This is a one-off injection in the lower spine which works quickly and gives sufficient anaesthesia for the length of the operation.

When an epidural has been used for pain relief in labour, this can usually be topped up to provide the anaesthesia required for an emergency caesarean. An epidural is sometimes used for elective caesareans but is becoming less common.

Both spinals and epidurals give regional anaesthesia so that you are awake while the caesarean is being done.

Around ten per cent of caesareans – both elective and emergency – are performed under general anaesthetic.[o] With a general anaesthetic you will not be aware of anything going on around you.

General anaesthetics are less safe than regional anaesthesia but may be used for various reasons. You may wish not to be awake during the operation, or you may have a medical problem which prevents the use of a spinal or epidural.

What happens if I need to have a caesarean?

The exact procedure varies with different hospitals and obstetricians, but in all cases you will be asked to sign a consent form, without which the operation cannot legally take place.

If you are having an elective caesarean, you will have some routine blood tests done. You may be asked to go into hospital the night before or early on the morning of the operation. You will usually be asked not to eat or drink for some hours prior to the operation, and to take antacid medicine to neutralize your stomach contents.

Before your operation, the final preparations will take place. These will involve: changing into a hospital gown; having a bikini shave if necessary; removing nail varnish, contact lenses and jewellery; and putting a name-band on your wrist. You may also need to take some clothes to the theatre for your baby.

You will then be taken to the operating theatre. If you are having a spinal or epidural anaesthetic, your birth partner will be able to stay with you during your caesarean and will have to change into theatre clothes. If you are going to have a general anaesthetic, your birth partner will usually be asked to stay outside the operating theatre.

If you are having an emergency caesarean, the degree of urgency will determine how much time is available for the above procedures.

What about the caesarean itself?

The procedure is similar whether the caesarean is an elective or an emergency.

There are likely to be a large number of people in the room with you. The medical staff may include: a midwife; the obstetrician and an assistant;

'I had a caesarean – I was surprised at the length of time of recovery. I had an emergency so I didn't have much time to think – but I was scared and was glad when it was over. The main disappointment was not being able to hold her immediately – luckily my husband held her quite quickly afterwards.'

a theatre nurse and an assistant; an anaesthetist and their assistant; and possibly a paediatrician.

You should not feel any pain at all during the operation although you may be aware of some sensations. Some women describe it as if 'someone is doing the washing up in your tummy'. If you have had a general anaesthetic you will not be aware of anything until you wake up after the operation.

Your baby will be born very quickly, during the first five minutes, followed by the delivery of the placenta. It will then take around half an hour to have your wound stitched.

If you are awake and your baby is well, you can have her handed to you straight away. If you have had a general anaesthetic, she can be given to your birth partner outside the theatre. If your baby needs any help breathing, or has other problems, she may need to be taken to the special care baby unit.

Your baby should be able to have skin-to-skin contact with either you, or your birth partner, as soon as she is born and some mothers have breastfed their babies whilst still in theatre.

Meanwhile, your wound will be stitched. There are several layers of tissues which need stitching. The stitches in the underneath layers will dissolve by themselves. Your skin will usually have one continuous stitch with beads, or special skin staples.

What happens after the birth?

Again, exact procedures will vary between hospitals and obstetricians. Typically, you would be moved out of the operating theatre to another room. A midwife will monitor you to make sure there are no problems until you have recovered sufficiently to be taken to the postnatal ward. If you have had a general anaesthetic, your birth partner and baby should be there with you when you wake up.

After the operation it is usual to be given a painkiller that lasts for several hours. It is also usual to wear tight stockings or be given medication to reduce the risk of getting thrombosis.

Are there any choices I can make for myself?

Many women are surprised by the scope of options available, even though a caesarean is surgery. Women who have had time to think about what aspects of birth are important to them, have often found it helpful to think through what they might like to have during their caesarean and state their preferences while discussing choices at the time.

Health professionals may be wary of discussing caesarean preferences until they realize these are not medical requests, but just environmental ones. For example, some women have chosen to have a commentary during the birth, music playing or silence; to have photographs or a video taken; see

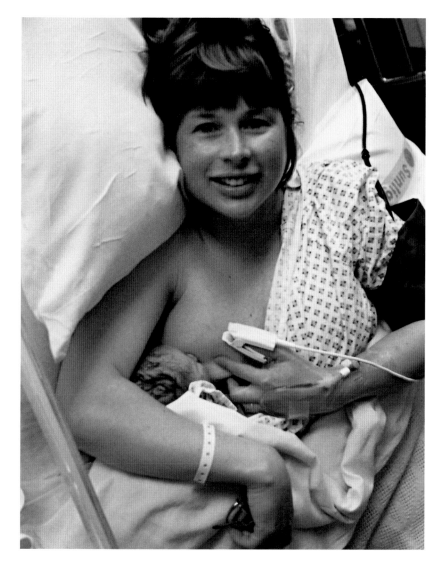

After a caesarean, you should still be able to hold your baby and cuddle skin-to-skin. Breastfeeding as soon as possible after the birth, if it's what you would like to do, is possible and some mothers have breastfed while still in theatre.

their baby born via a lowered screen or with a mirror; be the first person to greet their baby; discover the sex of the baby themselves or decide who they would like to give them this information.

If I have a caesarean, can I have my next baby vaginally?

VBAC (vaginal birth after caesarean) is accepted as a safe option for mother and baby. There is a very small risk of scar rupture, but caesarean section has risks too. Most mothers in this situation are able to choose either a VBAC or repeat caesarean with the next pregnancy.

A caesarean can be an extremely positive experience, when mothers feel confident it was the right choice for them and that their wishes were respected.

when a home birth is transferred to hospital

A much-wanted home birth doesn't turn out as planned

'Thanks to an amazing midwife who let us continue coping with the contractions, I felt in control, although unable to speak as they were coming every couple of minutes.'

'I had never considered home birth until I discovered that it was as safe as hospital, in a normal pregnancy. I felt relaxed about the labour even though my baby was in a posterior position and on the fifth day past my due date I went for a walk at 4pm. I had a show and contractions began at 10pm. The midwife discovered that I was 1cm dilated. The following day, at my antenatal appointment, I felt a gush of water – my waters had broken! Hospital policy was that a woman should deliver within 24 hours of her waters breaking to minimize infection risk, so a doctor was called.

'The doctor noticed a slowing of the baby's heart rate and recommended that I stay in. The baby was my priority, but I couldn't see any reason to be in hospital so my partner and I argued, which was stressful, but I stayed. I was then monitored, which was frustrating as I was trying to keep active.

'The following day, I had dilated to 2cm and on Friday, 3cm – I had progressed just 3cm in three days! I was given prostaglandin to move things along and the contractions increased. Thanks to an amazing midwife who let us continue coping with the contractions, I felt in control, although unable to speak as they were coming every couple of minutes. After a few hours, I was put on a syntocinon drip.

'This is when I opted for an epidural – after three sleepless nights I decided it would be hard to cope without. This shattered my dream of a natural birth but helped as the contractions became extremely painful.

'When the midwife examined me, she was amazed that I was fully dilated and the baby had turned into the correct position! I had to allow the contractions to move the baby down, as at this point I had no urge to push. The midwife became concerned that the baby was distressed so the doctor decided that he had to come out by ventouse. I was put in stirrups and pushed with all my might. Liam was born within five minutes.

'The cord was around Liam's neck which probably caused the slowing of his heart rate. He was whisked off for antibiotics. We were transferred to the Transitional Care Ward and spent a week being poked and prodded. Liam had trouble feeding, his blood glucose dropped and he had to be supplemented with formula. Luckily my milk came in the next day and I expressed all Liam's feeds. The doctors tested for meningitis and took Liam for a lumbar puncture. When the results came, nothing was wrong. This was hard to accept after everything Liam had been through.

'Eight days after his birth, we went home. Liam is thriving and I can almost see him growing! I do feel disappointed with the birth and given that nothing was wrong, I wonder whether I could have done it at home. Still, *I would do it all again!*'

a positive elective caesarean

'My first pregnancy was easy and my daughter was delivered vaginally after a 12-hour labour and a few whiffs of gas and air. When I became pregnant again, I thought I had this birth thing worked out. A check at 36 weeks threw a spanner in the works as the midwife discovered the baby was breech. A scan showed the baby was likely to be large. My daughter had weighed 9lb 4oz and this one looked similar so I was presented with the choice of trying a normal delivery or an elective caesarean.

'The decision wasn't easy; my instinct was for a natural birth but in the end I chose a caesarean. My husband and I weren't prepared to take the risks that can be associated with breech birth.

'Having decided, everything fell into place. We knew the baby's birthday in advance, which felt strange, but enabled us to book grandparents to look after my daughter and my husband knew when to book time off work.

The operation went well

'On the day of the operation we checked into hospital at 8.30am. I found it unreal; it was only when I heard a baby cry that it hit home why we were there! It was odd getting into a hospital gown and putting a sleep-suit on the radiator to warm when I felt completely normal. The operation went well: there was a relaxed atmosphere in the theatre and the staff were super. My husband saw our son being delivered, albeit accidentally. They asked him if he wanted to see the baby being born, but he didn't catch the last two words! The surgeon told us that Findlay had the cord wrapped around his neck. This would have made a vaginal delivery dangerous so any doubt about choosing a caesarean was gone.

'As the spinal block wore off, I was in a lot of pain. However the painkillers I was offered were effective and let me catch up on some sleep. I was told that it aided recovery to get up as soon as you can and I believe that's true. I went off for a shower on the morning after the op bent in two, but came back feeling a different person.

'I needed three nights in hospital and within a fortnight felt pretty much back to normal. It's 12 weeks since Fin was born and, apart from some numbness above the scar, I feel fine.

'I would still much prefer a straightforward vaginal delivery but in the same circumstances would be happy about choosing a caesarean. On the ward, the women having the most problems had emergency caesareans and were exhausted from long labours. I'm happy to say that an elective caesarean was not like I'd imagined. I'd had time to prepare for it emotionally and was quick to recover from it physically!'

'I thought I had this birth thing worked out. A check at 36 weeks threw a spanner in the works.'

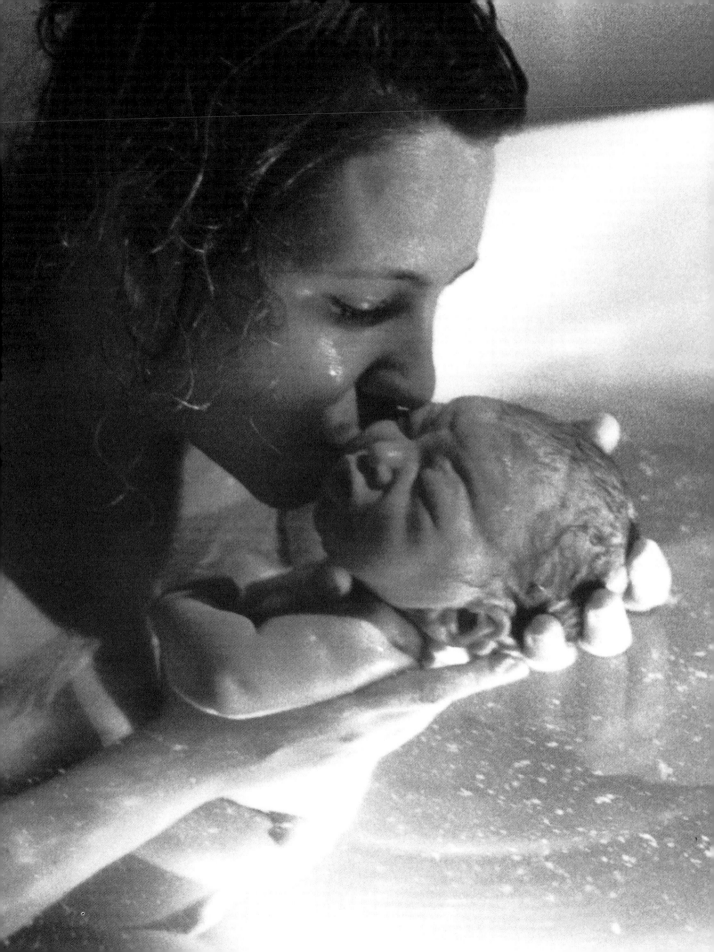

The birth

trust the process

Women have been giving birth since time began and all around the world they are doing so right now, as you read this book. The female body is designed for birth, thanks to profound changes that take place during late pregnancy and labour which enable the womb to open up and let the baby out.

Once really started, the process is unstoppable. Trust the process and go with it. Giving birth is an overwhelming experience and can be frightening, but it can also leave you with a feeling of exhilaration unmatched by any other.

This is how it works: during the last few weeks of pregnancy your body starts to produce its own natural pain-relieving chemicals called endorphins. These circulate in the body making you feel a bit 'out of it' – dreamy and forgetful. There are different theories about what triggers labour, but it seems that the

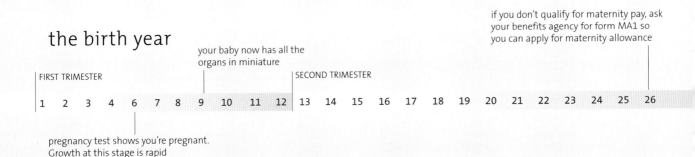

the birth year

your baby now has all the organs in miniature

if you don't qualify for maternity pay, ask your benefits agency for form MA1 so you can apply for maternity allowance

FIRST TRIMESTER

SECOND TRIMESTER

1 2 3 4 6 7 8 9 10 11 12 13 14 15 16 17 18 19 20 21 22 23 24 25 26

pregnancy test shows you're pregnant. Growth at this stage is rapid baby sends out a chemical message to the mother signalling readiness to be born. If the mother is also physically and psychologically ready, a biochemical switch is triggered. The hormone oxytocin pulses through the body, the great muscles of the uterus begin to contract and the exit from the uterus gradually widens. The contractions get more intense and more frequent and the body releases more and more endorphins. These bring about a dream-like state, enabling you to 'let go'. Gradually the womb opens to allow the passage of the baby. Once open, you are ready to work with the contractions to push the baby out into the world.

Certain things may get in the way of this magnificent process: if you are tense, anxious and do not feel confident in your surroundings, or with your support, the pain-relieving endorphins may not be so effective.

Just remember:

- You have nothing to fear: your body has been designed to give birth, thanks to millions of years of evolution.
- The intellectual part of you has to let go. The sooner you are able to let go, the quicker the labour will be.
- Take time to choose the right place and the right people to be with you during the birth – it's easier to let go when you feel safe.
- Having a baby isn't just a physical experience: it affects our whole self.

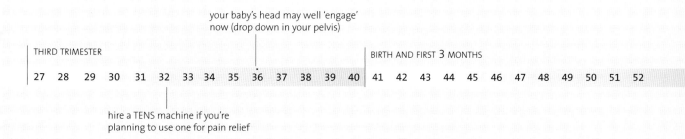

your baby's head may well 'engage' now (drop down in your pelvis)

THIRD TRIMESTER

BIRTH AND FIRST 3 MONTHS

27 28 29 30 31 32 33 34 35 36 37 38 39 40 41 42 43 44 45 46 47 48 49 50 51 52

hire a TENS machine if you're planning to use one for pain relief

the role of hormones

It is not known exactly what starts labour, but it is thought to be the baby. Oxytocin is transferred across the placenta to the mother's bloodstream, which suggests that both the starting and continuation of the birth process are influenced by the amount of oxytocin produced by the baby.

In a normal labour, the amount of oxytocin secreted by the baby is at the level used by doctors to induce contractions – that is, bring them on by artificial means. Oxytocin – 'the feelgood hormone' – is released into our bloodstream during labour. French obstetrician Michel Odent has suggested that natural birth releases a 'cocktail of love hormones'.[*] These hormones stimulate contractions, breastfeeding, the bonding between you and your baby, and they can take the edge off your pain.

Labour is controlled by the brain through your hormone system, which is in turn affected by how you feel. In order for a labouring woman to give birth instinctively, she must feel secure and comfortable in her birth environment. Different hormones released during the birth process – oxytocin, endorphins, prolactin, adrenocorticotrophic hormone (ACTH), – originate in archaic brain structures such as the hypothalamus and the pituitary gland. In other words, the most active component of the body of a woman in labour is the primitive part of her brain. Essentially, a labouring woman does not think rationally; she acts instinctively.

When the natural flow of labour is disturbed, adrenaline is released and this has the effect of delaying the birth, which is nature's way of protecting your baby. (If you don't feel that you are in a safe place, then it may not be safe for your baby to be born.)

This natural flow can easily be disturbed by all kinds of unnecessary stimulation, such as:

- bright lights
- being asked questions and being expected to respond
- feeling observed by others
- feeling unsafe or under threat
- loud noises
- invasive procedures
- too many strangers
- not enough reassurance.

Adrenaline and noradrenaline make your heart beat faster, constrict small blood vessels and increase your metabolic rate. A surge of adrenaline sends blood rushing to the brain and muscles to enable you to fight or run away, the so-called 'fight or flight' mechanism. The blood going to the brain and muscles is diverted from the digestive tract, the womb and other internal organ functions.

Adrenaline can make you panicky and raise your blood pressure. Your contractions will then slow down because adrenaline inhibits oxytocin production. Your body's natural response to what is seen as a threatening situation may then be diagnosed by medical staff as failure to progress with labour. Pain-killing drugs might then be given and a synthetic oxytocin drip set up, when simple steps like dimming the lights and providing privacy, quiet and an empathic carer could get the labour on course once more, just as effectively.

However, the hormones adrenaline and noradrenaline do play some positive part in the interaction between you and your baby immediately after birth. During the very last contractions of a natural birth, the levels of these hormones peak. One of the effects of this hormone surge is that the mother is alert when her baby is born. The baby releases his own hormones and so is also alert, with wide-open eyes and dilated pupils.

Gazing into each other's eyes is an important feature of the beginning of the mother and baby relationship, as it is when two adults fall in love. Oxytocin is also necessary for the natural delivery of the placenta because it causes the womb to contract. Oxytocin is also released when you put your child to the breast for the first time after birth.

The role of the brain

Different parts of the brain each govern different activities and functions in the body. The cerebral cortex acts as a processor of input from your senses, interprets and makes decisions, regulates your voluntary muscle activity and is concerned with memory, learning and reasoning. The thalamus passes sensory information on to the cerebral cortex. The hypothalamus is what co-ordinates the action of the endocrine glands (which produce hormones) and autonomic nervous systems (see box). It is also the control centre for food intake and water balance. The pituitary gland controls and integrates your hormonal activity.

Other hormones involved in birth

A number of other hormones are released during labour, along with those already mentioned. Oestrogen prepares your womb to contract by causing a dramatic increase in the number of 'oxytocin receptors' in the muscle of the womb towards the end of pregnancy.

Cortisol is produced by the adrenal gland. It releases fats and amino acids in your body to help you deal with the stress of labour. The surge of it produced by labour releases extra lung surfactant, something that in turn helps your baby to breathe at birth.

THE NERVOUS SYSTEM

The nervous system is divided into the 'somatic' and 'autonomic' nervous systems. The somatic nervous system controls the voluntary or skeletal muscles that you use to smile or walk, the ones you have control over.

In contrast, smooth muscle and cardiac muscle, as well as the muscle of the womb, is controlled involuntarily by the autonomic nervous system, which works automatically. This system also controls body functions such as circulation and digestion. The autonomic system is divided into the 'sympathetic' and 'parasympathetic' systems which balance each other out. The sympathetic system produces the 'fight or flight' reaction in response to stress or excitement. The parasympathetic system works to counteract this, and it is this system that dominates the body during sleep.

going into labour

As you approach your approximate date of birth, you'll start to get restless; eager to meet your baby yet increasingly anxious about labour. Try to relax. Remember that for most women giving birth for the first time, the move from pregnancy into labour is a slow and gradual process, and it's often spread over several days.

WAITING TO BEGIN

Increasingly in modern life we expect to know exactly when things will happen so that we can put a date in the diary, plan and be in control. Birth, however, is an event that is to some extent out of our hands.

It's not true that babies move much less, or even stop moving, before labour starts. Your baby's movements may gradually change in the last few weeks – but he should still be moving. If you think he is moving less, make sure you contact your midwife or labour ward the same day.

'PRACTICE' CONTRACTIONS

'Practice' or Braxton Hicks contractions (named after the obstetrician who first described them) are different from real contractions.

- Real contractions become gradually stronger, longer and closer together as time passes.
- The upper part of the uterus moves forward perceptibly during real contractions – you should be able to feel this movement if you put your hand on your bump.
- Each contraction builds up to a peak of intensity in the middle and then dies away again.

To help us track the journey through birth, it's officially divided into three stages. The first stage is when the cervix, or exit from the womb, unplugs and opens up wide enough to let your baby through. The second stage is the 'pushing' part, when you literally push your baby out into the world. The third stage is when the placenta is expelled. These three stages form one smooth, unstoppable process.

These first, second and third stages can be further divided into:
- pre-labour
- early labour (until the cervix is 3cm to 4cm dilated)
- strong labour (4cm to 10cm)
- transition (preparing to push)
- pushing
- birth
- delivery of the placenta.

Pre-labour

The countdown before true labour starts is known as 'pre-labour'. It can last for more than a day. You may notice a gradual increase in practice contractions, especially at night. These contractions should not be painful – but they can be uncomfortable and stop you sleeping.

Many women also start getting low tummy pains: colicky-like discomfort that comes and goes at odd intervals. The most likely cause of these pains is your cervix, softening and relaxing ready for action. The midwifery term for this is 'ripening'. You may also notice an increased flow of mucus from your vagina around this time, too.

Other signs of the cervix becoming more active include having a 'show' (when the mucus plug which seals the neck of the womb during pregnancy comes away, sometimes with a little blood) and loose bowel motions. On its own, having a show is not a reliable sign of imminent labour. Some women have repeated shows over a week (the mucus keeps being produced); others never have one at all. Similarly, if you get a touch of diarrhoea, it could be a sign that the cervix is waking up and tickling the nerves shared with the lower bowel – or it may be nothing to do with labour at all.

Before it can begin to open, your cervix has to change from a firm, tight tube 2cm to 3cm long, designed to keep your baby in, to a soft, stretchy disc ready to open and let him out. Midwives call this process 'effacement'.

During the pre-labour phase, contractions may be uncomfortable enough to stop you sleeping. However, unlike in 'real' labour, these contractions never seem to get stronger, longer, or closer together. If your midwife were to examine your cervix at this time, it would probably be closed or only 1cm dilated.

Early labour

Eventually, contractions start to increase until they are coming about every 20 to 30 minutes and lasting 10 to 40 seconds.

If you are planning to have your baby in a birth centre or hospital, there is no need to go in during early labour, unless you are worried or your midwife suggests this course of action. Swapping the comfort, privacy and intimacy of your home for a clinical, noisy, bustling hospital environment may make it harder to cope and accepting strong pain relief in the early phase of labour may also increase the risk of your baby being born by caesarean section.[©]

Here are some ideas for coping with early labour:

- If you're in bed, stay there. You need your rest. If this is labour, it will keep going. If it's not labour, at least you're resting.
- If it's daytime, carry on as usual. Send your partner off to work. Potter about, go for a walk, chat to a mate.
- Keep eating.
- Try simple remedies for the pain: a warm bath, a hot-water bottle, a small alcoholic drink, a dose of paracetamol.
- Be careful who you tell; other people may start to worry unnecessarily.
- Be positive. Think of this as a special time of gentle, private preparation.
- Ask for help if you need it. Phone your midwife or labour ward; your midwife may be able to visit you at home, or she may suggest you visit the labour ward for some professional reassurance.

How birth partners can help

- Be interested – but don't fuss. Give your partner time and space to get used to what is happening. She will involve you when she needs to.
- Look after her. Make tea, prepare food, run a bath, find clean clothes.
- Get ready and carry out normal tasks in preparation. If you are planning to give birth in a birth centre or hospital then make some sandwiches, fill a thermos flask, put bags in the car. If you are planning a water birth at home, check you have everything ready, but don't fill the pool just yet.
- Conserve your strength. In 24 hours' time, you will probably be more tired than you ever thought possible.

If you're in bed, stay there. You need your rest. If this is labour, it will keep going. If it's not labour, at least you're resting.

'I had been "niggling" as one of the midwives called it, for about 10 days before actual labour. Contractions started around 3.30pm, and I soon knew they were different to the 'niggles' I'd been having previously.'

established labour

The phase of labour when the cervix is dilating from about 4cm to 10cm is known as strong or 'active' labour. You will know when you are moving into this stage because the contractions will get stronger and closer together and the pain will become more intense.

Sooner or later, your labour will really get going. Your contractions will get longer, stronger and more frequent, until they are coming every five minutes, and lasting well over a minute. You will not be able to talk during contractions. Most women at this stage start withdrawing into themselves, becoming less aware of their surroundings or of time passing. These are all indications that you are moving into established labour.

Now is the time to call your midwife and ask her to come over if you are planning to have your baby at home, or to think about going to hospital.

'The quiet reassurance and comforting I received from Karen, my husband and the midwife was first-class, just enough and not too much to distract me.'

Why does labour hurt?

Contractions are like waves: they build up slowly, gaining in strength until they reach a peak and then fade away, losing their power before the next wave starts. Contractions start as small waves and get bigger and faster as labour progresses. At this active phase of labour, contractions can come every two to three minutes.

The pain of contractions seems to play a part in stimulating the release of

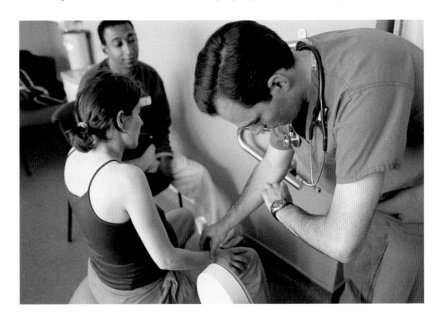

Your pulse and blood pressure will be checked throughout labour. Your midwife will monitor you to ensure that your labour is progressing normally, both for you and your baby.

the hormones necessary for the smooth progress of normal labour.[⊙] The increasing intensity of labour pain also makes a vital contribution to the way in which mother and newborn respond to each other when they meet for the first time.[⊙] By the end of a straightforward labour, both mother and baby are buzzing with nature's opiates, endorphins. Shortly before birth and fuelled by the expulsive contractions, both experience a surge of adrenaline. The mother is bursting with protective energy, while her baby is born alert, eyes wide open, ready to meet her gaze.

The pain of labour will probably be greater than anything you have ever experienced. But, unlike the pain of disease or trauma, labour pain is positive and productive pain. It also comes with built-in pain relief. When pushed to the limit, the human body produces endorphins (natural morphine-like hormones). Endorphins ease pain, change our perception of time, and make us feel good, giving us the will and energy to go on longer than we would have thought possible. Working with labour is all about using the power of endorphins – and letting your body get on with the job it is designed to do.

Occasionally, labour may not be straightforward. Things may not go as planned and the pain may just be too intense. If this seems to be happening, be kind to yourself. Accept the help that modern drugs and medical expertise can provide. What matters ultimately is that you do what's right for you.

Continuous care

A midwife should be with you throughout. At home, or in hospital, shifts may change but the support will remain. Apart from regular observations pertaining to the well-being of you and your baby, your midwife will be watching to make sure that labour is progressing normally. She will keep you and your partner informed of what is happening, encourage you when the going gets tough, and help you make any decisions regarding medical pain relief or other interventions. Your midwife is there to keep you safe and protected, so you can work with labour freely and intuitively. But it cannot be guaranteed that the same midwife will remain with you throughout.

How birth partners can help

- Be aware of what's happening. Your confidence in the birth process will make an enormous difference.
- Accept her pain. Seeing somebody you love in pain is very difficult and it is natural to want to stop the pain. Try to understand that in labour this response is not necessarily appropriate or even possible.
- Respect her. Keep her informed of what is going on and if something is not going as planned, explain clearly what the staff recommend to sort it out. Remember that your partner's consent is needed for every aspect of her care and treatment.
- Look after yourself. Take a short break every hour.

GROUP B STREPTOCOCCUS

Many people carry Group B Strep bacteria in their bodies without developing infection or illness. However, the bacteria can become deadly to people with weak immune systems and to newborn babies.

It's possible for pregnant women to transmit Group B Strep to their newborns at birth. Infection passed from mother to baby at the time of delivery can be very serious. If infection is found in the latter stages of pregnancy antibiotics are recommended and the use of these right up until the time of labour reduces the risk to the baby. In some areas of the country midwives are routinely testing pregnant women to see if this will reduce the overall risk of babies catching this infection.

The majority of infections can be prevented by administering penicillin at the onset of labour in those cases where the risk of Group B Streptococcus infection is highest. In practice, this means administration of an intravenous antibiotic to women with a raised temperature, prolonged rupture of the membranes, pre-term labour, an episode of Group B Streptococcus bladder infection during pregnancy or who have a history of a previous child that had a Group B Streptococcus infection.

working with labour

If you can help your body through this process, working with it, the pain of contractions can feel less intense. Move your body into positions that feel comfortable and right to you; concentrate on your breathing to stay calm, and create the space you need for this birth.

Left to follow their instincts, all creatures seek out a safe and private place in which to give birth. If you're having a home birth, it's easy to create the space you need. It may not be so easy in hospital. At the very least, all staff should knock and wait to be invited before entering a birthing room.

Once in your room, adjust the furniture to suit yourself. Close the curtains and turn down the lights. Consider using a birthing pool or bath. Water 'holds' you, surrounds and separates you. Many women find it really helpful in labour. Spend time in the bathroom or toilet – people tend to respect the privacy of a bathroom.

How birth partners can help
- Don't talk too much at this stage of labour. She needs to focus. Rational brain activity can interrupt the flow of endorphins.
- Care for her. She is working harder than she has ever done in her life before.
- Protect her. Help your midwife choose the best moment to speak with your partner. Keep your voice low so others will follow your example.

Stay upright
If your body is upright and leaning slightly forward during labour, your uterus forms an efficient column of contracting muscle. Your baby's head is pressed down centrally on your cervix so it opens evenly. As you approach the second stage of labour, your lower spine and sacrum are free to move back to give your baby room to descend. Staying upright also means you are free to move instinctively in response to the changing sensations.

An 'upright position' means any position in which your upper body is upright and your weight is off your bottom, be it standing, kneeling, all-fours, or sitting leaning forwards. The best upright position for labour is one which leaves your lower body free to move during contractions, but which supports you so you can rest in between.

If you arrive at hospital and continuous electronic fetal monitoring (EFM) is advised, ask why your carers have decided that it is necessary. 'Any interference with the natural process of pregnancy and childbirth should be shown to do more good than harm.'[o] Continuous EFM restricts freedom of movement in labour and may demand you assume certain positions (such as lying down).

If you agree to continuous monitoring, ask for this to be done whilst you remain upright. You may like to also ask if the unit has a 'telemetric' (remote) fetal monitor; a gadget that uses radio waves to transmit the ultrasound signals of your baby's heart to the base unit.

How birth partners can help

- Understand the importance of keeping upright during labour.
- Hold her while she leans against you.
- During pregnancy, think about whether you need to take any extra equipment into hospital – beanbag, extra pillows, small sturdy stool?
- Be practical. Is she really comfortable? How about a pillow under her head/thighs/feet/bump/knees? Can she reach her water bottle?
- Be prepared to rub her back for hours on end. Couples labouring in upright positions generally work up a wonderful rhythm of hip-wriggling and massaging.
- Tell her how well she's doing. Loving encouragement is what she needs.

Keep breathing

Breathing in a relaxed, measured way throughout your labour can really help you stay calm, as well as increase oxygen levels.

Holding your breath is a natural response to sudden pain – natural, but not helpful, especially in labour. If you hold your breath, your body tenses, and adrenalin levels rise. One of the effects of adrenalin is to divert blood from the uterus (and other internal organs) to prepare for 'fight or flight'. The muscle of the uterus therefore becomes short of oxygen, and contractions become more painful. Adrenalin may also upset the co-ordinated action of the uterus, adding to the pain.

Take time in pregnancy to become more aware of your breathing. With luck, when you start having strong contractions, it will feel natural to respond by breathing and relaxing rather than tensing up. Breathe in through your nose and out through your mouth, concentrating on the out-breath.

As labour progresses, there will come a time when you can no longer breathe smoothly through contractions. Don't panic and don't hold your breath. Just let your breathing naturally speed up – just as it does when you run upstairs or dash for a bus. Don't think about it; just let it happen.

If you breathe in this speeded-up way for more than a minute or so, you may feel an odd tingling sensation in your fingers and around your lips. This is caused by 'over breathing'; a temporary imbalance in the two gases involved in respiration: oxygen and carbon dioxide. The cure is very simple – just cup your two hands around your mouth and nose and breathe steadily for five breaths. This helps balance up the gases.

The support of a strong and reliable birth partner can help you withstand the pain of contractions.

good positions

To help your womb contract most effectively, try to stay upright and lean forward slightly. This will mean your baby's head is pressing firmly on your cervix and gravity is on your side. You'll probably find that it just feels 'right' to adopt the positions shown here.

Moving up and down stairs can help your baby move into a good position for birth and sitting on a toilet seat the wrong way round can be very effective too.

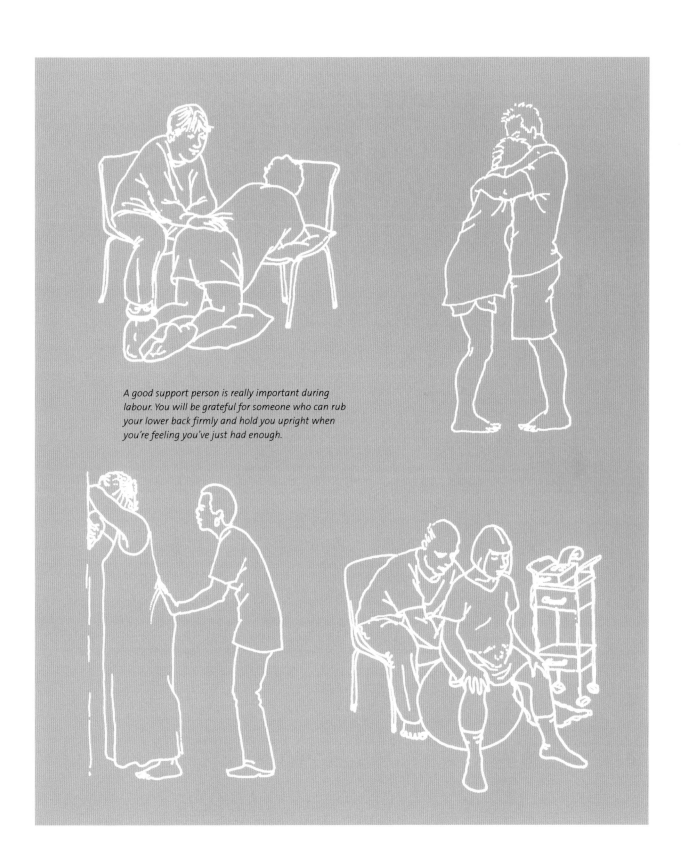

A good support person is really important during labour. You will be grateful for someone who can rub your lower back firmly and hold you upright when you're feeling you've just had enough.

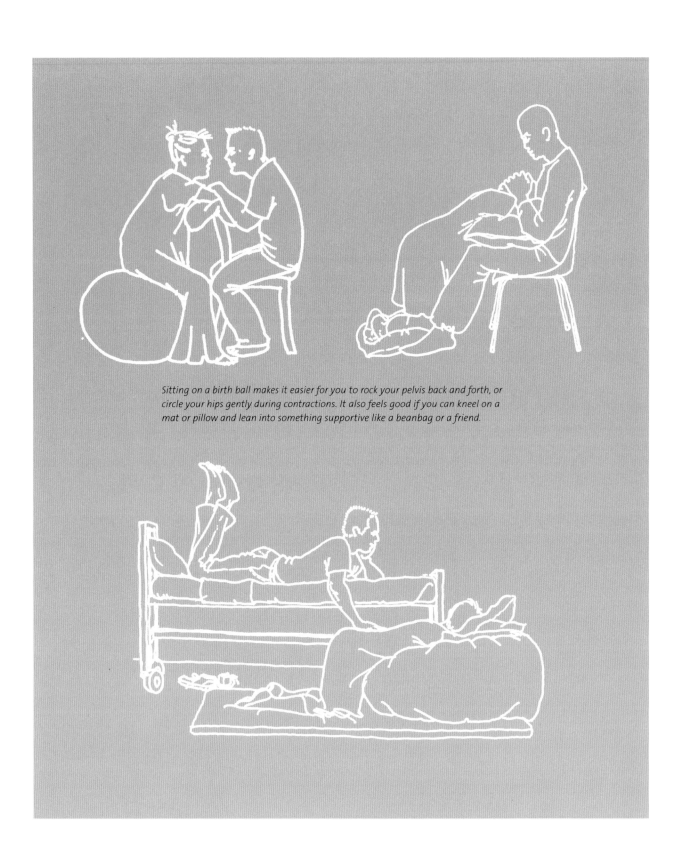

Sitting on a birth ball makes it easier for you to rock your pelvis back and forth, or circle your hips gently during contractions. It also feels good if you can kneel on a mat or pillow and lean into something supportive like a beanbag or a friend.

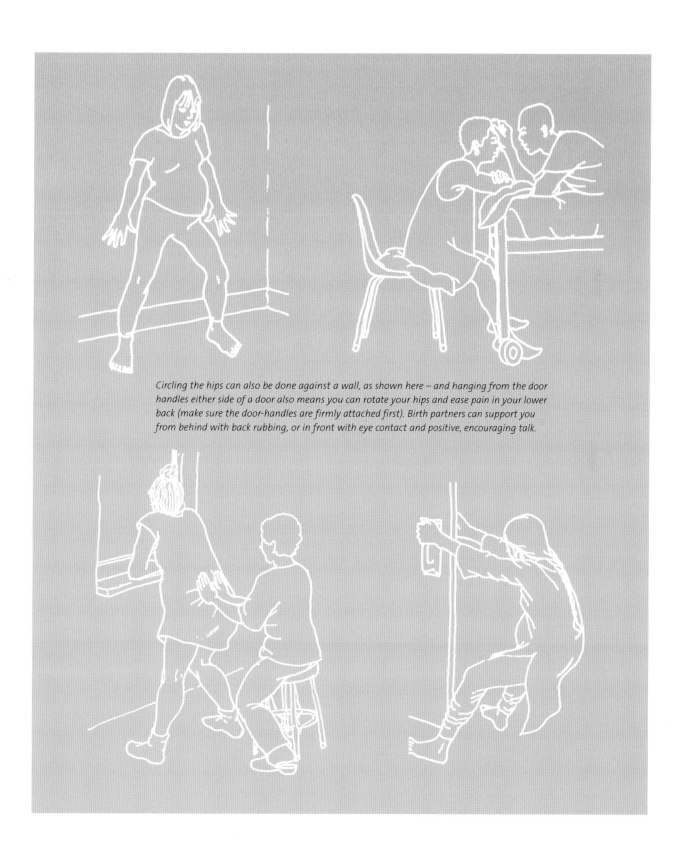

Circling the hips can also be done against a wall, as shown here – and hanging from the door handles either side of a door also means you can rotate your hips and ease pain in your lower back (make sure the door-handles are firmly attached first). Birth partners can support you from behind with back rubbing, or in front with eye contact and positive, encouraging talk.

dealing with the pain

Endorphins, the body's natural pain-relieving hormones, rise during labour and peak at the point of transition between first and second stage, when contractions can be at their most powerful. Instinctively, you will also find other ways to deal with the pain. Your midwives will be there too, giving support.

Make a noise

Many women find they get quite noisy during strong labour. Don't hold back. Making a noise can be really helpful, especially if you fit it in with the rhythm of your breathing.

How birth partners can help

- During labour, if she seems to be tensing up with contractions, remind her gently to keep breathing. Breathe with her if necessary.
- Keep your voice quiet and confident. If you find you are becoming snappy and irritable then take a break.
- Don't hush her if she starts making a noise. Just remind her quietly to keep the noise low and throaty.
- Help her relax by stroking down across her shoulders and upper arms, slowly and rhythmically, in time with her breathing.
- Tell her how well she's doing. If she starts saying she can't do this, agree that it's very hard work but she *is* doing it, and doing it brilliantly!
- Don't keep asking questions: she needs to switch off the thinking part of her brain. Instead, try to anticipate her needs.

Pain relief – using TENS

TENS stands for Transcutaneous Electrical Nerve Stimulation. TENS consists of four electrodes, attached to rubber pads taped to the labouring woman's back. The electrodes are connected by long wires to a base unit, which contains the small batteries needed to power the equipment, plus control knobs. When activated, TENS administers a mild electrical impulse to the area covered by the electrodes. The theory is that this impulse 'occupies' the nerve fibres serving the lower back, thus 'blocking' transmission of pain symptoms.

There is some proof that TENS can relieve the symptoms of chronic back pain. There is however no proof that TENS relieves labour pain.[*] This said, many women – and many midwives – believe TENS to be of value, particularly in early labour. You will need to hire a TENS machine in advance and it's worth trying it out before you go into labour. Ask your midwife, antenatal teacher or pharmacist about hiring a TENS unit.

Pain relief – using a birth pool

A birth pool is a large tub, much wider and deeper than a domestic bath, filled with warm water and ideally equipped with built-in thermostat and water heater.

When can I use it?

It is probably best to wait to use the pool until labour is well established. There is some (mainly anecdotal) evidence that labour may slow down or even stop should you immerse yourself in warm water too early.[◎]

What do I do?

Step into the warm water and get comfortable. Experiment with different positions: many women seem to prefer kneeling, legs well apart, with arms and head resting forwards on to the rim of the tub. You can use gas and air, provided somebody is with you.

Being in water will not stop the pain of contractions, but it will probably make them easier to cope with. We are not sure if this is due to the physical effects of immersion in water, the increased freedom of movement, or the privacy and intimacy of the surrounding. It's probably a combination of all these factors.[◎]

If you feel strongly that you want to get into the pool, you may well benefit from using it. If you feel you want to leave the pool, you should do so. Warm water can help if your contractions are coming quite strongly and frequently, or if your back is uncomfortable and you just want to relieve a feeling of pressure.

If your labour seems to be slowing down in the water, you might try moving into different positions or getting out of the pool for a while. Walking around can help. Squatting, kneeling on all-fours, or going up and down stairs can all help move the baby into a good position for birth.

Doing what 'feels right' is often best while you are in labour. You may choose to stay in the pool to give birth, or find, as many women do, that dry land suits you better when the moment arrives.

Practical points

If you hire a pool, it's useful to try assembling it and filling it in late pregnancy, or at least have one dummy run.

● Some pool hire companies recommend using a new sterile pool liner each time you use the pool. Other companies recommend simply sterilizing the liner yourself.

● Pools generally take about 30 to 60 minutes to fill.

● You can use Entonox ('gas and air') in the pool.

● You will usually be asked to leave the pool for any internal examinations (to assess progress in labour).

'Looking back, one of the most rewarding aspects of the water birth was the fact that I was so clear-headed afterwards as I didn't have to recover from the Pethidine or a lengthy labour and I managed to relax during the labour itself and that is all down to the fact I was in the pool'

What are the drawbacks to a birth pool?

- Floating in a tub of water is not compatible with electronic fetal monitoring. You will therefore be advised to get out of the pool should there be any concerns about your baby's well-being – although a hand-held Sonicaid can be used in a birth pool with a waterproof cover.
- You will also be asked to get out of the pool if you want Pethidine, because this drug may make you very sleepy.
- Epidural anaesthesia cannot be used with a birth pool.
- Getting too hot in the pool can cause problems. If your temperature rises, your baby's will also rise and this may cause him to become distressed.[○] Your midwife will keep an eye on your temperature, the ambient room temperature, and the water temperature. Help yourself by drinking at least a glass of water every hour and making sure that the water in the pool is not too deep; your breasts and upper body should be out of the water, to allow normal sweating and cooling.
- Many maternity units have strict policies on the use of water in labour – find out what these are during pregnancy. There's relatively little research available on the use of water in 'at risk' labours and so many units adopt an 'if in doubt, say no' policy. Remember, too, that pools are used on a 'first come, first served' basis and one may not be free when you need it. Many women prefer to hire their own pool and plan a home birth for that reason.

Other ways of using water

Use a normal domestic bath; run the water as deep as possible (block the overflow with Blu-Tack™) and lie or kneel. Stand under a shower. Ask your partner to hold a flannel wrung out in really hot water against your lower back and/or belly during contractions. You can use Entonox at the same time.

Pain relief – using 'gas and air'

Breathing nitrous oxide mixed in equal quantities with oxygen, helps to relieve pain effectively. Commonly called Entonox, it is used by three-quarters of women in labour.[○]

When can I use 'gas and air'?

Once again, it's probably best to wait until you are in advanced labour. Once you decide to use Entonox, it should be instantly available, either in a cylinder (at home) or piped (in hospital).

What do I do?

You can use either a mouthpiece or a face mask. The gas mixture takes 20 seconds to pass from your lungs into your blood and thence to your brain to take effect. This means that you must start to use it right at the very beginning

of each contraction. Breathe deeply as the contraction builds up. At the peak of the contraction, you can put the mouthpiece aside and concentrate on quick, light breathing, knowing there is plenty of gas in your system.

How much will it help?

Quite a lot – once you get used to it and provided you use it correctly. You can use Entonox standing, kneeling or on all-fours – provided there is somebody with you.

What are the drawbacks to 'gas and air'?

- Most women feel light-headed when they are using Entonox. The effect wears off within a minute or so. Some women like this feeling; some don't.
- Many women also feel sick when they first start to use nitrous oxide and oxygen. The nausea usually only lasts a few contractions so it's well worth perservering for a while.
- It is very important that you hold the mouthpiece or mask yourself. If you breathe too long and too deeply and take too much Entonox you will become drowsy. The mask will then slip from your face, so preventing you taking any more.

Other options

- Stand up and walk around – the increased pain could be a signal to change your position to help your baby on his journey.
- You could request a vaginal examination, if you think that knowing how far dilated you are will help.
- Consider using a birth pool.

Anything else I need to know?

When choosing your maternity unit, note the length of the Entonox pipes in the labour rooms. At least 3m means you can move around while using it.

Pain relief – using Pethidine

Pethidine is a powerful morphine-like sedative (sleep-inducing) drug with moderate pain-relieving qualities. It is usually given by injection into the large muscle of the thigh or buttock. The normal dose is 50–100mg. 'Pethidine' is actually a trade name; the correct generic drug name is 'meperidine'. Pethidine is used by around 40 per cent of women in labour.

'They gave me a small shot of Pethidine, which sent me to sleep and made me feel incredibly happy and relaxed.'

When can I use Pethidine?

Pethidine is best reserved for strong labour. Research suggests that the incidence of caesarean section birth is increased when powerful pain killers are given before labour is established.[⊙] Some authorities believe that contractions may slow down after a dose of Pethidine, especially if the drug is given before labour is in full swing.

About half of all women who have Pethidine say that it relieves their pain effectively and gives a welcome respite from the full tumult of labour.[⊙] Pethidine seems to take the edge off the contractions, reduce the muscular tension and anxiety that may contribute to pain, and help women relax and rest between contractions. Most women find they have to lie down once they have had Pethidine.

Other women find that Pethidine makes them feel remote and disassociated from what's happening without touching the pain; they fall asleep only to wake in pain with which they can no longer cope.[⊙] Research on the subject is not very helpful, concluding only that Pethidine is better than a placebo (pretend drug), and no better and no worse than other opioid drugs.[⊙]

What are the drawbacks to Pethidine?

Perhaps the most significant drawback is the effect of Pethidine on babies. Pethidine passes to the baby seven minutes after it is given to his mother, reaching maximum levels in 2–3 hours. The main effect is on the baby's behaviour after birth. Effects are minimal if the baby is born within an hour of the Pethidine being given, or after five hours.[⊙]

Babies who have been exposed to Pethidine may be slower than others to breathe at birth; the effects can be reversed by repeated doses of the antidote, naloxone hydrochloride (Narcan®). Pethidine babies may also be unusually sleepy for several days after birth. Getting breastfeeding going may be harder than usual,[⊙] although most difficulties can be overcome with patience and good support. Babies whose mothers have had Pethidine in labour may also be more prone to getting cold after birth.[⊙] The best way to keep a baby warm is to hold him skin-to-skin. If you are too sleepy to do this, your partner can slip his newborn inside his T-shirt.

How much would I need to take?

The effect of Pethidine, like all drugs, depends on the recipient; 100mg may be appropriate for a plump 20-year-old woman – but too much for a thin 40-year-old. Everyone's experience of the effects of drugs is different although most say Pethidine makes them 'woozy'. If you are undecided about using Pethidine, ask for 50mg initially and see how that works.

Anything else I need to know?

Pethidine makes two in three women feel sick,[⊙] so midwives often add an 'anti-emetic' (anti-nausea) drug to the syringe of Pethidine. Many anti-emetics are also potent sedatives that increase the soporific effect of Pethidine without contributing to pain relief. You may prefer to wait until you actually feel sick before accepting an anti-emetic.

Pain relief – using complementary therapies

The complementary therapies most often used in labour include:

- acupuncture
- aromatherapy
- herbal medicine
- homeopathy
- reflexology
- shiatsu.

All labour intervention should be treated with equal respect and healthy suspicion, and subjected to the same rigorous research standards. The research base for most complementary therapies as applied to childbirth is weak. More recently, however, a study analysed the effectiveness of five different therapies for labour pain: one each on acupuncture, audio-analgesia (listening to 'white noise'), music and aromatherapy – and three on hypnosis.[⊙]

It was found that both acupuncture and hypnosis were effective in reducing pain. In the acupuncture study, only 40 per cent of the women who received acupuncture required additional pain relief, while 87 per cent of the control group required it. The three hypnosis studies each had slightly different results, but taken as a whole, the findings suggested that women treated with hypnotherapy are more likely to have a vaginal birth, and less likely to have their labour speeded up. However, studies of the audio-analgesia, music and aromatherapy treatments showed no difference.

If you want to embrace a single therapy and use it to its full potential to ease your way through labour and prevent and treat complications, you need to contact a registered practitioner. (Don't forget to tell your midwife of your plans; some remedies may interfere with conventional care, and vice versa.)

'For my first baby I had a lovely lady who gave me reiki and massage during my labour, with special birthing aromatherapy oils. We got on straight away and it was lovely to have her there.'

birthing your baby

Although there is no sharp demarcation between the first and second stages of labour, many women experience a time of transition: a period of maybe an hour, during which the last circle of cervix melts away and the uterus and vagina merge into one continuous passage.

You may need to rest between contractions if your second stage goes on very long – lean into pillows or a beanbag.
Kneeling up supported by companions can be another good position.

Transition is often the most painful time in labour. Contractions are long and powerful, with very little rest in between. You may lose some blood from your vagina and (if they have not already broken) your waters may break at the height of a contraction. Your body senses that dramatic things are happening; many women are violently sick at this point, others start to shake, some have a fleeting sense of primitive dread or sudden fear. Your midwives will be expecting this and their reassuring presence will be deeply important to you now.

Pushing too soon

Occasionally things can get a bit muddled in transition, and you may get a strong urge to push before your cervix is fully open. If this happens, your midwife will probably tell you not to push because it is generally believed that if you push against an undilated cervix, the remaining tissue will become very thick and swollen, and even slower to open. Try getting down on all-fours, leaning on your elbows with your bottom in the air; this may help relieve the pressure. Keep breathing, emphasizing your out breaths – and don't panic; this time will pass.

Take your time

Full dilation of the cervix does not necessarily mean that it's time to start pushing. Your baby has to be ready; head low and turned, ready for the final part of his journey. Birthing your baby is generally much easier if you wait for signs that this has happened before starting to bear down. A strong, irresistible urge to push is a good indication. Your midwife will be looking for other clues and will guide you as necessary.

Pushing is not just about gathering your strength and bearing down during a contraction. It's also about letting go, relaxing the muscles around your vagina so your baby can pass through. This can be difficult: you probably haven't had your bowels open in front of another person for 20 years and pushing your baby out can feel a bit like doing just this. A calm, unhurried atmosphere, privacy, and support from people you trust will all help.

Try not to feel under pressure when you are pushing. Provided you and

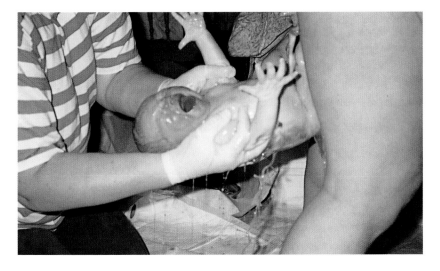

Giving birth standing up, or on all-fours, are good positions because your pelvis will open wider if your knees are lower than your hips.

'The second stage was amazing, I "knew" just what to do and when, and the midwives stopped coaching me and just encouraged/reassured me.'

your baby are well, progress is being made – however slowly – and you are happy to continue, there is no valid reason why you cannot push for up to three hours.⊙ If time goes by and your midwife has concerns, she should share these with you so you can make a joint decision about calling for obstetric help.

Crowning

As the birth approaches you may be aware of your midwife getting the room ready for your baby. Another midwife may enter the room. If you have decided that you don't want a natural third stage for delivering your placenta your midwife will prepare the hormone injection necessary for 'medical management' of the next stage. This will be given immediately after your baby is born.

Focus on the sensations of your body. Your perineum (the area between your vagina and back passage) will be stretched by your baby's head. The perineum is like foam rubber; soft and very stretchable. Help it stretch slowly by pushing until you feel the area stinging and burning, then ease off. Wait until the burning sensation fades, then push gently once more. You may find it helps to cup the top of your baby's head with your hand as he emerges – or you may not want to.

Your midwife will be close by, ready to suggest what to do should you falter. She may want to rest her hand lightly on your baby's head in order to control any sudden movement, or she may simply watch and wait; research suggests very little difference in the outcome of either approach.⊙

Within about five to ten minutes, your baby's head will be born. You can reach down and touch him. There may be a wait of several minutes for the next contraction. Your midwife will ask you to push hard and may help by guiding your baby out and up into your hands. You've done it!

EPISIOTOMY
Your midwife may suggest an episiotomy (a cut to enlarge the vaginal opening) for one of three main reasons:
- She suspects your perineum could tear badly.
- She thinks your baby is distressed and feels it would be better if he is born sooner rather than later.
- She can see that your perineum is unusually tough and unyielding.

meeting your new baby

Your baby will be warm, wet and slippery. Grasp his body under his arms, lift him up and hold him against your body. The moment you have been dreaming of for so long has finally arrived – your baby is here! Feelings of sheer relief can be overwhelming as you take your newborn into your arms for the very first time.

Your baby may not cry immediately and his skin may be bluish. This is normal. Cuddle him close and speak to him. Rub his head and body with a soft, dry towel. Your midwife will be watching closely and may place her fingers on his chest to check his heartbeat. Within a few moments, your baby will take a breath and the blueness will go. He may cry a little, but if he doesn't, it does not matter. Keep the lights dim and he will soon open his eyes and gaze up at you. Held in your arms, he can focus clearly on your face. Speak to him; he will recognize your voice.

Some babies need a bit of extra help to start breathing after birth. Home or hospital, your midwife will be trained and have the necessary equipment to clear his airways, administer oxygen, and help him breathe.

What will my baby look like?

Your baby may look a little odd immediately after birth. His head may be misshapen; pushed out at the back or pointed on top. This is due to 'moulding' – the normal displacement and overlapping of the soft skull bones. He will look better in 24 to 48 hours. He may also have a swollen lump on his head, caused by pressure during labour. His nose may be squashed, his face crooked, his ears crumpled – all this is normal and will soon straighten out. If he is born a little late, he may be covered in dark, tarry meconium. If he is born a bit early, he may be hairy and coated in white, sticky vernix. He may be streaked with your blood. You may not notice any of these oddities as you greet your new baby, exhilarated and with oxytocin, the natural hormone of love, coursing through your body.

Don't worry if you don't feel exhilarated, though. Your baby may look quite alien to you; completely different from the baby you expected. You may not feel anything much for him. If your labour has been long and hard, you may feel a bit detached and flat. Try not to worry. Hold him skin-to-skin for as long as possible. This will help you feel closer and more loving.

Depending on how you have chosen to deliver your placenta, sooner or later it will be time to cut your baby's cord. You, or your partner, may want to do this with scissors given to you by your midwife.

Continue holding your naked baby against your bare skin afterwards and

'They gave her to me, and it was love at first sight. I just couldn't believe how beautiful she was. She seemed so long. She had all this dark hair that was full of amniotic fluid and meconium, and therefore kind of green.'

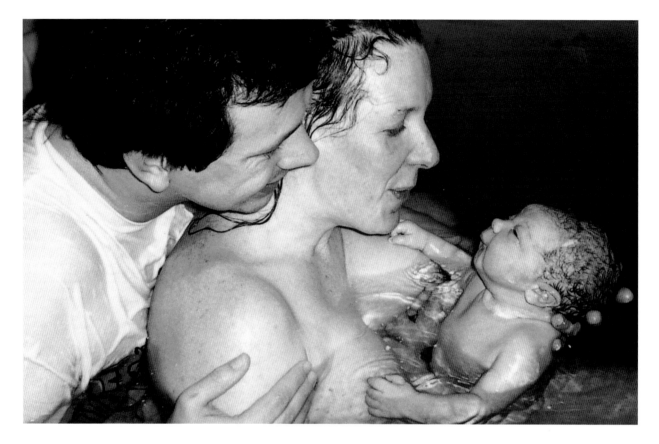

talk to him; hold him close and he will begin to learn your smell. Newborn babies lose heat very quickly after birth and holding him skin-to-skin will prevent this, provided he is dry (particularly his head) and the two of you are covered by a couple of dry towels or a warm blanket. Your midwife will continue to keep a close eye on both of you.

Keep the lights dim and your baby will soon open his eyes and gaze up at you. He can focus clearly on your face. Speak to him and he will recognize your voice.

First feed

Breastfeeding your baby within an hour or so of birth helps get feeding off to a good start.[○] Cuddling your baby skin-to-skin means that he is within sight and smell of your breasts. When he starts to look for your nipple, you will be able to respond immediately. Don't worry if your baby doesn't seem interested in breastfeeding for some time; video studies have shown that, left to their own devices, most babies wait nearly an hour before seeking the nipple.[○]

Please don't think that skin-to-skin contact is only for breastfeeding babies. If you have not yet decided how to feed your baby, cuddle him skin-to-skin and leave him to decide. He may seek your nipple and choose to breastfeed straight away. If you have chosen to bottle-feed your baby, make the first feed special by holding him skin-to-skin.

delivering your placenta

Most women don't even know that they have a choice when it comes to the delivery of the placenta because it has become usual in hospital for women to have a 'medically managed' third stage of labour. But there is another option.

'Active' or medical management has become the most common way of dealing with the third stage of labour, ever since it was introduced as a precaution against losing too much blood after birth. If there has been any medical intervention, such as a drip to speed up labour, it's also necessary to have a managed third stage. Now, this medically managed way of dealing with the delivery of the placenta has become so much the norm that most people don't realize that for women judged to be at low risk of blood loss, there is another, more natural, way of doing things.

'After 10 minutes of cuddles and suckling we got out and whilst nursing I delivered the placenta sitting in a chair.'

Natural delivery of the placenta

The third stage of labour is not just about getting rid of the redundant placenta. It's the time when the baby adapts to life outside the womb. Leaving the delivery of your placenta to nature is an integral part in this process.

After birth the umbilical cord is left intact; it is just long enough for you to hold your baby. Helped by a final boost of blood from the placenta, he will take his first breath – then another, and another. As his lungs expand, his heart and circulation will make the delicate adjustments necessary for independent life. Slowly, the flow of blood from the placenta will decrease, its job nearly over.

As you cuddle your new baby skin-to-skin, your system will be flooded with oxytocin, the hormone of love and labour; the hormone that will soon cause your uterus to contract and expel your placenta, and start the flow of milk from your breasts. Enclosed in your arms for the first time, this is a very special moment for you and your baby.

After a while, you may sense instinctively that it is time to cut the cord and you, your partner, or your midwife will do this. You will then probably want to spend time holding and admiring your baby. The room should be kept dim and quiet. It's important that you do not feel tense or watched, or adrenalin may interfere with the natural flow of events. Your midwife should stay close. If you wish, she may examine your perineum to see if you need stitches; she may even do these quickly for you whilst you are waiting for the placenta.

After 10 minutes or so (maybe longer, occasionally up to an hour) you should feel your uterus start to contract gently. After a short time, you

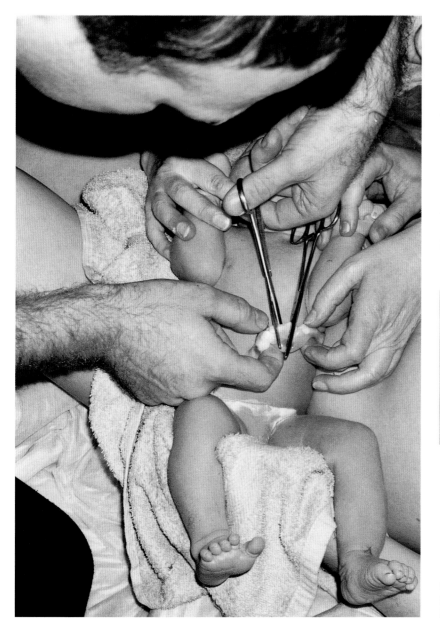

- Let mother and baby focus quietly on each other. This is a unique and private time. The hormonal side effect of these few uninterrupted minutes will help ensure that the third and final stage of labour goes smoothly.
- Don't rush away to make phone calls just yet. The outside world can wait for a while. Your partner needs to focus on her baby and the last few minutes of her labour.

YOUR PLACENTA

Examine your baby's placenta. It's a truly amazing organ – yet so sadly overlooked. The placenta legally belongs to you. You can do what you want with it – although most women ask the midwives or maternity unit to organize disposal.

There is no need to cut the umbilical cord immediately. Take time to gaze and hold your baby close.

should feel your placenta in your vagina and will push it out with a few small contractions. Your midwife will collect it in a container and place a hand on your belly to check that your uterus is well contracted.

Medical delivery of the placenta

The drug used in a medical third stage is usually 'syntometrine'; a mixture of syntocinon and ergometrine. This is generally given by injection into your thigh, either as your baby is being born or immediately afterwards. The main

Inside the womb, your baby was fed and protected by the placenta – the amazing organ that passes oxygen, nutrients and antibodies from mother to baby and prevents many harmful substances from reaching him.

effect of these two drugs is an extra-strong uterine contraction. Your midwife will immediately clamp and cut your baby's cord to stop him receiving an abnormal surge of blood from the squeezed placenta.

The contraction following the injection is strong, but not painful like labour contractions. This initial contraction causes the placenta to shear off the wall of the uterus; later, longer-lasting contractions will close the cervix – so it is important to get the placenta delivered in 15 minutes or so. If this does not happen, your placenta may have to be removed manually by an obstetrician in the operating theatre, generally under a spinal anaesthetic. It is not generally considered safe to simply wait.

Your midwife will wait for a few minutes for outward signs that your placenta has separated, before placing her left hand low down on your belly. She will then apply gentle pressure with this hand to hold your uterus in place, whilst she draws on the cord to extract the placenta. The procedure should be over in less than 10 minutes. Your midwife will then examine your perineum closely to see whether you need stitches.

Under the influence of the drug, your uterus will stay well contracted for several hours, thus controlling your blood loss. Once the injection has worn off, your own hormones should work to keep your uterus contracted, as it shrinks down over the next week or so.

Syntometrine has two significant side-effects:

- At least 6 per cent of women vomit violently about an hour after the injection.[*]
- The drug may occasionally cause a dangerous rise in blood pressure.[*]

These side-effects are minimized by using syntocinon alone, although this may not be quite as effective as syntometrine in controlling bleeding.[*] Due to drug licensing restrictions, syntocinon should be injected into a vein, rather than into a muscle.

Natural or medical – which way is best?

Medical management of the third stage has two apparent advantages. First, medical management is faster; an average of eight minutes against an average of 15 minutes for a natural third stage[*] – but at this point you will probably be focusing on your new baby and unaware of the time. Second, with medical management, you're less likely to lose a significant amount of blood (which means upwards of 500ml, approximately 1 pint). With medical management you have a 6.8 per cent chance of significant loss compared with 16.5 per cent if you do it naturally.[*]

The issue of blood loss may sound alarming, but needs to be balanced with the information that during pregnancy your plasma volume has increased by 50 per cent (plasma is the fluid part of your blood) and the number of cells in the blood also increases. A healthy pregnant woman therefore has a reasonable amount of blood to spare.

Some midwives think that the emphasis on blood loss at the time of the delivery of the placenta may be misleading, believing that women who had a medical third stage may actually lose the same amount of blood – but later on, when it is not measured accurately. This thinking is supported by research that shows all women tend to have a similar haemoglobin (iron level) three days later.[○] For some women though, there are health risks if they decide to have a natural third stage and for them, medical management has a significant role to play in ensuring outcome.

There are some women who cannot afford to lose even a moderate amount of blood in childbirth:

- very anaemic women
- the malnourished, unwell or weak
- those who have bled heavily during pregnancy.

Equally, there are some women who are already at greater risk of an above-average blood loss, and so may benefit from the 'protection' of a medical third stage:

- those having twins or very large babies
- women with blood disorders
- women who have previously had third-stage problems.

Finally, there is a group of women who may be steered towards medical management because the type of labour they have had may mean that the uterus does not work so effectively to expel the placenta and control bleeding:

- very long and exhausting labours
- very rapid labours (less than an hour)
- labours that have been started or speeded up with syntocinon
- labours where the woman has chosen to have Pethidine or an epidural.

All things being equal, it's up to you to consider the advantages and disadvantages of the two approaches and it really depends on your unique circumstances.

- Talk it over with your midwife
- Read *Delivering Your Placenta* a booklet published by the Association for Improvements in the Maternity Services (London: AIMS, 1999).

Research shows that women often know little about the third stage of labour. As the issues are complex, each woman should be able to talk about the third stage with a midwife and receive full and balanced information during her pregnancy. Women should not be expected to consider the pros and cons for the first time during labour.

While defining labour in terms of three separate stages may be helpful, there's a danger that we lose sight of the fact that all the stages are inter-related and combine to form a whole. How birth unfolds has an affect on the relationship between mother and baby, and how the mother feels about herself. This holds true for the third stage as much as any other part of the process and any approach should be as respectful as possible.

a wonderful twin birth in water

A midwife gives birth to two babies

'The water was lovely; it didn't take the pain away but helped me to cope. The buoyancy enabled me to change positions, setting into half-kneeling, half-squatting.'

'I approached the birth of my twins with excitement and trepidation. I had confidence to give birth following a water birth at home with my first child but discovering that my second pregnancy was twins added a degree of uncertainty. I resigned myself to a hospital delivery. I was lucky to have a wonderful midwife, Carole. I trusted her implicitly and without her support could never have achieved such a positive experience.

'I saw my consultant and emphasized that in the absence of complications, I wished to have privacy, minimal intervention and monitoring, an active birth using water and a physiological third stage. He was supportive and I was able to look forward to the birth. Both babies were head down.

'Labour started two days before my due date. The contractions quickly established between three and eight minutes apart. By 11.30pm, labour was established and Carole arrived to find me kneeling against Ian and concentrating on my breathing. We transferred to hospital where my room was warm, dark and quiet. The move was unsettling but once there, I switched off from the world and concentrated on giving birth.

'The pool was run and I had the fetal heart monitor held on by Carole for which I was grateful. I'd hoped my cervix might be 4cm dilated and was staggered when an examination revealed I was 9cm. The water was lovely; it didn't take the pain away but helped me cope. The buoyancy enabled me to change positions, settling into half-kneeling, half-squatting. I appreciated the privacy of the pool as twin deliveries often attract an audience. Carole, a supporting midwife, and my husband were my only attendants – the consultant and paediatrician hovering outside.

'My waters broke in second stage and I felt the first baby moving down. I didn't have a strong urge to push but doing so relieved the pain and after 20 minutes, my son was born into the water. I brought him gently to the surface. Knowing I had to do it again, the euphoria was overridden by pain and uncertainty.

'I left the pool to be re-examined. I was in pain so when I knew all was well, I didn't need asking twice to go back into the pool. The second waters broke spontaneously and I felt the baby coming. In spite of my protests, there was nothing I could do to prevent my daughter being born in two reluctant but easier pushes, 17 minutes after her brother. Again I brought her to the surface but she didn't cry and spent a moment being 'pinked up' with some oxygen. As I had minimal blood loss, I had a physiological third stage and pushed the placenta out nine minutes later.

'I had achieved a safe, natural twin water birth, which filled me with pride, gratitude to my carers, and love for my babies – a truly positive experience.'

a vaginal birth after three caesareans

'When I woke from the anaesthetic to find my first baby at my breast, I felt wonder at the creature my body had produced, but afterwards, started to blame myself for 'failing' by needing a caesarean. Two more unplanned caesarean births followed. We decided not to have more children and I had to accept that I would never know what it felt like to birth a baby.

'When I found I was pregnant again, my work as an antenatal teacher, and research I had read, made me certain that vaginal births after caesareans were not only possible but also safe. I knew that I needed to be at home with a wise woman. I knew of the independent midwife, Mary Cronk by reputation. Experienced in home births, she is down-to-earth, bolshy with uninformed medics and very knowledgeable. I resented having to pay for her care, not because I begrudge her, but because I believe this sort of care should be available to every woman.

'My previous labours had been long and slow, I couldn't believe this would be different so I was bemused one morning, 18 days overdue, to find I was having strong contractions every five minutes.

'I phoned Mary – my going overdue had interfered with her schedule and she had to be at a conference later so she'd reluctantly handed over my care to her colleague, Andrya, but wanted to know when it was happening. I phoned Andrya and then my friend Lesley sat with me while Raymond did the school run. Then Raymond rang Mary who came over until Andrya, and second midwife Sue, could get here.

'It was lovely to see Mary and soon all three midwives were in attendance. The pain was bearable although the thought of being still or prostrate was agonizing. Andrya's hand-held monitor and pulse-taking assured us that we were well. Eventually I sank into the pool – it felt like being hugged, a comforting, and safe place. I rocked through contractions and slumped through the intervals between. I retreated within myself to be with the pain, rocking and breathing.

'The pain increased, I felt the presence of God, loving and comforting me. Mary left quietly; though I could still hear her voice, encouraging me. At last the urge to push started and I was doing something other than enduring. I braced myself widthways across the pool, remembering not to grit my teeth but to go with the surges.

'In a flurry, Fergus was out: we did it! We did it! It was an affirmation of everything I know about the female body and spirit. On the day, I hadn't needed drugs or props, just my husband, my God, my home and three wonderful women who understood how birth works and how to help me make the final part of my own birth journey.'

An antenatal teacher finally births her own baby

'It was an affirmation of everything I know about the female body and spirit.'

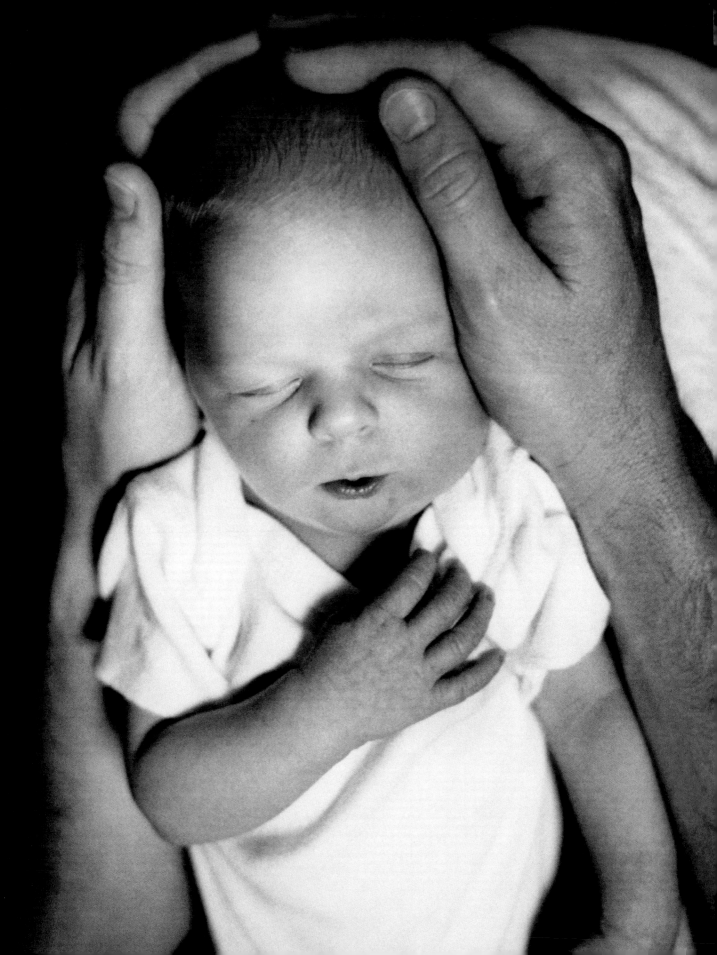

Babymoon

early daze

Having a baby is a major life event, something that changes your whole world. It's one of the life transitions known as 'thresholds' to anthropologists. When we pass through a threshold, we are allowed to withdraw from the rest of the community for a while into 'ritual seclusion'.

Centuries ago in England, the period immediately following the birth of a baby used to be a time when mother and baby were allowed their own protected space and were cared for by friends and family. In most cultures, seclusions are designed to last 40 days: a sacred period of time; a time to recover, reflect and readjust.© Just as a newly married couple enjoy a honeymoon, so your new family can enjoy a 'babymoon' – you, your baby and your partner at home together, preferably in bed for a while, with the rest of the world kept at bay.

the birth year

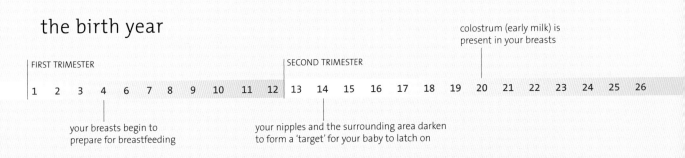

colostrum (early milk) is
present in your breasts

FIRST TRIMESTER

SECOND TRIMESTER

| 1 | 2 | 3 | 4 | 6 | 7 | 8 | 9 | 10 | 11 | 12 | 13 | 14 | 15 | 16 | 17 | 18 | 19 | 20 | 21 | 22 | 23 | 24 | 25 | 26 |

your breasts begin to
prepare for breastfeeding

your nipples and the surrounding area darken
to form a 'target' for your baby to latch on

In the UK, as new parents, you will receive care from a number of professionals. A community midwife will usually visit you regularly until your baby is 10 days old (or in some areas, up to 28 days). Some midwives don't come every day but you can ask for more visits if you'd like. Your midwife should give you a phone number where you can contact her, or the team, at any time.

You may have met your health visitor during your pregnancy and she will visit you at home when the baby is between 10 and 14 days old. A health visitor is a qualified nurse with special training in child development and health promotion. In the UK, every family with a baby aged under five has a named health visitor who can advise on all health matters as well as all sorts of other issues affecting new parents, from benefit rights to leisure activities. She'll let you know when and where you can visit her at the baby clinic and will also leave a phone number with you where she can be contacted.

You should be given an appointment to have a check-up at around six weeks after the birth. This is usually with your family doctor but sometimes with your midwife. You can raise any questions or concerns you have about whether your body is returning to normal and about how you are feeling. Remember to write down any questions you have in the days beforehand, and take the list with you to the appointment.

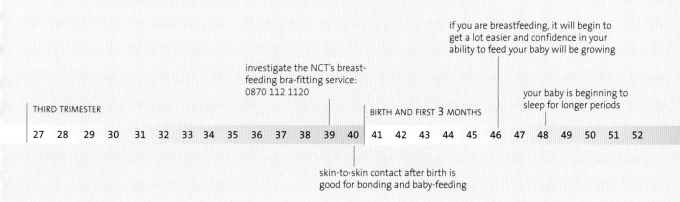

if you are breastfeeding, it will begin to get a lot easier and confidence in your ability to feed your baby will be growing

investigate the NCT's breast-feeding bra-fitting service: 0870 112 1120

your baby is beginning to sleep for longer periods

THIRD TRIMESTER

BIRTH AND FIRST 3 MONTHS

27 28 29 30 31 32 33 34 35 36 37 38 39 40 41 42 43 44 45 46 47 48 49 50 51 52

skin-to-skin contact after birth is good for bonding and baby-feeding

feelings after birth

It's not surprising that it takes some time to settle into the new role of mother. The overwhelming relief and thankfulness that many women feel after giving birth is hard to describe. It's an intensely emotional time – but feelings can be mixed too, possibly even sad.

HAVE I BONDED?

You may not feel instant and overwhelming love for your baby. Some women don't. Maybe she doesn't feel like yours yet – or you're just too tired.

Take each day as it comes. Keep your baby close to you. Hold her skin-to-skin. Feed her, care for her, and sleep with her. Act out love. It may take several weeks, but it will soon become a reality.

'I was bleeding copiously and shaking like a leaf. She was very very sleepy due to the Pethidine and I didn't really want to touch her. I was dumbstruck and rather shocked that I had a little girl when all who knew me had told me I was definitely having a boy!'

The overwhelming relief and thankfulness that many feel after giving birth is difficult to describe. It's an intensely emotional time.

For many, pregnancy is a very special time, a time when women feel nurtured and unique, on the verge of an exciting adventure. It is normal to feel a sense of regret – even loss – when this phase ends. Give yourself time. Tell other people how you feel, but don't be alarmed if they seem not to understand. Talk through the birth with whoever will listen, or write it all down. The nostalgia for pregnancy will gradually fade and you'll move on.

Some women may feel deeper distress. Maybe the birth was not as you hoped and planned. Perhaps things happened that you didn't want to

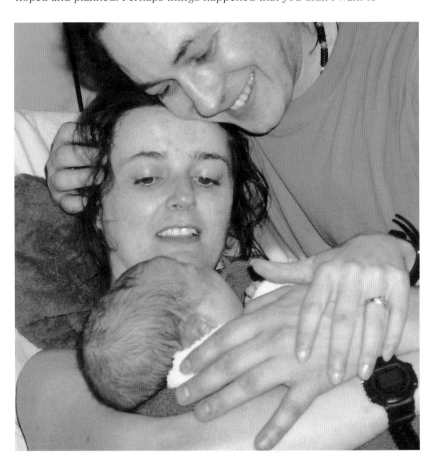

happen – an assisted delivery or unexpected caesarean section, maybe. Perhaps you feel let down – by your body or by other people. Maybe there were times of great fear and unbearable pain – or perhaps you can't remember much at all.

Talking about these feelings to others may be very difficult. Your family may not understand: after all, you have your baby – so do the circumstances of her birth really matter now? Your partner may even be part of the problem.

If you feel this way, act now. Your distress may fade, but it will probably not go away until it has been faced. Tell your midwife how you feel. Ask her to read through your labour notes, and explain what happened, and why. Better still, ask to speak with the midwife or doctor who cared for you in labour.

If you cannot talk things through with somebody in hospital, try to confide in somebody once you are home – your community midwife, maybe, GP, health visitor or antenatal teacher. Perhaps you would find it easier to talk to a stranger – the Birth Crisis Network runs a telephone helpline (see box).

What about your partner?

The early days can be hard for partners, too. They may also be affected by things that happened during labour, and overwhelmed by the enormity of change. They may feel sidelined by events, ignored by health professionals, excluded from the closeness developing between you and your baby. You may feel that your partner has become yet another responsibility. What you had hoped to be a time of shared happiness, becomes a time of increasing distance and tension. And with everything happening, there just doesn't seem to be the time or the opportunity to sort it out.

Tell him that you're having a difficult time – and you know that he is too. Try to use 'I' phrases ('I feel let down'). They're more effective and less blaming than 'you' phrases ('You're no help'). Try a row, or a cuddle, whichever works best for you, but you don't need to shoulder the burden of his feelings.

The 'baby blues'

Midwives reckon that 50–80 per cent of all new mothers suffer the 'baby blues' – a period of weepiness and irritability that sets in around the third to fifth day after birth and feels like 'coming down to earth with a bump'. Textbooks tell us that the 'blues' may last a few hours or 7–10 days.

It is sometimes thought that this change in mood is caused by the sudden fall in progesterone that occurs following birth. It may also coincide with the start of mature milk production, your baby becoming more unsettled, and your return home from hospital. But the 'blues' are not inevitable. Women who give birth at home are much less likely to experience them than women cared for in hospital. Others have found that the 'blues' tend to be worse amongst first-time mothers – especially those who haven't had much experience of babies beforehand.

NEED TO TALK?
If a 'listening' service is not available locally – or if you prefer to speak with somebody not associated with the place where you gave birth – contact Birth Crisis Network, a voluntary service offering telephone support across the country (tel: 01865 300266, e-mail: birthcrisis@sheilakitzinger.com, website: www.sheilakitzinger.com). Other women may prefer the complete anonymity of speaking with the Samaritans (tel: 08457 90 90 90, e-mail: jo@samaritans.org, website: www.samaritans.org). The Association for Improvements in Maternity Services (AIMS) is a voluntary organization that has supported many women following traumatic birth experiences (helpline: 0870 765 1433, website: www.aims.org.uk).

'I remember on the 3rd day in hospital being inconsolable, crying huge tears. "What's wrong?" asked the nurse. "I've got too many blankets on the bed and in the night they kept getting tangled up." I was still crying when my husband arrived.'

changes in your body

The female body has amazing powers of recovery. Already the dramatic changes of pregnancy are being dismantled as your whole body, having completed its task, is returning to the way it was before you were pregnant – more or less.

Within minutes of the birth of your baby and delivery of your placenta, your uterus contracts down to a grapefruit-sized pouch of tight muscle. Squeezed shut in the middle of this muscle is the wound left by your placenta when it detached in the third stage of labour. Already, bleeding from this wound has stopped and the area is beginning to heal itself, although you will continue to lose blood in the lochia, or discharge after the birth.

Meanwhile, the soft lining of your uterus is being washed away in your lochia (vaginal loss) and a new lining is being built up. The powerful uterine muscles are beginning to shrink; in six short weeks the weight of your uterus will reduce from 1000g to just 60g. This process is called 'involution'.

You will probably find yourself going to the loo frequently in the first few days as you lose the 2–8 litres of extra fluid that you carried during pregnancy. At the same time, your heart, lungs and circulation will be quietly returning to normal.

As your placenta leaves your body, its job finally completed, levels of pregnancy hormones fall rapidly. Smooth muscle tone throughout your body improves quickly – heartburn gets better, constipation is relieved and varicose veins improve, although backache and the risk of injury remain potential problems for several months.

'I feel a new respect for my body which is nothing to do with the way it looks. I'm a much stronger woman now, and that's reflected in all areas of my life.'

Your breasts

As pregnancy hormones fall, so levels of prolactin rise. Prolactin is the main hormone responsible for milk production. Whether or not you choose to breastfeed, your breasts will begin to make mature milk to replace the colostrum present throughout most of pregnancy. If you are breastfeeding, feeding your baby in response to her needs will ensure that your breasts continue production.

Your back

It takes quite some time for the joints of the pelvis and spine, softened by the hormones of pregnancy, to return to normal; back discomfort and the risk of injury may persist for three to five months following birth. The abdominal muscles, stretched to twice their normal length during pregnancy, regain

Contact your midwife urgently if, at
any stage, your discharge:
• becomes suddenly heavier
• is bright red in colour
• contains lumps of tissue
• has a nasty smell.
These may be signs that your uterus is
not contracting down well enough.
There may be small pieces of placenta
left inside and an infection brewing.

*Take time to get to know your baby. Keep
her close to you, hold her skin-to-skin and
care for her. If you didn't bond with her
immediately, act out love – it will soon
become a reality.*

their tone within a couple of months. Paying attention to your posture and
regular, gentle exercise which you enjoy, will help build up the strength of
these important muscles. In the meantime, be aware how you move and lift
things carefully.

Blood loss after childbirth

This is what to expect:

Days 1–3 Heavy, dark red discharge that may contain fragments of amniotic
membrane and large clots (formed as blood pools in the vagina). This is

mainly blood from the placental site. Your loss will be heaviest when you first stand up, after emptying your bladder, and while breastfeeding.

You will probably have to change your pad every time you go to the toilet. Call your midwife urgently if your loss seems to be heavier than this, or if you feel dizzy and weak. You may need tablets or an injection to help your uterus contract down to stop the bleeding.

You may also experience uncomfortable 'after pains' for a few moments each time you feed your baby in the first few days. These are caused by a surge of the hormone oxytocin, stimulated by your baby's suckling. Oxytocin is responsible for the 'let down' (release) of your milk. It also causes your uterus to contract, and so speeds up vaginal discharge.

Your midwife will feel your uterus at each visit to check that it is well contracted, and is involuting normally.

Days 4–10 Brownish discharge. The placental site is beginning to heal so there is less red blood and more serum (the watery part of blood).

Days 10–21 Much lighter, yellowish or clear discharge. The lochia now mainly consist of leucocytes (white blood cells involved in healing and fighting infection) and cervical mucus. Your lochia may be finished by three weeks, or may continue off-and-on for up to six weeks.

Caring for stitches

Stitches may cause pain in the first few days afterwards, and you may have some bruising. The following ideas can be helpful:

- Some women find that homeopathic arnica tablets taken during, or soon after birth reduce swelling and bruising.
- Re-start pelvic floor exercises as soon as possible after the birth. They help reduce swelling and speed healing by improving the circulation to the area. You may find it difficult to feel when you are doing them at first. Start them when you are lying on the bed with your knees bent. You can then progress to practising while sitting up.
- Walking will also prevent stiffness and help reduce swelling.
- Lying on your side, putting an ice pack, or frozen packet of peas wrapped in a tea towel over the painful area for a maximum of 20 minutes, may reduce swelling. This can ease the pain. You could do this in the first three days but no longer because ice packs do not aid healing and may in fact prevent it.
- When opening your bowels press a clean sanitary pad over the stitches to prevent straining. Sit well back on the toilet. Drink plenty of fluid and eat plenty of high fibre foods like bran, wholemeal bread, dried fruit and fresh fruit and vegetables to prevent constipation.
- After emptying your bladder, pour a jugful of warm water over the vulva or use a bidet to help prevent stinging. A few drops of pure essential lavender oil, which is an antiseptic, could be added to the water.

- Find a comfortable position for feeding your baby – perhaps lying down in bed on your side.

After a week or two, if you have continued problems with stitches, ask your midwife or health visitor to refer you to an obstetric physiotherapist.

If you find sitting up uncomfortable, don't sit on a rubber ring as it makes the swelling worse. You can try two pillows, one under each thigh, or better still hire a Valley Cushion (find more information on page 247). A Valley Cushion is a specially designed cushion for women with a painful pelvic floor, haemorrhoids (varicose veins around the anus), or a sore coccyx.

Midwife checks

At each visit, your midwife will check:
- Lochia and the height of your uterus – to ensure that your loss is normal, and your uterus is well contracted and 'involuting' (shrinking).
- Legs – to check for signs of thrombosis. The risk of thrombosis increases if you have had surgery, or are confined to bed for any reason. Tell your midwife immediately if you experience any pain, swelling or redness in your legs.
- Breasts – for nipple soreness or breast pain, or other signs of difficulties.
- Perineum – to monitor the healing of any trauma. At the same time, she will probably ask if there are any difficulties with passing urine or having your bowels open.
- How you are feeling generally. Do use this time to ask questions or talk about worries.

She may also check:
- Temperature and pulse – a raised temperature and rapid pulse may be a sign of infection or, more rarely, a thrombosis (blood clot in your leg). A rapid pulse may indicate anaemia.
- Blood pressure – particularly important if you suffered pre-eclampsia during pregnancy. A few women develop high blood pressure for the first time after delivery.

What to eat

Eat whatever you feel like eating. Simple nutritious snacks for the early days include sandwiches, bowls of breakfast cereal with milk, bananas, apples, crackers and cheese. If constipation is a problem, snack on dried fruit and try to drink a lot of water. Breastfeeding is thirsty work and you will probably find you need to drink a lot of fluids. You may not want to spend a lot of time walking to the loo, but this will get your circulation going.

It can take a bit longer to start eating again after a caesarean section. This is because any big abdominal operation does interfere temporarily with the working of your bowels and it may take some time for your gut to start moving freely again.

after a caesarean

Although caesarean births are becoming more and more common (more than one in five births) a caesarean section is still a serious operation and it can help to look at your recovery in terms of weeks and months, not days. Don't feel you have to get better quickly or try to be Superwoman – take your time and be kind to yourself.

What to expect in the first few days

Pain relief will be necessary initially, and different methods include an intravenous drip (you may be able to control this yourself), injections, suppositories (inserted into your back passage), and liquid or tablets taken by mouth. Many women progress quite quickly to taking paracetamol only.

If you feel the pain relief is not strong or frequent enough, discuss this with your midwife. Pain that is allowed to build up can be more difficult to bring under control again. So being 'brave' is not a good idea because it can lead to more pain and less mobility.

You should have a call bell that you can reach easily. Caesarean mothers need more help and you should not feel bad about asking for help as often as you need it.

You will usually be helped to get up on your feet very soon after delivery and certainly within 24 hours, to improve blood circulation. To begin with, moving around, getting in and out of bed, standing and walking can be difficult. It is usually better to try to stand as upright as possible and the more you can move around the easier it will get.

Many hospitals have an obstetric physiotherapist who offers specialist advice on postnatal exercises. Ideally, you should be able to see the physiotherapist personally and some units provide post-caesarean exercise sheets.

Your scar

Your wound will be about 15–22cm (6–9in) long, generally on a horizontal line in your upper pubic hair, and covered by a dressing. A midwife will usually remove your stitches or staples around five days after you have had the caesarean.

Postnatal infections are more common after a caesarean and include infections of the wound, urinary tract or bladder and uterine infections. These are usually treatable with antibiotics.

On the postnatal ward

You may have a catheter (thin tube) draining your bladder which can commonly be left in place for up to 24 hours, and you should then be able to pass urine as normal. If you do not have a catheter, you may be expected to use a bedpan in bed. Many women find this very difficult. Ask if you can use a commode at the bedside or, better still, be helped to the toilet.

Opening your bowels again for the first time can also be difficult. The timing varies considerably from woman to woman, and often does not happen for a week or more.

It is usual to be given only fluids after surgery, then a soft diet, however, research shows no disadvantage in allowing women to eat as soon as they are hungry, if they wish to do so.

It is usual to leave hospital after 3–5 days. You might like to discuss with your carers what would be best for you.

Will I find breastfeeding difficult?

A caesarean should not alter your choice of feeding or your ability to produce milk. However, you may find it more difficult to sit or lie comfortably and you may need to experiment with positions to avoid pressure or strain on the wound. Breastfeeding can be very important for mothers who feel they have been deprived of a vaginal birth, and some who have found breastfeeding difficult have referred to it as a 'double failure'.

Difficult feelings

Many women are able to accept or feel very positive about a caesarean. Others, however, are left with nagging doubts, or even anger, resentment or feelings of violation. Some women who experience negative feelings do so straight away, while others may not do so for months or even years.

The way you feel can be very much affected by the circumstances of the caesarean (and any labour), including such things as whether you were involved and comfortable with the decisions made, whether you had sufficient information and whether you were treated with respect. Women often wonder what they may have been able to do differently.

For some, a caesarean may give rise to postnatal depression or post-traumatic stress disorder – these women may need significant support during recovery.

People cope in different ways: some are able to move on, leaving the experience in the past; others wait until they are ready to deal with their feelings; and others have a need to sort feelings out immediately.

Finding the right information and support can be difficult, but may be available from the hospital, your GP or health visitor, from voluntary organizations such as NCT, AIMS or the Birth Crisis Network (see page 245) or via the internet and e-groups.

Many mothers who have extreme negative feelings work through the experience to gain new confidence and assertiveness, and many go on to have very good birth experiences in subsequent pregnancies, as a result.

MAKING YOURSELF COMFORTABLE
- Whether sitting or lying, experiment with pillows to support you and your baby so you're both comfortable.
- Keep the pressure off your scar with high-waisted knickers (available from NCT Maternity Sales see page 247).
- Some people find peppermint tea (or ginger) helps to release trapped wind.
- Ring your bell and ask for help if you are in pain when you need to reach or hold your baby.

DRIVING AFTER A CAESAREAN
You will usually be advised not to drive for up to six weeks, although there are no clear restrictions to stop you. If you feel well enough to drive, and you are capable of doing an emergency stop, check that your insurance is valid. This may require medical clearance from your obstetrician or family doctor.

your new baby

Throughout pregnancy, your baby was nourished and sustained by the placenta. Floating in a protective environment, cocooned in warm fluid, sound-insulated, temperature-controlled – all her needs were met in the womb. But at birth, the supply line is cut; and your baby has to adapt to life on her own.

'It was amazing. I lifted her on to my tummy. I remember her eyes were still full of water from the womb. I bonded with her the minute I looked into her eyes.'

When your baby's umbilical cord is cut, she is immediately forced to adapt to life without her placenta. The way her body does this is extraordinary: within just a short space of time, breathing, circulation and digestion are established and your baby is out there on her own – a separate little being.

Before birth, the placenta acts as your baby's lungs – delivering oxygen and removing carbon dioxide. Although she has been practising breathing movements since the eleventh week, her lungs contain fluid rather than air during pregnancy. This fluid helps keep the tiny air sacs open, ready for her first real breath.

As she passes down through the birth canal, your baby's chest is squeezed and this fluid is eased out of her lungs into her mouth and throat. Her lungs are now poised ready to breathe. When her body slips out of yours, the pressure on her chest is released, her lungs expand and air is drawn in. The respiratory control centre in her brain clicks into action and she continues to breathe.

The fluid squeezed out of your baby's lungs will drain quickly away. Some midwives like to use a little suction gadget to remove this fluid, but this can be distressing for the baby, and is generally not necessary.

Immediately she is born, it can be a good idea to keep your baby on her side or front, either across your tummy or in your arms. She may cough and splutter for a few seconds (and may swallow some of the fluid) but this will not hurt her. Cover her with your hands to keep her warm, and maybe rub her back gently. She will soon start breathing properly.

Your baby's cord stump

Your baby's umbilical cord was literally her lifeline throughout pregnancy. Then, within minutes of her birth, it was clamped and cut. The clamp is there to make sure that no blood is lost from the cord. Provided it has been correctly fixed, it will not slip off. (The only way to remove it is to cut through the hinge. Your midwife will remove this clamp when your baby is three days old, and the risk of bleeding is past.)

Your midwife will tell you how to clean the cord stump, since the exact technique varies from hospital to hospital. You will probably be told to

OPPOSITE *For the first few days, your baby's body will be curled up as it was in the womb. Her cord clamp will be removed after three days and the stump will fall off after about a week.*

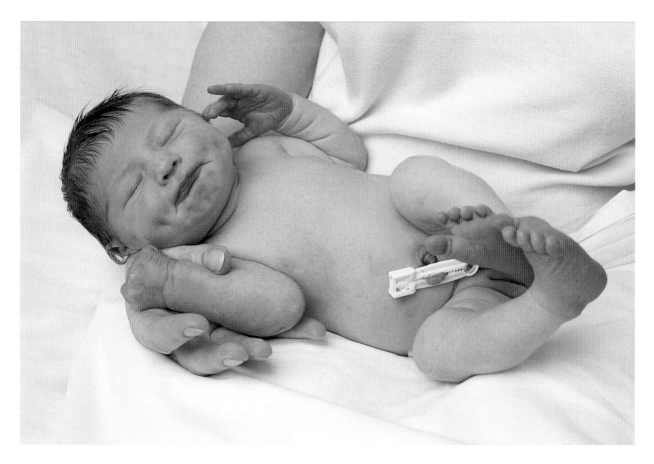

simply wipe the stump with clean water and dry with a cotton wool ball each time you change your baby's nappy.

If possible, it's a good idea to try and keep the cord stump and clamp outside your baby's nappy. You may have to fold the top of the nappy over to do this. This will stop the stump getting wet with urine – especially if you have a baby boy.

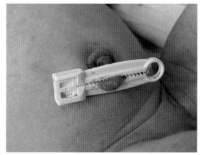

The short length of cord left will dry and shrivel over the next few days, until it detaches when your baby is about a week old. There may be one or two specks of blood when this happens, but it will not hurt your baby. She will then be left with a normal looking 'tummy button'.

Continue to keep the cord clean until it falls off and tell your midwife if your baby's cord stump bleeds, looks sticky or has an unpleasant smell. These may be signs of infection.

Baby health checks

Soon after delivery, your baby will be checked over by your midwife. A few days later a slightly more detailed examination will be performed by a paediatrician (children's doctor). If you had your baby at home, your GP may

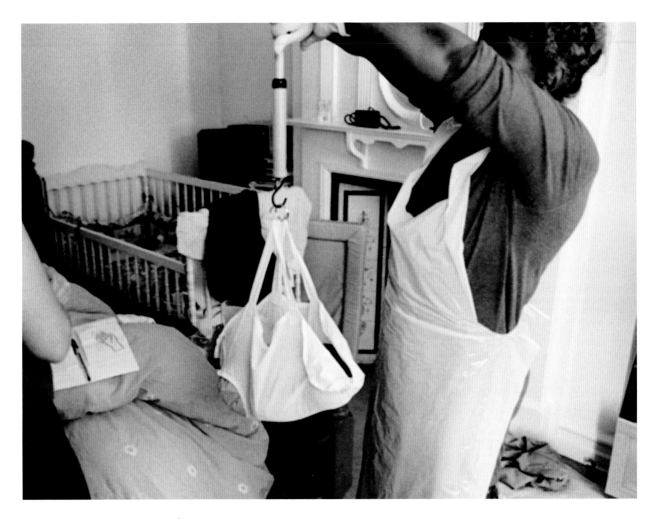

Midwives who visit you at home will often weigh your baby in a special sling.

visit to do this check. Your baby will probably be examined lying in her cot or on your bed. You should have a clear view and there should be plenty of time for the midwife or doctor to answer your questions.

Your doctor or midwife will:

- observe your baby for general signs of good health
- check for abnormalities
- listen to her heart and lungs to ensure all is well
- feel her tummy and check her external genitalia (sex organs)
- watch her movements and check her reflexes
- check for congenital dislocation of the hips by gently holding her legs and moving her hip joints
- ask you about feeding and your baby's behaviour
- ask you if you have any worries or questions.

Jot down any questions you might have beforehand as this will help you remember to ask them.

Your baby's nappies

1–2 days Your baby has been passing urine for several months whilst in your uterus. She will have her first wee in the outside world within 24 hours or so of birth. If her nappies are still dry after this time, don't panic. It may simply mean that she passed urine during delivery and it was missed in the general excitement. She will probably not pass much urine at all during the first few days.

During this time your baby will pass 'meconium' – a thick, greenish-black, tarry substance. Meconium has been accumulating in her bowel since about 16 weeks of pregnancy. It contains mucus, skin cells, swallowed amniotic fluid, and various digestive products. Oddly enough, it has virtually no smell. Your baby may have one or two very large poos, or several smaller ones. Colostrum helps your baby to pass the meconium.

Meconium can be very messy. It may be a good idea to apply plenty of barrier cream, to your baby's bottom when she is first washed or bathed after delivery. This will make it easier to wipe her skin clean after each poo.

2–5 days Provided your baby has started feeding, meconium will gradually become greenish-brown in colour. This is because waste products from her food are beginning to pass through her system. Midwives call this sort of poo a 'changing stool'. Your midwife will probably ask at each visit what colour your baby's poos are. A changing stool is a useful sign that your baby is beginning to feed well.

5–6 days onwards If breastfeeding is going well, your baby's poos will now be very soft and bright yellow in colour. They will have a sweetish, rather pleasant smell. Once you are producing mature milk, your breastfed baby will probably pass 4–5 motions a day. (After the first few weeks, and as your baby's digestion matures, the frequency of poos may well decrease. She may pass just one poo a day – or one every week.)

The poos of a formula-fed baby are more solid, bulky and pale yellowish-brown in colour. They smell rather unpleasant, and at first, are passed less frequently than those of a breastfed baby.

Often your baby's nappy will be wet, rather than dirty. She will now be passing urine regularly. Her urine will be pale in colour.

Soft, yellow poos and 6–7 wet nappies in 24 hours, are welcome signs that your breastfed baby is getting plenty of milk. An artificially fed baby may have fewer, more solid, poos, but should also have 6–7 wet nappies. Formula-fed babies are more likely to become constipated. If your baby seems to be straining and having difficulties filling her nappy, talk to your health visitor; your baby may need more water.

Very frequent, greenish poos (after the first five days) and an unsettled baby, may be a sign that your breastfed baby is not feeding effectively. This may happen if she is not well latched on to the breast during feeding, or is being taken off the breast before she has had what she needs.

KEEPING YOUR BABY SAFE

- Don't let your baby get too hot (or too cold). Feel her chest or back to check her temperature.
- Don't let anyone smoke in the same room as your baby.
- Be very careful not to have any hot drinks or boiling water anywhere near your baby.
- It's not safe to fall asleep on a sofa with your baby.
- Place your baby on her back to sleep.
- Put her in the 'feet to foot' position if she is in a cot so she can't slip any further down.

WHEN TO CALL THE DOCTOR

You should contact your doctor immediately if:

- You think your baby is ill, even if there are no obvious symptoms.
- Your baby has a fit or convulsion.
- She turns blue or very pale.
- Her breathing is quick and difficult, or grunting.
- She is exceptionally hard to wake or unusually drowsy or does not seem to know you.
- She has glazed eyes and does not focus on anything.
- You see any sign of bruising or bleeding.
- Your baby is not feeding or is reluctant to feed.
- She has a rash that doesn't fade when you press a glass against it.

Very infrequent poos, few wet nappies, and dark, scanty urine may be a sign that your baby (breast or formula fed) is not getting enough to eat. (It may sometimes be hard to tell whether or not your baby has had a wee, because a disposable nappy may absorb the urine without trace. You will soon learn to tell though, by the relative weight of the used nappy in your hand.)

Heel prick blood tests

When your baby is six to ten days old, your midwife will offer to do a blood test to screen for various metabolic disorders (meaning disorders arising from faulty chemical processes in the human body). If you agree to this test, the midwife will take a small sample of blood from your baby. This will then be sent to a specialist laboratory for testing.

Your midwife will tell you what conditions are screened for in your area. Usually, the following are included:

- Phenylketonuria (disease resulting from a defective gene that interferes with the regulation of an amino acid).
- Congenital hypothyroidism (a disorder of thyroid activity).

A set of scales can be brought to a home birth too, for weighing your baby.

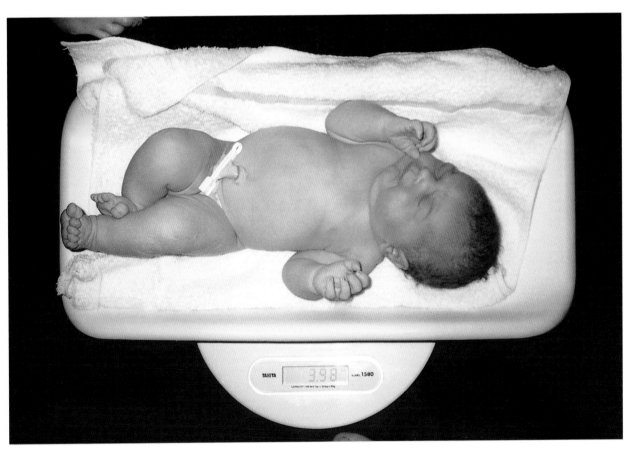

Left untreated, these two conditions may lead to mental retardation and other developmental problems. Early diagnosis and prompt treatment will prevent future handicap.

- Cystic fibrosis (an inherited disease in which a number of body tissues produce an abnormally thick mucus).
- Hereditary blood conditions (these are not routinely tested for in every area; ask your midwife what the policy is and if you feel your baby is at risk, ask to speak to a specialist).

The results of the test will be sent to your health visitor and GP within a few weeks. You will be contacted earlier than this if the test needs to be repeated or a problem has been found.

The midwife will take the blood sample by pricking your baby's heel and allowing the blood to drip onto circles of absorbent paper. Your baby may react to the initial prick as it may feel painful for a short time, but the rest of the test should be painless.

Here are some things that may make the test easier:

- Keep your baby's feet warm with socks until the last moment. This will speed up the collection of the blood. Some midwives use warm water to the same effect.
- Hold her so that her feet are hanging downwards. This, too, will make the blood collection easier.
- Breast or bottle-feed your baby as the midwife is doing the test. She may stop and cry for a moment when her heel is pricked, but will be instantly comforted by feeding.

Some hospitals offer infant hearing tests which are quick to perform and give results without a long wait. A hearing screener will place a special device called a transmitter in you baby's ear and the ear produces an echo. A computer analyses your baby's responses and thus detects any hearing loss. Experts agree that early diagnosis and treatment of deafness play a big part in minimizing the problem.

The 6–8-week check

When you are given your postnatal check, which is usually – though not always – carried out at your GP's surgery, your baby will also be examined. You'll be asked about any concerns or worries you may have, so it's worth writing down a list and bringing it to your appointment.

- Your baby will be weighed and measured.
- You will have time to discuss any feeding problems.
- Her heart will be listened to.
- Hip joints will be manipulated to check again for signs of dislocation.
- Your baby's reflexes will be tested.
- Baby boys will be checked to make sure the testicles have descended.
- Plans for vaccination will be discussed.

minor baby ailments

Spots, rashes, marks and minor imperfections can all mar your beautiful baby's looks. Your midwife or health visitor should be able to suggest treatment and if you need to know more about the condition, you will find a list of useful organizations at the back of the book.

Many new babies arrive with minor physical abnormalities, most of which can be dealt with swiftly by experts with specialist knowledge.

Club foot

Club foot usually refers to a newborn's foot which turns inwards and downwards. This can be detected in an antenatal ultrasound screening test and does run in some families. Minor degrees of this condition are common at birth and are a result of pressure on the foot while the baby is in the womb. Most are treated by physiotherapy. Babies with more marked deformities may need to have their feet treated by splints and a few may need surgery. All newborns are examined for club foot at birth.

Cleft palate

A baby's palate forms in two parts which join together as the baby develops inside the womb. Very rarely the palate does not join together and there is a gap which is visible inside the baby's mouth. The condition can also affect the upper lip and some babies may have both a cleft palate and a cleft lip. Clefts of the lip are often found at an antenatal ultrasound screening test. There are now centres across the UK specializing in the treatment of this condition and you should be referred to a specialist team.

Treatment is by surgery but in the early days the main problem for the baby is how to get enough milk as the gap interferes with the sucking process for breastfed babies. Bottle-fed babies are not so badly affected as the sucking mechanism is different. It may be necessary for you to express your breastmilk and feed your baby with a bottle.

Tongue tie

A baby with tongue tie cannot make her tongue stick out beyond her lips. The tongue is tied by the frenulum which is a membrane holding the underside of the tongue to the floor of the mouth. Breastfed babies find it very difficult to suck and it can affect some bottle-fed babies, too. Tongue tie can be a cause of failure to gain weight in the more marked cases. Doctors are divided in their opinions on this subject. Traditionally tongue tie was left

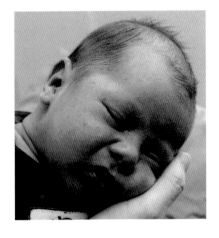

At around four to six weeks of age, a baby's sweat glands start to work which can result in a spotty face. Wash your baby's face with a squeezed out cotton wool ball which has been dipped in cool, boiled water and pat dry with a tissue.

until the baby was older, as most will partly resolve and won't interfere with speech. However it is possible to see a specialist who will divide the frenulum if the tongue tie is interfering with breastfeeding.

Birth marks

There are a number of different blemishes, known as birth marks which can appear on a newborn baby's body.

Mongolian blue spot

Dark-coloured, blue-black spots found singly or in groups on the lower back or buttocks at birth, are common in black or Asian children. They fade by the time the child is three or four years old.

Stork marks

So-called stork marks (red or purple patches) are on the forehead, upper eyelids and on the back of the neck. They are more obvious when the baby is crying. Stork marks, especially those on the upper eyelids, fade within two years. Those on the forehead may take up to four years to fade. The ones on the back of the neck usually persist.

Strawberry marks

A strawberry birth mark (haemangioma) is bright red, appears in the first few days after birth and can grow during the first few months. They nearly always shrink and fade after this although the process may take a few years. Approximately 1 in 20 babies have haemangiomae, and they tend to be more common in girls, twins and premature babies. Most are best to have no treatment at all. Most will completely disappear leaving little or no mark on the skin by the age of five.

Port wine stains

These are a darker purple colour and usually don't fade. Recent new advances have revolutionized the treatment of port wine stain with excellent results and minimal side effects.

Jaundice

Many perfectly healthy babies develop jaundice at about 2 to 5 days after birth. Their skin and the whites of their eyes will turn a yellowish colour, because their immature livers are struggling to break down bilirubin, a by-product of the destruction of red blood cells no longer needed after birth.

If your baby becomes jaundiced, keep feeding her. Don't wait for her to cry, offer feeds when she seems interested because feeding will encourage her to excrete bilirubin and her jaundice will start to fade.

Occasionally, babies will need phototherapy (light treatment) which will help their bodies break down the bilirubin. Your baby will be placed in her cot, naked except for a nappy and an eye mask, under the warm light of a phototherapy unit. Treatment will continue for anything from a few hours to one to two days.

NEONATAL HEARING TESTS

Neonatal screening to check newborn babies' hearing is being rolled out across the UK. It will allow those babies who have a hearing loss to be identified early.

Early detection also means support and information can be provided to the parents at an early stage. Babies who miss the test at birth for any reason will get another opportunity when they are a few weeks old.

A trained hearing screener or health visitor will place a small transmitter in the outer part of your baby's ear, which sends clicking sounds down the ear. When an ear receives sound, the inner part, known as the cochlea, usually produces an echo. This is called the Otoacoustic Emissions test (OAE). Using a computer, the screener can see how your baby's ears respond to sound. The test only takes a few minutes. The results will usually be given to you at the time of the screening test.

what a new baby needs

Every baby is born with certain reflexes: the ability to suck, to turn her head if something touches her cheek, to follow a moving object with her eyes and to close her fist around anything that touches her palm. Without these involuntary responses to stimulation, she wouldn't survive.

'It was weird – I was so exhausted by the birth I thought I would sleep for days, but in fact I was on such a high that I just stayed awake the whole night, watching my baby! I couldn't believe he was really here at last – it was sort of unreal. The next night I was really tired, yet Billy suddenly started to feed all the time, so the midwife showed me how to feed lying down, and she tucked us up in bed together. It was lovely.'

Did you know that your baby is born with lots of skills to make sure she can survive: she's even able to start breastfeeding without any help?

If you hold a newborn baby upright, with her feet in contact with something, she steps as if she's trying to walk. This reflex puzzled scientists for many years, as newborn babies' necks and backs are not strong enough to support them in walking properly. However scientists in Norway recently discovered that if a baby is placed onto her mother's tummy after birth, she will 'walk' up her tummy until she reaches the breast.

Once she gets there, another reflex – the rooting reflex – comes into action, and she turns her head from side to side, with her mouth wide open, looking for your breast. You may have noticed during pregnancy that your areola – the dark skin around your nipple – has got bigger and darker. It's like a target for your baby to aim at.

If she finds the breast, she latches on, and the third reflex – suckling – comes into play. When the roof of the baby's mouth is stimulated, she starts to move her jaws in such a way that she will milk the breast.

Of course these reflexes are for emergency survival, so even though your baby could do it all by herself, you'll want to help her.

Cuddling your baby 'skin-to-skin'

When she's born, you can cuddle her close to your breast, and the chances are that she will latch on well during this cuddling time. If she's not in the mood, then simply holding her 'skin-to-skin' will start to stimulate your milk supply, as well as giving you both a chance to get to know each other.

Sleep and rest in the first day

Although babies are generally quite alert for the first hour or so after birth (unless affected by drugs you had during your labour, such as Pethidine), your baby may well then sleep for long periods in her first day. This is not surprising, really, as birth is also tiring for her. Although you may feel worn out, you may also be feeling 'high' and probably unable to sleep. You might find yourself spending hours just watching your baby – at last you know what she looks like!

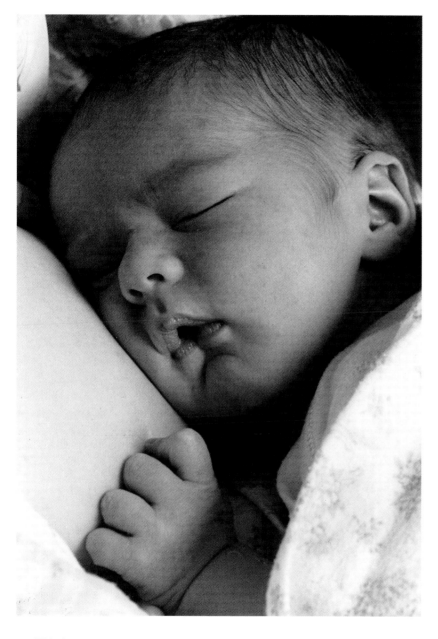

SKIN-TO-SKIN

Research indicates that when newborn babies are cuddled close to the breast with their skin touching their mother's skin, breastfeeding is more successful. You might want to request this early 'skin-to-skin' contact on your birth plan so that hospital staff don't whisk your baby away for routine tasks during this crucial time.

If you intend to formula-feed, you might still like to have this early 'skin-to-skin' contact, as it will help you and your baby bond. It's a way of getting to know each other.

Both you and your partner can cuddle your baby against your bare skin – it creates all sorts of benefits for all of you.

This is a great time to rest, recuperate, and cuddle your baby. It's fine to tuck up in bed together if you can; if you are in hospital you can ask the midwife to tuck the bedclothes in around both of you, and to show you how to feed lying down. You and your baby need to be close, to get to know each other and to bond, as well as to build up a milk supply if you're breastfeeding.

Her sleep will seem quite erratic at first; she will not discover the difference between night and day for about six weeks. In the early days therefore, it makes sense to rest when your baby sleeps, if you can. As you

Play with your baby during her daytime alert periods, but at night-time let her know that sleep is what's required.

start to recover from the birth, and as your baby becomes more alert, you can begin to show her the pattern of night and day. Keep night-times calm and quiet, avoiding changing her nappy if possible.[○]

Early feeding

At first, your baby will feed little and often.[○] Her tiny tummy, which is only the size of a walnut, can't hold much. Also she is learning how to feed and at the beginning she will find this quite tiring, so feeding will occupy much of your time until she gets the hang of it.

Don't worry too much if your baby doesn't seem interested in food at first, but do spend as much time as you feel you want to in skin-to-skin contact, which is always beneficial, offering her the breast or bottle during her brief moments of alertness.

Your midwife may suggest waking your baby to feed her, as sleepy babies can get lethargic and 'forget' to feed. You may particularly need to wake a small baby, or one who has been born after a labour with Pethidine or other drugs, to make sure she is getting enough to eat.[☉]

Jaundice is due to an excess of a pigment called bilirubin, and is common in newborn babies. It may even be normal, to some extent. Bilirubin is a by-product of the breakdown of excess red blood cells after birth and often babies' livers are not quite ready to process this. Breastfeeding or bottle-feeding as often as possible helps jaundice pass, but again you may need to wake your baby to feed as jaundice does make babies sleepy.[☉] Your midwife will be able to tell whether the jaundice is severe and needs treatment, or whether it is mild.

Unsettled

If your baby seems unsettled and unhappy in these first few days, it is worth thinking about her experiences so far. All she has known is the inside of the womb, where she was held, she was warm, and where she could hear your heartbeat and your voice. She was never hungry, didn't have to worry about keeping warm, or worry if you had left her; she knew you were there. It makes sense, therefore, that the safest and most comforting place for her now will be next to you.

Even though your baby is now out in the world, you are really still interconnected; she is just as dependent on you and your body as she was during the last nine months. Not only does she need you to feed her, she needs you to watch over her, keep her warm and comfortable, and she needs you to help her feel safe and secure.

The effects of labour on feeding

- If you were given Pethidine during labour, especially within a few hours of the birth, it can depress your baby's suckling reflex for several days.[☉] This can mean breastfeeding will take longer to get established, so in the meantime, have skin-to-skin contact as much as you can. If you are bottle-feeding, you may need to keep waking your baby to feed as she will be very dozy.
- A caesarean section shouldn't affect your baby's ability to feed, but it may make it harder for you to hold her in the correct position if you are breastfeeding. Many women find an underarm hold works well, and lying on your side can also be comfortable. You also need help to sit up after a caesarean if you are formula-feeding.
- An assisted delivery – forceps or ventouse, can give your baby a headache, and being held in certain positions or even suckling could be painful for her. She will need you to be patient, perhaps experimenting with different positions.

what a new mother needs

Having a baby can be an overwhelming experience and it's only recently that researchers have really started to look at the impact it has. Your body will have gone through massive changes, and you may experience feelings that you weren't expecting. No one adjusts to motherhood overnight – remember that it takes time.

When your baby is asleep, or settled with somebody else, do something that makes you feel good. Often this may be taking a nap yourself. Alternatively, you may feel better if you wash your hair, phone someone who always makes you feel happy, or catch up on your favourite TV programme. Do whatever cheers you up.

Above all, new mothers need mothering themselves – so they can, in turn, learn to mother their babies.

Plan ahead. Who is going to mother you when your baby is born? Who will cook, clean, shop, wash, fetch and carry, hold your baby whilst you bathe, shield you from visitors, make endless hot drinks and snacks, dry your tears, give you a cuddle, accept your grouches, tell you you're great – yet expect very little in return? Is this really a one-man job?

Care from other women

There's still a strong tradition that a new mother's own mother should be there to support, nourish and care for her daughter after birth. She may even do things for her daughter that she hasn't done since she was a child: run her a bath, wash her hair, prepare her favourite meal.

As the sheer hard work of looking after a baby hits home, a typical comment from new mums is: 'I'm now beginning to appreciate how much my mother did for me.'

It has been said that motherhood is like a craft, and that all apprentice mothers need a more experienced woman who has had children herself and knows what's involved, to be around and available to support and guide her. Often, this may be your own mum, but if that's not possible, you may find you are drawn to other mothers in your area and seek them out. A new mother needs contact with other mothers. This is more than a social pleasure – it's a psychological necessity.

Handling visitors

Be ruthless with company (or, better still, get somebody else to be ruthless on your behalf.) State a time limit for their visit at the onset. Be polite but very firm. Tell them that you need to rest. Wearing nightclothes for the first

Try to relax when your baby is sleeping. You may be tempted to rush around catching up with housework – but it's better to get someone else to do that.

few days at home will reinforce this message. Say that you will phone, send a photo, or return the visit 'when we've got organized'.

Make lists – of snacks to eat, questions to ask your midwife, people to phone, items to buy, things to do. Put stars by things that other people can do, and pin the lists up somewhere obvious. Maybe visitors will take the hint!

Many women describe the early days after their baby's birth as a roller coaster – amazing highs, horrible lows – and no chance at all to get off and just stand still. The days seem to rush by – an endless succession of feeding, nappy changes, visitors, washing, clothes sorting and tidying. There is so much to do, yet nothing ever seems to get done properly. You may feel selfish and unreasonable wanting it otherwise, yet increasingly aware of the tension and anxiety building within you.

Here are some ideas that may help:

- Lie in the bath. Feed your baby first then get somebody else to hold her, take a piece of fruit, cup of tea or glass of wine with you, go into the bathroom and shut the door. Run a warm, deep bath and lie back in it.
- Go for a walk. Exercise stimulates the release of endorphins. A brisk walk will clear your mind of worrying thoughts and niggling anxieties. Carry your baby in a sling, or leave her with somebody else whilst you walk round the block or go to the corner shop. Swing your arms and breathe deeply. You will come back feeling refreshed.
- Start a journal. It need not be particularly detailed: just jottings about how you're feeling, what you're doing and how your baby is progressing. If you don't feel like writing, draw little faces to show your mood each day.
- Have a laugh – it really does help. Watch a funny TV programme, hire a video, or chat to a friend who you know will make you laugh. Like exercise, laughter releases endorphins, releases muscle tension, and deepens your breathing.

When you're tired

If you have an answerphone, use it. Turn the volume on the phone down, or unplug it, and let the answerphone take messages when you feed the baby or take a nap.

Just stay in bed with your baby. It's safe for your baby to sleep with you, unless you or your partner smoke, have drunk alcohol or taken any drugs or are extremely tired. Make sure your baby doesn't get too hot and don't let her head get covered by the bedding.

Don't skimp on your own meals. Keep them simple, but nourishing. Sandwiches, fruit, salad and a yoghurt, a bowl of soup with bread and cheese or baked beans on toast make good, quick meals.

Ask your partner to look after your baby in the evening while you get some sleep – or ask a visiting relative or friend, so you can both have a rest.

> **NEW MOTHERS NEED:**
> - rest
> - a good, well-balanced diet
> - support with feeding
> - help with looking after the baby
> - a listening ear
> - contact with other mothers.

'I thought, I'll have the baby, I'll take the maternity leave, and I'll go back to work in six months, no problem. But when it happened it was just like a landslide, a physical and emotional landslide – and nothing prepares you for that!'

how breastfeeding works

Before birth, your baby is nourished by your placenta; after birth, your breasts take over the work of feeding your baby. Breastmilk is the best food your baby can have. It costs you nothing and is freely available – as long as the interaction between your baby's demands and your own body is allowed to work freely.

Once again, hormones are in charge and direct your body to make milk. Progesterone and oestrogen develop your breasts during pregnancy. The beta-endorphins circulating in your blood to help you during labour, also help the release of prolactin, the milk-producing hormone. In addition, beta-endorphins are present in your colostrum, the early milk you produce in the first few days after delivery (see page 202).

Prolactin and oxytocin work together in a complementary way to make sure your baby gets the benefit of your milk.

Prolactin – the mothering hormone

Prolactin is the hormone essential to milk production. It aids the action of progesterone and oestrogen and is essential for the complete development of the milk-producing cells in your breasts. When you put your baby to your breast, her sucking sends messages through the nerves via the hypothalamus (the hormone control centre of your brain) to your pituitary (the master gland, the most important of the endocrine glands) which then releases prolactin.

The more your baby sucks, the more your pituitary gland will be stimulated to produce prolactin. Levels of the hormone start to rise within 10 minutes of sucking. This delay in prolactin-release means that when your baby feeds she is 'placing her order' for the next feed rather than stimulating milk production for the current one.

Frequent feeding of your baby in the early days is important as, the more the baby sucks, the more 'prolactin receptor sites' are developed within your breast. Prolactin levels naturally rise in sleep and night feeds help maintain a high level.[©]

Oxytocin – the love hormone

The tingly feeling that you get when you put your baby to the breast is the milk-ejection (or 'let down') reflex and is caused by oxytocin. Oxytocin is released in short bursts in immediate response to a stimulation such as thinking about your baby or hearing her cry. This means that milk can spray out of your breast into your baby's mouth before she begins to suck. In the early days of breastfeeding, it may take several minutes, for the first let-down to occur and you may not feel it to begin with. (Some women never feel it.) The pulses of oxytocin, brought on by feeding, stimulate contractions of your womb which are known as 'after pains'. These help your womb to return to its original size after pregnancy. If these pains disturb your baby's early feeds, you could try taking paracetamol half an hour before a feed.

Sexual stimulation also induces the release of oxytocin so you may find that some milk is ejected during orgasm. Feeding your baby before making love will reduce this effect.

Structure of your breast

Each breast is divided into lobes or 'alveoli', like bunches of grapes, where milk is produced and each of these contains 15 to 20 ducts or tubes to conduct the milk towards the nipple. The lobes are made up of glandular tissue, each one sub-divided into lobules (or 'grapes'). Each duct widens on its way to the nipple to form a collecting sac, where the milk gathers just behind the areola (the dark area surrounding each nipple) before it is expressed. Collagen, the connective tissue, acts as a packing material, supporting the glands. This glandular tissue is surrounded by fat and it is the fat that determines the size and shape of the breast.

Infra-red photos of lactating breasts show that they grow hot in response to a baby's cry, which is when blood rushes to the breasts, bringing blood sugars to the milk glands. With sucking, oxytocin is released into your bloodstream, causing star-shaped muscle cells around your milk glands to

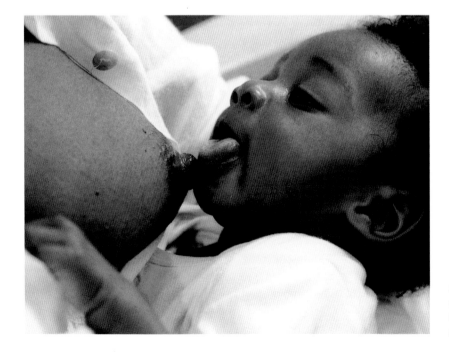

Nipple-stimulation increases the flow of oxytocin in your bloodstream, which in turn triggers the 'let down' reflex and leads to more milk being produced.

contract and squeeze out sweet-tasting milk. This again, is the 'let-down reflex' and it is this reflex that must be stimulated for the milk supply to build up. Eventually, baby and breast are working in harmony, with your milk supply matching her hunger.

Getting ready for feeding

In the first three months of pregnancy, the internal structures of the breast begin to grow, which may make your breasts feel rather uncomfortable in early pregnancy. Near the end of the sixth month, your body will able to produce early milk or colostrum, but the development of the mature, milk-releasing cells doesn't take place until the last three months. During pregnancy, the pigmentation around your nipple darkens and it has been suggested that this may act as a visual guide or 'target' for the newborn baby, to help her latch on. The sebaceous glands around your nipples enlarge. These provide lubrication and protection for the sensitive skin of your nipples. Your nipples also enlarge and become more prominent. Blood-flow to the breasts doubles, so your breasts will look as though they are 'marbled' with blood vessels.

What's in breastmilk?

Breastmilk has exactly the right blend of protein, fat, carbohydrate, minerals and vitamins needed for the rapid growth and development of your baby. The make-up of breastmilk is individual to you as a mother and changes from feed to feed. The minerals in it are easily absorbed – for example, only 4 per cent of the iron in formula milk is absorbed compared with 49 per cent from breastmilk.[º] Breastmilk provides immunity for your baby in many ways. For instance, it builds a lining on the walls of her digestive tract, her throat and her urinary tract, which then protects her from invading organisms. Gastro-enteritis is unusual in breastfed babies.

Colostrum is the first milk that your breasts produce in the early days after your baby is born. It is thick and cream to yellow-orange in colour due to high levels of beta-carotene. It has higher concentrations of sodium, potassium, chloride, protein and fat-soluble vitamins than mature milk and has a laxative effect that helps empty meconium from your baby's bowels. (Meconium is a dark substance which forms the first faeces of a newborn baby and if this is retained it can lead to neonatal jaundice.) Colostrum also helps your baby's gut start up slowly after birth and assists with the growth of beneficial bacteria, which form a protective coating on the gut lining.

Transitional milk comes after colostrum. It may continue for up to two weeks. Concentrations of immunoglobulins, total calories and protein have decreased while lactose and total fat have increased.

Mature milk appears as early as three days after the birth. Breastmilk supplies everything that your baby needs, including water.

Get yourself comfortable with pillows under your head and maybe behind your back. If you have generous breasts, you will find it helps to have the short end of a pillow under your ribs – so that your lower breast is not squashed against the mattress.

Line your baby up with your breast. When she looks for the nipple and her mouth is open wide, slide her swiftly on to your breast, making sure that her head is not curled forwards.

You may need someone to guide you the first few times, as it's not easy to see when you're in this position.

Foremilk and hindmilk: every breastfeed from now on is made up of foremilk at the beginning of the feed, which gradually changes into hindmilk. Foremilk is high in volume but low in fat and is good for satisfying your baby's thirst. It is available for the first few minutes of a feed but gradually changes to hindmilk – lower in volume but higher in calories, so it meets your baby's hunger. A baby needs a balance of both foremilk and hindmilk for a satisfying feed. When your baby latches on, at first she enjoys a drink, and then she gets down to a satisfying meal of hindmilk. If she wants the second breast, she can have another drink and as much hindmilk as she needs.

A living fluid

Not only does your milk change during each feed, it also varies with circumstances. For instance, in hot weather, if your baby feeds as often as she wants, she will take more foremilk, allowing her to quench her thirst and replace lost fluids without needing bottles of water.©

Because your baby's immune system is immature during her first year and she cannot fight infections as well as you can, your body will produce antibodies to pass onto her through your breastmilk.

Babies are meant to feed often. The volume of milk you produce increases to meet demand and, as long as feeding is regular, you can go on producing milk for several years. Most studies suggest that the average daily volume of milk produced is about 800ml, but there is great individual variation and mothers of twins will produce about twice as much milk. The World Health Organization recommends that you give your baby nothing but breastmilk for the first six months after birth and then carry on breastfeeding as long as you want, while also giving solid foods.©

breastfeeding your baby

Breastfeeding has health benefits for you and your baby. It protects you against bone disease and certain cancers. Breastmilk is more than just a food: it's a living substance that protects a baby from infection as her immune system develops, and contains everything she needs for the first six months of her life.

PHONE 0870 444 8708
You can call the NCT Breastfeeding Line any day of the week between 8am and 10pm and speak directly to an NCT breastfeeding counsellor.

A GOOD LATCH
- Your baby's chin is firmly in contact with your breast.
- Her nose is clear of your breast, or lightly touching.
- Her cheeks are rounded throughout the feed – her jaw and tongue are massaging the milk out of the ducts behind your areola.
- The whole of her lower jaw is moving. You can see the muscles working right back near her ears.
- It isn't painful for you.

With a good latch, your baby will feed happily at your breast, quickly at first, to stimulate the let down reflex, then more slowly as she enjoys the flow of milk. She will stop feeding spontaneously when she's had enough and will be settled afterwards (although she may want to feed from the other breast soon).

All it takes is one really good feed and you and your baby will soon become experts. It's worth getting it right from the start.

Breastfeeding step by step
Gather together all the things you may need: a drink for you, tissues, perhaps your watch, if you need to know the time.

Get yourself comfortable first. You'll soon find breastfeeding positions that suit you and your baby. If you prefer to sit up, make sure your back is upright. Sit straight on a straight-backed chair, with your feet flat on the ground (or supported on a low stool or telephone directory) and your back supported by pillows. Pillows on your lap will bring your baby up to the level of your breasts.

(You won't need these pillows forever, but they are useful in the first few weeks while you and your baby are both learning.)

The next step is to get your baby comfortable.

Calm her if she has been crying. Talk to her and tell her what is happening. You may find it helps to wrap her securely in a cot sheet for the first few feeds, but make sure she doesn't get too hot. Later, she'll prefer to have her hands free so she can touch and stroke your breast.

Lie her on your lap, on top of the pillow, holding her close and turn her whole body towards you, without twisting her neck. Keep her back and head in a straight line.

Nose to nipple: notice how your breast hangs in its natural position and line your baby up so that her nose is level with your nipple. In this position, it means that she will have to tilt her head back slightly to reach for your nipple. This gives her room to open her mouth really wide and get a good latch on to your breast. (Imagine how hard it would be for you to eat an apple with your chin tucked down against your chest.)

Let her head move freely. Support her head but don't have it wedged in the crook of your arm. She needs to have room to tilt her head back and drop her lower jaw so that she can open her mouth wide enough to latch on.

Touch her lips with your nipple. Wait for her to open her mouth as wide as a yawn in response. This may take a few minutes. She needs to open her mouth wide, so that she can take in not only your nipple but a good proportion of your areola (the coloured part around the nipple) as well.

Draw her close. As soon as your baby's jaw drops and her mouth opens wide, quickly draw her closer, moving her whole body, not just her head. Once she gets a good mouthful of breast, with her tongue underneath, she will draw your nipple further back into her mouth and start sucking. It may get several attempts to get this right. If you don't get 'a good latch' your nipples will soon get very sore.

Sore nipples

Many women have sensitive nipple skin for the first week after birth, and combined with the unfamiliar, strong sensation of your baby's feeding action, it can feel uncomfortable. As long as your nipples are not damaged or distorted in any way, it will quickly pass. When your baby latches on, wait for 30 seconds, and if you still feel uncomfortable, take your baby off your breast by inserting a clean finger into the corner of her mouth to break the suction, and try again.

Practise relaxation at the beginning of the feed, and try to latch your baby on when she is just waking up and her sucking action is not so strong, before she gets really hungry.

If your nipples become damaged, then it will be painful, although they heal quickly. Now it is even more important to keep asking for help until you find someone who can show you a more comfortable position for holding your baby. Do keep feeding your baby if you can, as you need to keep stimulating your breasts to maintain your supply. If the pain is worse on one side, it might help to start a feed off on the other side, and swap once your baby is feeding less hungrily. Alternatively, you could hand express milk to feed your baby, as well as to keep your supply going.

It may be suggested that you use a nipple shield to prevent further damage and to protect your nipple, although suction through the nipple shield can still open the cracks. If feeding does not feel possible without a shield, then this may be one option. The main problem is that using them may reduce your milk supply, and seems to alter your baby's sucking action. Many women find it hard to get rid of nipple shields afterwards – their babies sometimes seem to prefer the super-stimulation of this artificial nipple.

If you do have a cracked nipple, you might find it helps to use a pure, hypoallergenic lanolin ointment after feeds until your nipples heal. This ointment prevents scabs forming and keeps the nipple skin moist while it heals. Women also find it soothing. Pat your breasts dry before applying it. You don't need to remove it before the next feed.

Line your baby up 'nose to nipple'.

Wait for a wide open mouth.

Move her swiftly onto your breast with tongue down.

A good latch means she's drawing on your whole breast, not just the nipple.

As your baby feeds, your brain responds by releasing prolactin, the hormone that gives the signal to make more milk. In effect, your baby 'places her order' for the next feed while she's at your breast.

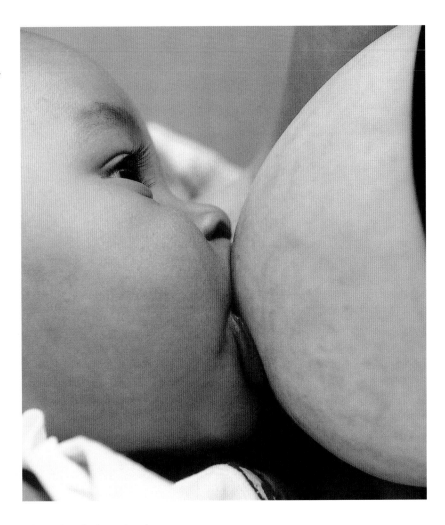

'She knew what to do within 10 minutes of being born. I was supremely confident after being a breastfeeding mum for such a long time before. Overconfident as it came out. I had forgotten that newborns needed positioning carefully as their mouths are so small.'

Thrush of the nipples

Another, less common cause of sore nipples is thrush (*Candida albicans*), a fungal infection. Consider this if you have had thrush during pregnancy, are prone to thrush, or if you or your baby have recently taken antibiotics. Thrush causes nipple pain, and sometimes deep breast pain; your nipple skin may look pinker than usual and shiny, and your baby may have white patches on her tongue or in her mouth. Women describe the pain as sharp and stabbing, like needles, and it often continues between feeds. It is important that both you and your baby are treated by your family doctor or pharmacist with anti-fungal treatment, even if only one of you has symptoms, otherwise you can re-infect each other.

Sore breasts

Two to five days after the birth, your milk 'comes in'; which happens whether you are breastfeeding or not. Your breasts become hot, swollen and uncomfortable, and it can be hard for your baby to latch on. We call this 'engorgement' but your breasts are not full of milk; they are swollen with excess fluid due to an increased blood supply. This usually passes within 24 hours; in the meantime, feeding your baby frequently will help. Many women find warm water on their breasts before a feed, or ice cold flannels afterwards, brings relief. If your breasts become engorged when your baby is older, perhaps because she's missed a feed, you can express some milk to relieve the discomfort, otherwise you could develop a blocked duct, or even mastitis. As your ducts are always filling up with milk, your breasts will vary in size and shape all the time, and lumps will appear from time to time. These should never last long because whenever your baby feeds she normally drains them. If you have a lump that seems persistent, it may be the beginning of a blocked duct, especially if it feels tender. Feed your baby with her lower jaw as near to the lump as possible, so if it occurs on the outer side of your breast, try feeding underarm on that side, for instance. You might also find it helpful to massage the lump gently towards your nipple while your baby is feeding.

Mastitis

Most women have heard of mastitis, but don't worry – not many end up getting it. If you are unlucky enough to develop mastitis, you will feel fluey, may have a temperature, and your breasts will be sore. Try to rest and drink plenty of fluids. It is important to keep feeding your baby, as stopping breastfeeding will make the problem worse. Usually mastitis results from insufficient drainage of the breast – from delayed feeds, attachment which is not quite right, blocked ducts or untreated engorgement. If you can correct the problem, the mastitis will ease, and will not require medication.

Your GP may prescribe antibiotics but most cases of mastitis are not caused by infection, so antibiotics here are preventive. However, in a few rare cases, mastitis does result from an infection which can lead to an abscess and will require antibiotics. Alternatively, your GP may prefer to prescribe an anti-inflammatory drug to reduce the inflammation. Neither of these will harm your baby, though antibiotics may upset her tummy, and you will then need to watch out for thrush.

If you can identify why you got mastitis, you can probably prevent it happening in the future, so talk it through with a breastfeeding counsellor.

How much? How often?

Research shows that your body will make the right amount of milk for your baby, if you let her feed when she asks.[⊙] If you try to impose a feeding pattern that suits you, your body will produce the amount of milk you let it, which may not be enough for your baby. Only your baby knows how hungry she is, and how much breastmilk she needs for her hunger to be satisfied.

BLOCKED DUCTS

If you are getting recurring blocked ducts, think about where on your breasts they happen, and therefore what might be restricting the flow of milk.
- Does your bra fit well?
- Is something restricting your milk flow during a feed, such as your hand or your baby's hand?

OUT AND ABOUT WITH YOUR BREASTFED BABY

One of the fears that some new mothers have is about breastfeeding in public places. While you may feel self-conscious feeding in public at first, within a couple of weeks, you may well find you are both able to feed pretty much automatically, and then it will be easier to go places with your baby. Many shopping centres now have specific spaces for feeding babies, but don't feel you have to use them. You might find it helps to wear a loose top or drape a scarf around both of you while you feed, and avoid button-through tops.

- Your baby needs milk at night because she simply can't store enough food during the day to keep her going when she's little.
- Breastfeeding at night is lovely and comforting, helping her get back to sleep.

Benefits for you

- Breastfeeding at night in the early weeks helps your milk supply get established. The more you feed, the higher your prolactin levels, and therefore the more milk you will make.
- You may well find you wake frequently anyway. It's natural to want to check her when she is so little. Breastfeeding gives you a cosy time together.
- When you breastfeed at night, prolactin helps you get back to sleep: a big advantage over bottle-feeding. You probably found sleeping difficult in the weeks leading up to the birth. This may have been your body's way of preparing you for these disturbed nights. Now you have a good way of dozing off again.

Comfort feeding

Some mothers worry that their baby is 'just comfort feeding'. They wonder how they can tell when she's sucking at the breast because she's hungry, and when she's sucking for other reasons, such as wanting some reassurance.

For a baby, breastfeeding is not just about nutrition, it is also about warmth and closeness and learning to be a social human being. Researchers notice that breastfeeding babies interact with their mothers, pausing while she talks, replying by sucking. They believe that feeding a baby teaches the give and take of communication and forms the basis of learning human speech.[⊙]

Although your baby has to feed during the night, you might also want her to learn how to get back to sleep again quickly. It can help if you:

- Avoid putting on a light. Use a low light if you need to see what you are doing.
- Try not to chat or interact with her if possible – low murmurs and gentle, soothing cuddles are best.
- Don't change her nappy unless she is smelly, has a sore bottom, or has wet clothes.

If you want to start cutting down on the number of night feeds, it works best to drop one at a time. Initially, you will need to help her get back to sleep without that feed. Try to become aware of when her cry means 'I am tired and want to sleep' or when it means something else, like 'I am hungry/ cold/ frightened.' It is better if someone else can go and comfort her until she is used to doing without a breastfeed every time she wakes.

Breastfeeding twins

It's perfectly possible for a woman to breastfeed two, three or even four babies concurrently[⊙] and many mothers of more than one baby breastfeed exclusively or combine breast and bottle-feeding successfully.

Twins, who can sometimes be small at birth, can enjoy all the benefits of breastmilk and once you've got breastfeeding well-established, you too will appreciate the comfort and practicality of having your babies' food instantly available with no bottles and powder to worry about.

Breastfeeding in a 'rugby ball' hold works well. Your babies can rest on pillows at either side of you, with their legs pointing behind you, your arms around them and their heads cradled in each of your hands as you hold one at each breast.

If you're the mother of twins, you'll sometimes want to feed both twins together, sometimes one after the other – it's up to you. Experiment with different set-ups so you feel comfortable and find out which is easier for you. You may find you prefer feeding them together, only to discover that at times, one twin is very hungry while the other stays fast asleep.

It can help to learn to express milk at least occasionally, as this gives you the option, when it's convenient, of allowing one of your helpers to bottle-feed expressed milk to one baby while you feed the other 'direct'.

Talking to other twin parents about what worked for them is a good way to get ideas, and the twins association, TAMBA (see page 245) has helpful leaflets suggesting ideas to support breastfeeding and showing different ways of holding your babies.

The Baby Friendly Initiative

Certain hospital practices – known as the Ten Steps (see box) – have been found to be helpful for women who want to breastfeed, and maternity units who follow these practises are called 'Baby Friendly' if they have achieved standards set by the UNICEF Baby Friendly Initiative. It is worth trying to find out if your local hospital is Baby Friendly as you are much more likely to get expert help and to avoid conflicting advice. There is a Community Baby Friendly award given for any community facilities which meet UNICEF's standards in supporting breastfeeding.

THE TEN STEPS
Every facility providing maternity services and care for newborn infants should:
- Have a written breastfeeding policy that is routinely communicated to all health-care staff.
- Train all health-care staff in skills necessary to implement this policy.
- Inform all pregnant women about the benefits and management of breastfeeding.
- Help mothers initiate breastfeeding soon after birth.
- Show mothers how to breastfeed, and how to maintain lactation even if they are separated from their babies.
- Give newborn infants no food or drink other than breastmilk, unless medically indicated.
- Practice rooming-in (allow mothers and infants to remain together 24 hours a day).
- Encourage breastfeeding on demand.
- Give no artificial teats or pacifiers (also called dummies or soothers) to breastfeeding infants.
- Foster the establishment of breast-feeding support groups and refer mothers to them on discharge from the hospital or clinic.
See www.babyfriendly.org.uk

Always bring baby to breast, not breast to baby. Don't try to put your breast into her mouth. Wait for her to take it by moving her close, keeping body and head in line.

formula-feeding

Breastmilk is the healthiest option for your baby, but there are many reasons why parents might not breastfeed. No one should pressurize you to breastfeed or formula-feed – all that is reasonable is to give you the information and let you make your own decision. Feeding your baby, however it's done, should be a source of joy.

The sad fact is that many parents who do want to breastfeed end up formula-feeding, due to lack of information, support and practical help. If you are unsure, it's actually better to start with breastfeeding and see how you feel about it – you can always switch to formula if it's not for you and your baby, but it is much harder to switch to breastfeeding if you start with formula.

Formula-feeding – how to do it

There is a huge choice in formula-feeding – it can be difficult to decide what to buy. You will need at least six bottles and teats, some method of sterilizing, plus of course the formula. It is probably best to be guided by your health visitor or midwife about which formula to start your baby on. She should also show you how to prepare a bottle at least once, but you must make sure that you read the instructions on the tin carefully, as it is important the ratio of water to powder is correct. Don't ever be tempted to make the milk thinner or thicker than instructed.

Formula-feeding – step by step guide

1　It saves time if you make up all the bottles you need that day, so get everything ready beforehand.
2　Wash everything thoroughly, and then sterilize everything you are going to use – bottles, teats, measures, knife.
3　Boil more fresh cold tap water than you need, and allow it to cool.
4　Fill each bottle to the correct level, using the cooled, boiled water.
5　Using the spoon provided in the tin of formula, take a scoop of formula, and level it with the knife. Don't pat it down or compress it.
6　Add the powder to the bottle, put the top on and shake thoroughly.
7　Place in fridge until you want to use it.
8　When you want to feed the bottle to your baby, she won't mind it straight from the fridge. Heating milk risks too many burns and scalds.
9　Sit comfortably, and hold your baby close, with her body across your lap, sitting her a little upright if you can.
10　Keep the bottle held up at an angle, so the teat is always full, to avoid your baby swallowing air bubbles.

Keep it calm

Try to feed in a calm and restful atmosphere.

- Gather together all the things you need – bottle, tissues or bib, drink and snack for yourself.
- Choose a comfortable chair with good back support. A small footstool or a couple of big books may be useful to raise your knees and level your lap. Pillows under your arms will make you more comfortable.
- Some babies like to be wrapped cosily in a shawl for feeding. Others prefer to be able to move their arms, touch and explore.
- Experiment with feeding positions but make sure her head is always slightly higher than her tummy. You may prefer to hold her tucked in close to your body with her head resting in the crook of your arm. Or you may prefer to hold her slightly away from you, with her head in your hand and her feet touching your tummy – you may both enjoy the more direct eye contact that is possible in this position.
- Touch your baby's lip gently with the teat and wait for her to open her mouth. Don't try and force the bottle into her mouth – she knows when she's hungry.
- Hold the bottle up at an angle so that the teat remains full of milk and she doesn't suck in any air. Don't jiggle the teat around if she stops to rest. Bottle-feeding is hard work for a baby.
- If she starts spluttering, take the teat out of her mouth and sit her upright to catch her breath. When she's calm, start again. Using a slow-flow teat will prevent her being overwhelmed with the flow of milk and will encourage active sucking.
- When she stops sucking and seems contented, resist the temptation to make her finish the bottle. If she doesn't want any more, throw any leftovers away.

Your partner will enjoy feeding his baby too, but try not to let others share this pleasure at first.

Bonding with your formula-fed baby

It is true that breastfeeding and bonding seem to go naturally together, because you're the only person who can breastfeed, but you will still bond with your baby if you are formula-feeding.

You can formula-feed on demand, which is one way of staying in tune with your baby and fulfilling her needs.

Cuddle your baby skin-to-skin – ie with your bare skin next to hers, and co-sleep with your formula-fed baby if you want to. This will help your baby bond with you, as well as meeting her needs for contact.

Don't sleep with your baby, though, if either you or your partner are smokers or have been drinking or taking drugs or are extremely tired. And try not to fall asleep on a sofa with your baby as this can be dangerous.

Breastfeeding is recommended for at least the first six months. Even if you want to change to formula, or combine breast and bottle later, it is important to give your newborn baby breastmilk. Colostrum, the first milk your body produces, is a very important source of antibodies and builds up your baby's immune system.

Methods of sterilizing

As your baby does not have a good immune system, and milk allows germs to grow easily, it is important that everything is thoroughly sterilized; otherwise you put your baby at risk of illnesses like thrush or gastro-enteritis. There are two ways to sterilize your feeding equipment; heat or chemical, and both are fairly easy once you've got the hang of them.

Heat sterilizing – steam

If you are using a steam sterilizer, just follow the instructions, add water to the unit, plug it in at the mains and switch on. The water boils and steam then sterilizes the feeding equipment. You can also heat sterilize by immersing all your baby's bottles etc in a large saucepan of water, bringing it to the boil, and letting the water boil vigorously for 20 minutes. Make sure that everything is completely covered by water.

Heat sterilizing – microwave

You can buy special microwave sterilizers, which also work by killing germs through heat. Make sure you follow the instructions, according to the strength of your microwave oven.

Chemical sterilizing

Sterilizing tablets are available from any chemist. Dissolve them according to directions, in a deep container of water, leaving everything to soak in the solution for a certain length of time – usually 24 hours. This means you need to have enough equipment to have some soaking and some in use.

You will need to sterilize everything that comes in contact with milk, for at least your baby's first year.

Out and about with your formula-fed baby

Although formula-feeding in public might seem easier than breastfeeding, in fact it can be just as hard to find somewhere suitable to sit and feed your baby, and you will also need to transport the bottled milk safely. You need to keep the milk cool until just before you use it, so you will probably need an insulated cool bag, with some ice blocks, to make sure the milk doesn't get warm when you're out and about.

If the bottle no longer feels cool to the touch when you take it out of the bag, don't use the milk. Bacteria thrive in warm milk.

Some restaurants will heat a baby's bottle on request, and some mother and baby changing rooms also have places to heat bottles. You can also feed your baby formula without heating it.

Winding your baby

If your baby seems to need to bring up wind:

- Sit her upright on your lap with your hand under her chin, keeping her back as straight as possible. Your baby will probably be leaning forward slightly and you will need to support her head at first. Then you can pat her back quite firmly.

Alternatively:

- First put a good absorbent towel over your shoulder reaching well down your back, then
- prop her over your shoulder, so she's upright, her chin is resting on your shoulder and her tummy is stretched out full length against your chest,
- now stroke her back and sides firmly and slowly upwards towards her neck several times. Quite firm pressure is needed, like stroking a cat really hard, backwards!

If your baby seems very windy, you could experiment with different types of bottle or teat, perhaps trying a teat which slows down the milk flow. You could also feed your baby in a more upright position, with frequent pauses to allow trapped air to escape.

soothing a newborn

Most babies have fairly simple needs — they need to be fed, to feel comfortable and safe, they need human company and they need sleep. They cry to let you know there's a problem because that's the only way they can get help, and all they expect is that you will deal with the problem.

It can be hard to find a way of comforting a baby who's not hungry. Your baby won't cry 'just to annoy you', or from any other complicated motive, so do respond to her cry. Most research suggests that babies whose cries are answered, cry less, and grow up to be more independent.[◎]

Most babies seem to enjoy anything which reminds them of being in the womb, where they were warm, held, rocked and moved around in constant contact with you.

- You can buy 'womb noise' tapes, but the sound of a tumble drier, extractor fan, running water, vacuum cleaner or hairdryer works just as well, as does playing the radio when it is not tuned to any station, so you hear the static.
- Many babies love music, and we know that they remember the music they heard during pregnancy.[◎] Playing your favourite music (CDs you listened to during pregnancy) can sometimes help soothe a crying baby.[◎]
- If your baby is not one for loud music, try singing lullabies to her. She will probably particularly like it if you hum or sing softly while resting your head against hers.
- Get into a warm bath with your baby, but make sure that the water's not too hot and that someone is around to help you get out.
- Babies love to be in motion. You can dance with your baby, jiggling round the room in time to your favourite music, you can take her for car rides, perhaps en route to see other new mums in a postnatal support group, or to have a good walk in the park or the country with your baby in a sling, back pack or pushchair.
- Getting out for a walk with your baby every day is a good idea; it's healthy exercise, you both get lots of fresh air, and getting out of the house will help you avoid developing postnatal depression.
- If your baby wants to be held or jigged around a lot of the time, get other people to hold her too. She won't mind who is doing the carrying. Invest in a good sling; the ones with lots of different positions will probably last you longer, but ask around for recommendations and borrow a few to try out. Some slings don't have enough support and your baby will outgrow them very quickly.

- You can recreate the feeling of the restricted space inside the womb by swaddling your baby, although make sure she doesn't get too hot when wrapped like this.

Helping your baby to sleep

Young babies are not capable of deep sleep. Many drift in and out of sleep fairly ineffectively, depending on their ability to soothe themselves.

Research into sleep training consistently shows that the most effective strategy early on is to find a way of establishing the difference between night and day,[⊙] and this involves two things:

- When you feed your baby at night, keep lights dim, talk quietly – avoid too much interaction – simply communicate that this is sleep time.
- Establish a bedtime routine to let her know it is time to sleep.

Bedtime routines

It doesn't really matter what you choose to do; a bedtime routine is basically about keeping things predictable. It should involve winding down, so

SWADDLING

To swaddle your baby, use a large baby blanket: lay it in a diamond shape, folding the top point over to create a flat edge for her shoulders to lie along. Fold one side over her body and tuck under her bottom (keep her arms bent up). Then bring the bottom point up to tuck into this wrap, thus immobilizing the feet. Wrap the other top corner around her and secure this corner in the material at her neck. Leave her hands free so that she can find them.

If you 'swaddle' your baby in a cot sheet or blanket, make sure she has access to her hands and don't let her get too hot.

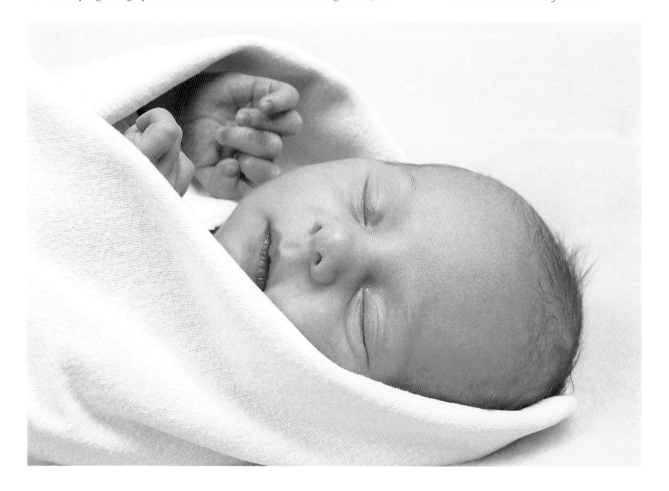

CRANIAL OSTEOPATHY

This is popular with many parents and there's some evidence that it helps soothe babies who cry a lot.[⊙] Cranial osteopaths look for disturbance in the bones of the skull, and remedy these with gentle massage. The theory is that during labour, the baby's skull is compressed, distorting and overlapping the skull bones. Normally this moulding is reduced in the first few days after birth by crying (which raises intracranial pressure) and by suckling, which also moves the bones of the jaw and face.

If the moulding is extreme though, through a very slow, difficult or assisted delivery, then the compression stays, makes the baby more irritable; perhaps to the extent of giving the baby a headache. She cries a lot and prefers being held upright as this decreases pressure on the head. It is also suggested that the nerve to the tongue can be affected so suckling is less effective, and the baby tires before she has had enough milk, so feeding is frequent and erratic.

Cranial osteopathy treatments are only available privately, and a baby usually needs somewhere between two and six treatments, depending on the severity of the problem.

perhaps a bath, clean nappy and a milk feed and finally, tucking her up in her cot – don't put her in an adult bed alone.

Where should my baby sleep?

Our society tends to believe that it is better for babies to sleep alone, and that separate sleeping encourages independence, but in fact there is no research evidence to suggest that babies who sleep on their own are less dependent on their parents.

When scientists have observed bedsharing in the laboratory, they noticed that mother and baby tune into each other, and their cycles of arousal and sleep come together. Research has also found that when mothers and babies sleep together, they face each other, close enough to inhale each other's breath, suggesting that perhaps the mother is stimulating the baby to breathe more regularly.[⊙]

Bedsharing mothers do wake more often, but they actually spend just as much time asleep overall as mothers whose babies sleep in another room, and tend to feel less disturbed,[⊙] because the baby who sleeps in a separate room has to cry to attract attention, and in the process, gets agitated and upset.[⊙] You have to get out of bed to respond to your baby, so you both wake up fully, and thus it takes longer to get back to sleep again. In addition, babies will not feed as effectively if they are already crying and upset.[⊙]

The Foundation for the Study of Infant Deaths (FSID) advises that having your baby's cot in the bedroom with you for the first six months is safer. The most recent and comprehensive research into cot death in this country has concluded that sharing a room with a parent halves the risk of death.[⊙] The study also found that bed-sharing is fine when certain precautions are met.

Safe bed-sharing

- You need to make sure your baby can't fall out of bed. You could use a guard-rail if it can be placed flush against the side of your mattress. You can buy sidecar cots where the side drops down and the cot mattress can be raised to the same level as your bed.
- Put your baby on her back to sleep.
- Don't put your baby to sleep alone in an adult bed.
- Avoid large pillows or cushions, and don't sleep with your baby on a couch or water bed, as these are too soft. Surfaces should be firm.
- Make sure that your duvet or pillows cannot cover your baby's head.
- Don't fall asleep with your baby on the sofa.

It's better not to bed share if:

- You or your partner are smokers.
- You have been drinking or taking drugs (this includes prescribed drugs such as sedatives or strong painkillers).
- You are extremely tired.

Safety in the cot

- Use a mattress completely covered with PVC or another wipe-clean surface. It doesn't have to be new as long as it's firm, clean and dry.
- Make sure the mattress fits without any gaps.
- Put your baby on her back to sleep.
- Don't use pillows, duvet or other soft bedding which could pose a risk of suffocation. Use one or more layers of light blankets for babies less than a year old, tuck the covers in firmly and make the cot up from the bottom – so your baby sleeps 'feet to foot'.
- Avoid overheating the room or overdressing your baby.

During the first six weeks, a baby's circadian rhythm, which governs heart rate, temperature and activity level, matures. This means that she will begin to develop a pattern that will help her to be more firmly asleep or awake – rather than drifting in and out of these two states. Somewhere between one and three months of age, she should begin to sleep less frequently but for longer periods. You will start to learn to anticipate her sleepy times and she will begin to recognize your signals that it's time for bed.

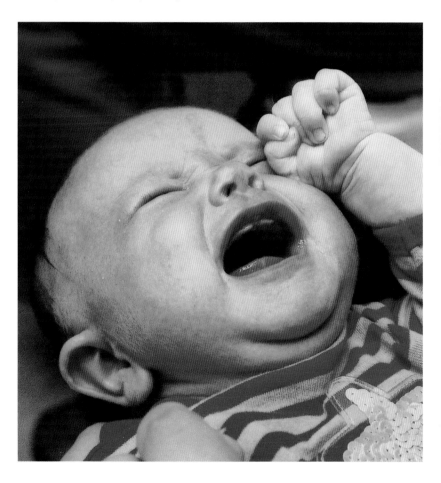

BACK TO THE WOMB

Some mammals can get up and walk straight after birth. In comparison, human newborn babies are very dependent on our care. One theory is that evolution has made our brains grow so enormous that we have to be born early, otherwise our heads would be too large to fit through the pelvis. As a result, some say that all human babies in a sense are born premature. They could do with another three months inside.

It's certainly true that recreating the sensations of life in the womb can make a baby feel secure – holding, rocking, shushing noises can all help soothe a crying baby.

One study compared infants sleeping in an ordinary cot, with those sleeping in a cot specifically designed to feel similar to the womb: it moved, made noises and held the babies firmly. The babies with the special cribs cried significantly less during the study period, slept for longer at night and slept through the night sooner, too.⊙

Most people can tune out all sorts of noise, but the sound of a baby crying is very difficult to ignore and your baby's appearance – smooth skin, big eyes – is designed to make you want to pick her up and cuddle her straight away.

expressing breastmilk

You may need to express your breastmilk if you or your baby are ill. You may also want to do this if you are returning to work or leaving your baby for any other reason. Try hand expressing first as it's easier because you don't have to keep sterilizing a pump.

There may be times when you would like to give your baby your own expressed breastmilk. It's usually easier to do this after breastfeeding has been established – around six weeks works well.

If your baby only feeds from one breast at a time, it can be a good idea to express from the other side at the same time, using a hand pump you can work with one hand only. If your baby has long gaps between feeds (three hours or more) you could try expressing between those times. Alternatively, you can express what is left after your baby has finished a feed.

You'll need to experiment to find the best time and the best method for you, but you may find it's quicker in the morning and gets easier.

Before you start expressing, there are several things you can do to help:
- try to be as comfortable and relaxed as possible
- have your baby, or a photograph of your baby, close by
- have a warm bath or shower, or lay warm flannels on your breast
- gently massage your breast towards the nipple

How to hand express
- Sterilize a wide-necked bottle or bowl to catch the milk.
- Hold your breast, with your thumb on top and your fingers underneath, so that your little finger is against your rib cage, and your first finger and thumb are opposite each other, making a big 'C' shape round the whole of your breast.
- Your milk comes from deep within your breast, so your finger and thumb need to be well away from your nipple, back behind your areola.
- Squeeze your thumb and first finger gently together, hold and release, and keep doing this without changing the position of your fingers, until you see some drops of milk appearing. This may take a few minutes.
- Some women find they can do this more effectively if they gently push their whole hand back towards the ribcage, before they squeeze.
- If the flow of milk starts to slow down, you can move your hand round, keeping that 'C' round your whole breast, so that you are 'milking' a different section of your breast each time.
- You can swap from side to side to increase the amount of milk expressed.

Benefits for premature babies

Expressing your milk is not a lot of fun; it's hard work and you'll need all the support and encouragement you can get – but it's worth it if your baby is unwell or unable to feed from you for any reason. Many mothers find it very comforting to provide breastmilk for their pre-term baby because it's the one thing they alone can do.

Breastmilk is especially suited to pre-term babies because of their immature digestive systems. It contains factors that protect against infection and allergy, and research has even shown that the milk from mothers of premature babies is higher in protein than the breastmilk of mothers of full-term babies. Breastmilk also protects babies from the very dangerous bowel disease, necrotizing enterocolitis.

Long-term expressing

If you want to express milk for all your baby's feeds – for example if she's very premature, you will probably need to borrow or hire a hospital-grade electric breast pump. When pumping exclusively for a newborn, it's important to imitate a baby's feeding pattern as far as possible. This means pumping about every three hours for the first few weeks, including once during each night.

Storing expressed breastmilk

Expressed breastmilk (EBM) keeps well if refrigerated or frozen. It will last for 3–5 days stored in the coldest part of the fridge (below 4°C, 39°F – usually the back or the bottom of the fridge, NOT the door). Freezing only causes minor changes to the nutrients and anti-infective properties. Frozen EBM stored in a deep-freeze is best used within three months.

You will need to freeze EBM in sterile containers. You may prefer to buy special EBM polybags (available from chemists) as they have no harmful chemicals. Label and date the bag, and then pour the milk straight into it from the pump or bowl, if you are hand expressing.

Chilled expressed milk can be added to milk which is already frozen, as long as you don't add more than half as much again. As milk will expand on freezing, don't fill containers to the top.

When feeding EBM to your baby, use fresh first and the oldest batch of frozen next. The fat in EBM often separates – simply give it a good shake.

Breastmilk is best defrosted slowly. Milk that has been defrosted in the fridge will keep for 24 hours. You can thaw milk quickly by standing the container in hot water, but you must use it immediately. You can heat EBM in a bowl of hot water – don't heat it directly in a pan or microwave, as this will destroy some nutritional benefits. Microwaves heat unevenly and hot spots could scald a baby. Milk does not have to be at body heat – babies don't mind it cool or at room temperature.

organizing your day

Gradually, after the first few weeks, a pattern will emerge and you will begin to feel as though things are settling down. The excitement of the early days may fade but now you'll start to find time for simple pleasures like taking a shower that lasts longer than two minutes or eating a meal without a baby at your breast.

'I think it's really important to get out and see as many different people as you can, because there are certain people you click with and others who you don't. I go to all the groups on offer.'

Everyone will tell you that the chaos of the first weeks with a new baby does not last long – so remember that when you're finding it hard. Anyway, you may find that you love this stage, when your baby's greatest pleasure is to be cuddled in your arms and to gaze up at your face. If you lower your standards, and you've got the right support, you can relax and really enjoy this special time. At this stage, a little organization can help a lot.

Rationalize your home

- Hang a stocked-up baby-changing bag ready to go by the front door. Include nappies, wipes, nappy-cream, a change of clothes, changing mat, hats and toys etc.
- Keep a 'baby changing station' with nappies, wipes and a change of baby clothes in every room you use on a regular basis.
- Pack away fancy clothes and just keep easy-care separates to hand – comfortable trousers, wash 'n' go tops, stretchy skirts and comfortable shoes.
- Keep one complete outfit including tights, shoes and fresh underwear, hanging up in a dry cleaner's bag at the back of the wardrobe so that you can slip it on if you need to look good in a hurry.

Getting help

- Accept all offers of help – ironing, cooking and shopping – and promise to do the same for your friends when it's their turn.
- Ask visitors to stop off and pick things up for you on their way over – a loaf of bread, milk, nappies, whatever you need.
- Perhaps you could find a neighbour or local teenager to pop in a couple of times a week to help you with washing or cleaning, and use some of your new Child Benefit to pay for it.
- Contact your nearest further education college and see if any trainee nursery nurses would like to get some work experience by helping you out.
- Get to know your health visitor – every new mum in the UK has a named health visitor to give support and friendship. Health visitors are ideally placed to form a relationship of trust with mothers. Research has shown that, if you're feeling overwhelmed, a health visitor can be more help

than a psychologist.[®] Let her know how you're feeling. She will understand what you're talking about, and can offer useful ideas.

- HomeStart provides help on an as-needed basis. It's a voluntary organization that has over 200 branches across the UK offering support and practical help to families with pre-school children. They send experienced mothers out to help and support new mothers and it doesn't cost a thing. (Contact details on page 245.)

The talking cure

It always helps to talk through how you're feeling. If you don't have someone close you can talk to, seek out other new mothers through your local baby clinic or NCT branch. New mothers can get very lonely when they stop work and it can feel worse if you have mixed feelings about being at home with your baby. If you can make friends with others in the same situation, it's good for you and the whole family. A happy mother with a social outlet of her own is a definite asset for her baby, who will thoroughly enjoy her mother's happiness and the variety of new faces that she'll see.

In the early weeks it sometimes seems an achievement to get the curtains open by lunchtime, let alone get out of the house and socialize with a whole new group of people, but as soon as you are able to, making friends with other mothers can help to reduce the loneliness. You might find that problems you thought were unique to you are in fact shared by many others, and that discovery alone – plus the opportunity to take the long view – puts things into perspective.

FEELING STRESSED?

- Get into bed with your baby, breastfeed her and sleep whenever she sleeps.
- Get someone (partner, your mum, a friend) to take her out for an hour or two in the buggy to give you a break. If this is a success, make it a regular arrangement.
- Go out to a mother & toddler group, even if the other babies are much older than yours. A new baby is always a conversation-opener and it's good to talk to other mothers who will understand how you're feeling and will be able to sympathize.
- Light some candles and run a warm bath. If your baby has been fed and she still won't sleep, have a candle-lit soak in the tub with her. (Ask someone else to bring you warm towels.)

Getting out of the house and meeting new people is good for you – all mothers need to find time to be with other new mums.

see also

postnatal depression

Postnatal illness was once a taboo subject – but now it's recognized that motherhood can turn us upside down. New mothers are expected to carry on as though nothing has changed, when in reality their lives have changed forever.

GIRLS AREN'T BORN MOTHERS

And neither are boys born fathers. Looking after a child is a skill we have to learn like any other. We get thrown in at the deep end when we have our first baby and it's not surprising that we find this hard.

Sometimes it can feel as though you'll never cope, but remember that the time when your baby is very new really does pass by in a flash. Enjoy it as much as you can because when it's gone there's no way of turning back the clock.

All life-changes mean extra stress and strain, but they also offer enormous potential for growth. A time of change is both a period of heightened vulnerability and heightened potential. If we can be aware of how we are changing, and can reflect on what we are doing, thinking and feeling at this time, it can help us grow in strength.

Postnatal depression (PND) is more than just feeling low some of the time after the birth of your baby. After all, 'off' days are a part of normal life and no one expects sunshine every day. Postnatal depression is longer-lasting; it usually presents within the first six weeks after the baby's birth and 60 per cent of women with PND will experience symptoms before six months, although it may be a long time before this is recognized.

Textbooks on the subject generally quote studies which put the numbers of women affected at between 10 per cent and 15 per cent of all new mothers. However, other studies reveal higher totals of as much as 27 per cent.[⊙] A practical definition of postnatal depression is that it is a depressed mood which lasts, which overwhelms more positive feelings, and which becomes evident in the first weeks and months after childbirth.

Have I got postnatal depression?

You may have PND if:
- you are often sad, and find it hard to see the funny side of things – some women feel so low they avoid meeting people, and some cry easily
- you feel you are the only mother who can't cope
- you feel a failure, and guilty because of it
- you feel anxious and irritable, maybe worried over world problems you can't influence
- you find coping with your baby's crying very difficult
- either you can't sleep even though you are exhausted, or you endlessly crave sleep
- you feel as if you hardly ever have enough energy to do things
- making decisions, even about simple things, is very hard.

Edinburgh Postnatal Depression Scale

The Edinburgh Postnatal Depression Scale (EPDS) is a brief questionnaire, normally used at 6 to 8 weeks after the birth and/or 6 to 8 months after the birth. It asks a mother what her moods and feelings have been in the last week. It's simple to use and doesn't pry into personal experiences but does identify women who could do with help and gets it for them.

Caring for someone with PND

Living with a depressed partner places a considerable burden on the other partner, whatever the cause of the depression – new motherhood or anything else. Fathers who are trying to support a mother who is very needy can feel desperately lonely themselves. So it's important for supporters to get help too, and if friends or family members are not able to provide what you need, your family doctor will be the best person to talk to.

The good news is that PND responds well to treatment, especially if you seek help from your doctor early.

Health visitors, too, are trained to spot postnatal depression and can offer counselling as well as practical support and suggest medication. Antidepressants are sometimes prescribed, so do ask about any possible side-effects, to help you decide whether or not to take them and tell your doctor if you are breastfeeding. There are several different kinds and some have been shown to be safe to take while breastfeeding.

For many women, antidepressants have helped their unpleasant symptoms fade until they have gone completely. Women come off them gradually, as they recover.

Other strategies that really do make a difference are spending regular short periods of time away from the baby, doing things you enjoy. And relaxation tapes can be helpful. Ask your health visitor if she has tapes she can recommend. Talking to a supportive friend or counsellor can make a real difference, too, but not all women will find this works for them.

How friends can help

- Show you care – without feeling loved, she may find it hard to get better.
- Listen, let her tell it in her own way – she may need you to listen to the same story many times before she can make sense of it all.
- Let her express her bad feelings as well as the good ones – don't say things like 'you don't mean that'.
- She may worry she doesn't have feelings for her baby, but these will emerge as her depression lifts.
- Persuade her to give time to herself – she needs it.
- Encourage her to seek help if she hasn't already done so.

Puerperal psychosis

This is a very serious illness – it affects 2 or 3 women in every 1000. It usually starts within the first six weeks of birth with a dramatic change in personality. Often a woman becomes extremely agitated, her thoughts race and her ideas are chaotic. At other times she seems severely depressed.

It's important to get medical help straight away for puerperal psychosis, which can only get worse untreated. With the right treatment most women make a full recovery.

'I believe, looking back, that when I had my own child, the child in me became scared again. How could I protect and care for my own child properly when I felt so unprotected and scared myself?'

'I had PND with my first, but it took a long time to acknowledge that's what it was. I just didn't feel like myself: that all this was happening to someone else. I found it hard to cope at times but getting out was better than staying at home. I remember hiding my utter horror when others cooed over newborn babies… for me having a new baby was absolute hell in every way possible…'

baby massage

During her last weeks in the womb, your baby was firmly held and continually caressed by the muscular walls of your uterus. No wonder then, now that she is born, firm holding and stroking continue to calm and soothe her. Babies need touch as much as they need food.

Your health visitor will be able to give you information about baby massage classes in your area. These provide an excellent way to meet other mothers, bond with your baby, and learn a skill that will enhance your life. For all ages, the physical touch of massage encourages good blood circulation, relaxes muscles and nerves, improves the functioning of the lymphatic system and has a relaxing effect on the mind.

Good for both of you

In a study recently conducted at Queen Charlotte's and Chelsea Hospital in London, a group of depressed mothers who attended five baby massage classes each showed a remarkable improvement in mother–baby interaction and were 'back as normal mothers enjoying their babies… and relating to them' after learning how to do the massage.[o]

The research involved two groups of postnatally depressed mothers who were allocated randomly – to attend either infant massage classes plus a support group – or the support group only. Each group attended five weekly sessions. Measures of depression (the Edinburgh Postnatal Depression Scale (EPDS) and mother–infant interaction (a video recording)) were made at the beginning and the end. The EPDS scores decreased in both groups but most significantly in the massage group. The massage group also showed marked improvement in mother–infant interaction. This was not apparent in the non-massage group.

Massage can be tried out at home as well as learned in classes. Many fathers in particular find it rewarding to massage their baby. Massage is especially good for a second or third baby who may not get much special time alone with you, apart from feeds. Remember that you don't have to do a full massage every time – if you're in a hurry, just do the favourite bits.

Stroking and caressing your baby is something you will probably do almost without thinking from birth. For the first six or seven months of life, massage is most effective. Once your baby is mobile, she may be too busy to lie still, but massage can still be part of your daily routine.

Use firm but gentle pressure with either the flat pads of your fingers or the whole palm of your hand. Keep one hand on your baby at all times. If

'I didn't have a lot of time for my second baby, because my first was still so young. Massage sessions with the new baby gave us time to focus on each other.'

you need to reach for a tissue, for example, keep the other hand on your baby's skin for reassurance.

How to begin

Have everything ready before you start. Find a warm, quiet place where you won't be disturbed and have everything you need to hand – massage oil (a simple vegetable oil such as almond), tissues, a clean nappy and a clean set of clothes. The massage can be done on the floor, with the baby laid on a towel on top of a changing mat or folded blanket.

Remove any rings or bracelets you may wear; make sure your fingernails are short and wash your hands in warm water. Dry them, then rub them together to make them nice and warm.

Undress your baby and lay her on her back. Kneel or sit facing her, and taking about a half-teaspoonful of oil, rub it over the palms of your warm hands. Use just enough oil to let your palms glide smoothly over her skin. Talk to your baby, make eye contact and tell her what you are going to do.

A greeting

Place your hands, side by side, palms down flat on the baby's tummy and stroke gently upwards around the shoulders and smoothly back down to the toes. Repeat this a few times, talking or singing gently and letting your baby's response guide you.

CAUTION

- Don't give a massage near feeding time. One hour before or after is best.
- Never wake a baby up for a massage.
- Aromatherapy oils designed for adults should be avoided.
- Never use deep pressure when you massage a baby.
- Always be guided by your baby's response. If your baby's not happy being undressed and massaged, leave it for a while and perhaps try again another day.

Research shows that baby massage is good for mother–infant interaction. It's a fun thing to do and can cheer you both up.

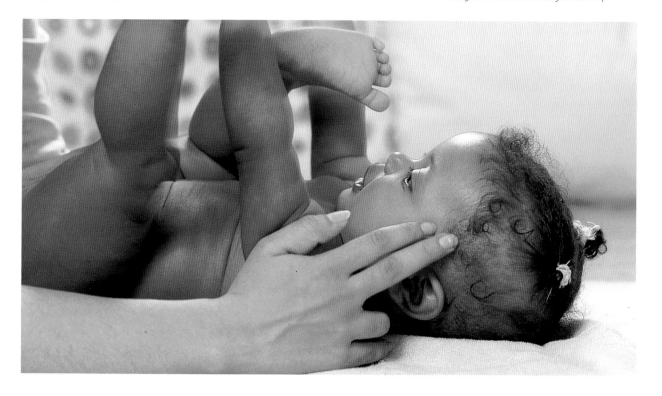

Chest and arms

Without applying any more oil to your hands, place them together, palms down, side by side on the baby's chest and gently press them down, round the chest and up again. From the same starting position, stroke up around the shoulders and down again, stroking the arms down towards the wrists. Repeat this movement two or three times, without getting any massage oil on the baby's hands (it will irritate her eyes if she rubs them).

Tummy

Put a little oil on your hands and make clockwise circles over the tummy with one hand and then, with the pads of two fingers, make small clockwise circles around the colon (beginning just up from the right groin, upwards to just under the ribs, across to the other side and down). Repeat a few times. This sometimes helps colicky babies. Then repeat the 'hello' strokes you began with, running your hands around the shoulders and back down to the toes. Ask your baby if she'd like to turn over.

Legs

Apply a little more oil to your hands if needed and, starting with hands at either side of the base of the spine, stroke up to the shoulders and back down to the toes a few times before smoothing each leg in turn.

Hold one of your baby's ankles in one hand, and with the other hand, take hold of the top of the leg on the other side. Pull down gently but firmly and as you get to the ankle, move your other hand up to the top of the leg on the same side, pulling down in the same way while the first hand takes over holding the ankle. Repeat this 'leg pulling' motion several times.

Go through the same massage on the other leg, and then running both hands up both legs at the same time and gliding right back down to the ends of the toes. Repeat this finishing stroke a few times.

Use a simple vegetable oil such as almond and a firm, but gentle stroke, letting your baby's response be your guide.

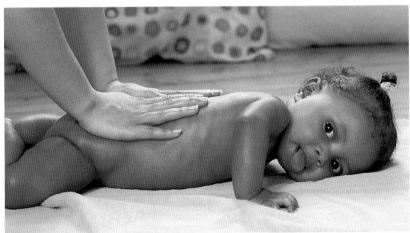

Massage is a delightful way of getting to know your baby. A parent's loving touch shows children they are lovable, and a happy baby shows parents they're doing it right.

Feet

With your thumb, rub small circles on the base of your baby's foot (anti-clockwise circles are supposed to be calming). Repeat on the other foot and then rub up and down the legs as before.

Back

Starting with hands at either side of the base of the spine, stroke up to the shoulders and down to the toes. Glide your hands back up the legs to either side of the base of the spine, and repeat the movement. Do not touch the actual spine itself, just massage at either side. With the flat of the hand, make large anti-clockwise circles around the base of the back. Finish off with a few strong stroking movements, up the back, around the shoulders and back down to the toes.

Finally wrap your baby in a warm towel and give her a cuddle.

one year on...

Becoming a mother has turned everything on its head. It's now 12 months since conception and the last year has seen you develop enormously as a person, as you and your partner faced the challenge of new parenthood. The year ahead will have its challenges too.

Strengthening your body

In the first year of life, a baby moves rapidly from dependent newborn to active toddler and you may find you have trouble keeping up! If you're planning to go back to work, this next year will probably be the busiest of your life to date and will stretch your organizational skills to the limit – but you will also find life immeasurably richer now that you both have the responsibility of your baby to care for.

As at any other challenging period in life, it's important to eat well, stay fit and take care of yourself.

After a month or two, you could ask your health visitor or sports centre if there's a postnatal exercise class being run near you. Make sure the class is run by a teacher qualified to teach postnatal exercise.

It should be noted, however, that no high-impact exercise should be undertaken until at least three months after your baby is born – no matter how fit you were before getting pregnant. High-impact exercise, such as running and jumping, puts a great deal of strain on the pelvic floor and this is an area you will want to get back into condition as soon as possible. Continue with your pelvic floor exercises until you feel those muscles are completely back to normal. The exercises will help stitches to heal more quickly too. Doing them for the rest of your life will help prevent problems later on, such as a prolapsed uterus or bladder.

Strengthening your relationship

After the birth of a child, the majority of couples experience a change in their sex lives, usually for the worse. Tiredness, physical discomfort and loss of libido are just some of the problems that impact on sex. But simple caresses help a lot – whether you're being stroked and cuddled or doing the stroking, both ways make you feel better.

A new baby obviously needs an awful lot of nurture from her mother. This puts a big strain on you and means you'll want more love and attention in turn, from your partner. On the other hand, he's deprived of your usual emotional support during this time and if he can't cope with a lot less cherishing than he's used to, he can't help you when you most need it.

KEEP FIT CAUTION

Pregnancy hormones will have loosened your ligaments to accommodate the growing baby and for some time after the end of pregnancy, your joints will remain loose and prone to injury.

When you exercise, never lie flat on your back and lift both legs in the air. This can do damage when you've just had a baby and your muscles are still weak.

Never lie flat on your back and do sit ups with your feet held down, either. This could damage your back if your abdominal muscles are still weak.

Keep talking, spending time together, listening to each other and considering each other. You're parents now: you depend on each other and need to take care of each other.

It can be helpful to think of your ability to give love and affection as an 'emotional storecupboard' that needs to be kept stocked up if you are to draw from its supplies. Who's filling up your storecupboard? Everyone needs love and support from different places; from friends and family as well as their partner. Spread the load and remember that no one can really give love unless they're getting it too.

Is there sex after childbirth?

The National Childbirth Trust ran a survey to see how well couples were able to adjust their sex lives in the year following a new baby. Nearly 1300 people returned the questionnaire and the results make interesting reading. According to this, the time a couple takes to resume sex varies a great deal. A few couples (20 per cent) begin before their baby is a month old. The majority (around 45 per cent) begin at between four and eight weeks, but quite a few (18.6 per cent) wait for three to four months and 15 per cent chose to wait until at least five months after the birth, and in some cases much longer.

Most women (61.4 per cent) felt that they had started at the time that was 'right for them' but some would have liked sex to have started earlier (17.1 per cent) and some later (18.6 per cent).

Tiredness was pinpointed as the main culprit responsible for loss of libido. For some, the interest was there but not the energy. Men too, will have been affected by the birth and may find that it impacts on their libido. Talking it through can help. If something more is needed, Relate is an organization that can offer effective psychosexual counselling.

Better or worse?

Although about half the couples in our survey thought having a baby had made their sex-life worse, almost a third (27.5 per cent) thought it had stayed the same and 16 per cent felt it had got better. These women listed as the new improvements:

- being more relaxed
- having a better body image
- physical improvements
- a better relationship
- feeling less inhibited.

You don't need to wait for the six-week check-up to make love providing that both you and your partner feel ready. (Remember that breastfeeding may not give you full contraceptive protection.) As the survey showed, many women wait several months before making love with penetration. Stitches

THE KEYS TO HAPPINESS
Researchers in the USA collected data from 21,501 couples, some happy with their relationship and some not. They gave all the couples a list of 195 statements and asked them to tick the ones that most applied to them. When the mass of data was analysed, the researchers discovered that certain statements were ticked a lot more by happy couples, so these could well be goals worth working towards in your relationship:

- I am very satisfied with how we talk to each other – 90 per cent.
- My partner understands my ideas and opinions – 87 per cent.
- We are both equally willing to make adjustments in the relationship – 87 per cent.
- We find it easy to think of things to do together – 86 per cent.
- Our sexual relationship is satisfying and fulfilling – 85 per cent.

New mothers need contact with other mothers: a happy mother with a social outlet of her own is a definite asset for her baby, who will thoroughly enjoy her mother's happiness and the variety of new faces that she'll see.

'After nine months of breastfeeding I felt I had done all I wanted to, stopped and three days later my sex drive returned like a storm.'

can be problematic, in which case, there are many ways of reaching orgasm without penetration. Your doctor will check your stitches at the six-week check, but if they continue to give trouble, make another appointment to have them looked at.

Breastfeeding

Of the 138 women in the survey who specifically mentioned loss of libido, several linked this to breastfeeding. When foreplay triggers milk production, many couples find this off-putting and vaginal dryness can be caused by breastfeeding. If this affects you, it's worth mentioning it to your GP as there are creams that can be prescribed to help. Using a Femidom contraceptive also makes intercourse easier. Many women found that their libido returned as their babies were weaned.

In the meantime, feeding your baby before making love will make your breasts less likely to leak and your baby more likely to sleep soundly.

Talk to each other

Intimacy can be achieved in many other ways than sex. Talking about your feelings, and listening to your partner talk about his or hers, is of course another way of getting close. Most happy couples would probably put their success down to 'being there for each other' – making time to listen and sharing hopes and concerns.

As your birth year closes, think back to where you were at this time last year and reflect on how much has changed since then. An enormous physical, emotional and spiritual shift has taken place and you have emerged from that upheaval, transformed into deeper, stronger people who know that now you are parents, life can only get better.

You're a mum and dad now and your relationship is the root out of which your future happiness will spring, giving your children all the security they need in order to grow and flourish.

a–z glossary of terms

The following list covers many pregnancy and childbirth-related terms and conditions. If you have any queries, remember your midwife or antenatal class teacher is always available to give information too.

AFP Test (see *screening test*) Blood test carried out between 16 and 18 weeks of pregnancy. Measures the amount of alpha-feto-protein in the mother's blood to assess the risk of the baby having spina bifida or Down's syndrome.

AFTERBIRTH (see *placenta*)

AFTERPAINS Contractions occurring in the first few days after the baby is born. Can be painful, especially during breastfeeding. More common after second babies than first. They help the womb regain its pre-pregnancy size.

AMNIOCENTESIS (see *amniotic fluid*; *diagnostic test*) Diagnostic test usually carried out between 16 and 18 weeks of pregnancy. A needle is passed through the mother's abdomen and a small amount of amniotic fluid is withdrawn from her womb. Cells which have come from the baby can be extracted from the fluid and used to diagnose spina bifida, Down's syndrome and other genetic abnormalities.

AMNIOTIC FLUID The fluid surrounding the baby during pregnancy. Also called 'waters' and liquor'. At eight months, there is about 0.5 to 1.5 litres. Too little amniotic fluid (oligohydramnios) may indicate problems with the baby's urinary tract; too much (polyhydramnios) could indicate problems with the oesophagus or spinal cord.

AMNIOTIC SAC The 'bag' which contains the baby and the waters. It consists of two membranes lining the womb, the chorion and the amnion.

ANAEMIA An iron deficiency of the blood which causes tiredness, breathlessness and pallor. Can be treated by eating a diet containing foods rich in iron and/or by taking iron tablets.

ANALGESIA (see *Entonox*, *epidural*, *Pethidine*) Medical word for drugs or treatments which provide pain relief.

ANTENATAL CLASSES Classes run by midwives, health visitors, physiotherapists and childbirth educators to prepare women and their partners for labour and parenting. Classes are often provided in early pregnancy and then during the final two months of pregnancy.

ANTERIOR POSITION When the baby is lying with the back of his head towards the front of the mother's pelvis at the end of pregnancy. The technical term is occiput anterior or OA. Labour tends to be shorter and less painful when the baby is in the anterior position.

ANTIBIOTICS Drugs used to fight bacterial infections, but which cannot be used against viruses. Antibiotics must be prescribed with caution during pregnancy as they may have adverse effects on the baby.

ANTIBODIES Proteins made by the body to fight off infections. The mother's antibodies cross the placenta and provide the baby with protection against infections such as German measles (rubella) and chicken pox during the first few months of his life.

APGAR SCORE A score indicating how strong the baby is at birth. The midwife assesses the baby's heart rate, breathing, muscle tone, reaction to stimulus and skin colour on a scale of 0 to 10. Typical Apgar scores might be 7 at birth and 10 five minutes later.

AREOLA The coloured circle of skin around the nipple. Raised areas on the areola are called Montgomery's tubercles and secrete substances which keep the nipples supple. When breastfeeding, most of the areola should be in the baby's mouth.

AROMATHERAPY The use of essential oils made from plants to treat pain, illness and states of mind. Essential oils can be inhaled, used for massage or added to the bath. Many are dangerous during pregnancy and labour, so always consult a qualified aromatherapist.

BIRTH BALL A large ball, similar to those used in gymnastics, which the mother can sit on or kneel over during labour to help her keep mobile.

BLOOD PRESSURE (see *pre-eclampsia*) An important indicator of the mother's and baby's health during pregnancy. The blood pressure consists of two readings, recorded as a higher figure over a lower figure (eg 120/70). Raised blood pressure may be due to pre-eclampsia.

BRAXTON HICKS CONTRACTIONS Contractions of the womb which occur in late pregnancy. The mother's tummy goes very hard but the contractions are not painful. Some women have frequent Braxton Hicks while others have none.

BREECH POSITION When the baby's bottom, rather than his head is in the pelvis at the end of pregnancy.

BROW PRESENTATION When the baby's head is tipped backwards, so that his brow would be born first. This can make labour very difficult because the brow is much wider than the back of the baby's head which normally comes first. A caesarean section may be necessary.

CARPAL TUNNEL SYNDROME The carpal tunnel carries nerves from the wrist to the hand. Fluid retention during pregnancy can narrow the tunnel and this puts pressure on the nerves, causing pins and needles and numbness in the fingers. Exercising the hands and wearing wrist splints can help. The condition usually disappears after birth.

CEPHALIC (abbreviation: ceph) Describes a baby who is lying upside down, with his head in the mother's pelvis. The usual position at the end of pregnancy.

CEPHALO-PELVIC DISPROPORTION (CPD) When the baby's head is too big to pass through the mother's pelvis and he has to be born by caesarean section.

CEREBRAL PALSY A condition involving varying degrees of physical and mental disability caused by lack of oxygen during pregnancy or at birth.

CERVICAL INCOMPETENCE (see *cervix*; *Shirodkar suture*) When the muscles that close the neck of the womb (cervix) are weak. The weight of the baby may cause the cervix to open in the fourth or fifth month of pregnancy. A stitch called a Shirodkar suture, can be put around the cervix in the early stages of pregnancy to keep it closed.

CERVICAL MUCUS (see *menstrual cycle*) Lubricates the vagina. The mucus changes in quantity and consistency during the menstrual cycle. Women can be taught how to examine their mucus to determine when they are fertile.

CERVIX The neck of the womb. It is long, hard and tightly closed during pregnancy. At the start of labour, it becomes softer and shorter and then opens to 10cm to allow the baby to be born.

CHLAMYDIA A sexually transmitted infection that can be treated with antibiotics. Although the mother may have no symptoms, the presence of the bacteria in the vagina can lead to premature labour and the baby may become infected.

CHLOASMA A slight darkening of the mother's forehead, nose and cheeks during pregnancy which makes it look as though she has a butterfly mask on her face. Disappears after the baby is born.

CHORIONIC VILLUS SAMPLING (CVS) Diagnostic test carried out from 11 weeks of pregnancy to find out whether the baby has Down's syndrome or another genetic abnormality. A needle is passed through the mother's abdomen under ultrasound guidance, and a tiny sample of the placenta taken. This is analysed in a medical laboratory.

COLOSTRUM The milk that is in the mother's breasts immediately after birth. It is thick, yellowish and rich in antibodies which protect the baby against diseases such as German measles. Colostrum is replaced by mature milk after about three days.

CONSTIPATION A common problem in pregnancy, caused by hormones slowing down the passage of food through the large bowel. Iron tablets can make it worse. Treatment includes eating plenty of fresh fruit, vegetables and cereal.

CONTRACTIONS Sometimes called labour pains. The muscles of the womb tighten to open up the neck of the womb (cervix) and push the baby out through the vagina.

CORDOCENTESIS Specialized antenatal test which involves taking blood from the baby's umbilical cord under ultrasound guidance. The blood is examined to see if the baby has haemophilia, anaemia, problems with his immune system or other abnormalities.

CRAMP Leg cramps are common during pregnancy. Drinking plenty of milk may help reduce the frequency of attacks. Flexing the foot at the ankle and then circling the ankle vigorously relieves the spasm.

CYSTITIS An infection of the bladder which makes passing urine painful, with a burning sensation. There is a need to go the toilet much more frequently than usual. Cystitis should be treated with antibiotics to prevent the infection from spreading to the kidneys.

DEEP TRANSVERSE ARREST A problem occurring during labour. The baby cannot get past the two bony projections (the ischial spines) that stick into the pelvis. Changing the mother's position can help, but sometimes a caesarean is necessary, or forceps may be used to help the baby's head pass the spines.

DIABETES Condition where the pancreas does not produce enough insulin and sugar accumulates in the blood leading to extreme thirst, drowsiness and eventually coma. Some women develop diabetes during pregnancy (gestational diabetes). Babies born to diabetic mothers can be very large.

DIAGNOSTIC TEST (see *screening test*) A test such as chorionic villus sampling or amniocentesis which can confirm whether the baby has a congenital abnormality such as spina bifida or a genetic condition such as Down's syndrome.

DOULA A Greek word meaning 'wise woman'. Used to describe an experienced mother who supports another woman during labour, and helps her care for her baby during the first few days at home.

DOWN'S SYNDROME Sometimes called Trisomy 21, this syndrome is caused by an abnormal twenty-first chromosome. People with Down's syndrome are below average intelligence and may have heart and lung problems. The degree of disability varies greatly.

DUE DATE (see *EDD*) The due date is calculated as nine months and one week from the first day of the woman's last menstrual period. Most babies are not born on their due date.

ECLAMPSIA (see *pre-eclampsia*) A serious medical condition, usually preceded by pre-eclampsia, when the mother has major epileptic fits. These can occur during pregnancy, labour or in the postnatal period. Both mother and baby are at risk.

ECTOPIC PREGNANCY A pregnancy where the baby develops outside the womb either in the Fallopian tube, or occasionally, in the abdomen. If the pregnancy is in the Fallopian tube, the mother may experience severe pain on one side of her abdomen and shoulder pain. If an ectopic pregnancy is suspected, the mother should contact her midwife or GP immediately.

EDD – ESTIMATED DATE OF DELIVERY (see *due date*)

ENDOMETRIUM (see *uterus*) The innermost layer of the womb (uterus). The endometrium is shed each month during a period and then regenerated.

ENGAGEMENT When the baby's head or bottom sinks down into the pelvis during the last month of pregnancy. If the baby is four-fifths engaged, the midwife can feel only one-fifth of his head above the bony cage of the pelvis.

ENGORGEMENT When the breasts feel hot, hard and uncomfortable due to a surplus of milk. Generally only a problem during the first few weeks of breastfeeding, after which the breasts adjust to make the amount of milk required by the baby.

ENTONOX A mixture of 50 per cent oxygen and 50 per cent nitrous oxide which can be inhaled by the mother during labour for pain relief.

EPIDURAL (see *mobile epidural*) An anaesthetic injection into the spine which numbs the nerves supplying the uterus and cervix so that the mother can no longer feel contractions. Also removes sensation from the legs and feet.

EPISIOTOMY (see *perineum*) A cut made through the tissue stretching between the back wall of the vagina and the back passage. Helps the baby be born more easily. May be necessary so that forceps can be placed around the baby's head.

EXTERNAL CEPHALIC VERSION (see *breech position*) A procedure carried out in the final weeks of pregnancy to turn a baby who is in the breech position into a head down position. The doctor places one hand on the baby's head and one on his bottom and pushes him round. It is now considered best practice to try to turn breech babies because it reduces the likelihood of the mother needing a caesarean section to give birth.

FALSE LABOUR (see *Braxton Hicks contractions*) Braxton Hicks contractions can easily be interpreted by the woman as the start of labour. However, labour is not properly diagnosed until the contractions are regular and painful and the cervix is opening up.

FETAL SAC (see *amniotic sac*)

FETAL SCALP ELECTRODE A tiny monitor that is clipped onto the baby's head during labour to check that he is not becoming distressed.

FIRST STAGE The first part of labour when the cervix or neck of the womb opens up from 0cm to 10 cm. May last a few hours or a few days, but generally takes from between 12 to 18 hours for a woman having her first baby.

FLUID RETENTION (see *pre-eclampsia*) Sometimes called oedema. The blood volume and the amount of fluid in a woman's tissues increase considerably during pregnancy. The ankles, hands and face may become puffy. A small amount of swelling is generally normal, but should be mentioned to the midwife as it is occasionally a sign of pre-eclampsia.

FOLIC ACID Vitamin that helps prevent spina bifida. Women are advised to take 400mcg a day from the time they start trying to conceive to three months after becoming pregnant. Women who have given birth to a baby with spina bifida should take a higher dose when trying for their next baby.

FORCEPS Sometimes described as stainless steel 'salad servers'. Forceps are used to help the baby be born when he is lying in an awkward position and the mother cannot push him out. They may also be used if the mother's pushing is ineffective because she has had an epidural or is very tired.

FOREMILK (see *hindmilk*) The thin, watery milk that comes at the beginning of a breastfeed. The foremilk is designed to quench the baby's thirst.

FUNDUS (see *engagement*) The medical term for the top of the uterus. The fundus reaches the mother's belly button by 20 weeks of pregnancy, the diaphragm by 36 weeks and then drops down again as the baby engages in the pelvis.

GAS AND AIR (see *Entonox*)

GENITAL HERPES Painful ulcers (similar to cold sores) on the cervix, vagina and vulva. If the ulcers are 'active' and weeping at the end of pregnancy, it is safer for the baby to be born by caesarean section rather than vaginally as the ulcers may infect his eyes causing blindness.

GERMAN MEASLES The popular name for rubella. If the mother catches German measles for the first time in early pregnancy, the baby's heart, brain and eyes may be affected. If caught later in pregnancy, the baby is less at risk although his hearing may be damaged.

GINGIVITIS Medical term for inflammation of the gums. Common in pregnancy and can lead to tooth decay. Always floss carefully.

GLUCOSE TOLERANCE TEST A test for diabetes. Blood is taken after the mother has fasted for six hours. She is then given a glucose drink and more blood is taken. The blood sugar level should rise and then quickly return to normal.

GUTHRIE TEST (see *phenylketonuria*) A blood test performed around the fourth day of the baby's life to detect a rare disease called phenylketonuria. The baby's heel is pricked with a needle and a small drop of blood squeezed onto a specially prepared card.

HAEMOGLOBIN (see *anaemia*) The iron-containing part of the blood that makes it red. Lack of haemoglobin causes anaemia, although it's normal for haemoglobin levels to drop slightly during pregnancy. Haemoglobin levels are tested at the first pregnancy visit, and at 28 and 36 weeks.

HAEMORRHAGE (see *third stage*) Medical term for excessive bleeding. Bleeding may take place before the baby is born when it is called an antepartum haemorrhage, or after the baby is born – postpartum haemorrhage. A postpartum haemorrhage can occur when the placenta is being delivered or up to 10 days following the birth.

HAEMORRHOIDS (see *piles*) Varicose veins in the back passage, often extremely painful and may bleed heavily. Constipation makes them worse so it is advisable to have a diet rich in fibre and to drink plenty of water. Ointment can be prescribed to help shrink them.

HCG – HUMAN CHORIONIC GONADOTROPHIN The hormone measured in antenatal tests. From 16–18 weeks of pregnancy, the level of HCG in the mother's blood can be used to estimate the risk of her having a baby with Down's syndrome.

HINDMILK (see *foremilk*) The creamy, satisfying milk that comes with the 'let down' reflex.

HOMOEOPATHY An alternative therapy based on the theory of treating like with like. Remedies derived from plants, minerals and animal sources are given in minute quantities. In large quantities, these remedies would cause the symptoms they are designed to treat. Consult a qualified homoeopath before taking any remedies in pregnancy.

HYPNOTHERAPY An alternative therapy which induces a state between waking and sleeping when emotional problems and irrational fears can be more easily understood and overcome. Women can be taught self-hypnosis as a means of controlling pain during labour.

IMMUNE SYSTEM (see *antibodies*; *immunization*; *vaccination*) The immune system is a complex defence mechanism which operates throughout the body to protect us against infections and toxins. The bone marrow, thymus, spleen and lymph nodes are important parts of it.

IMMUNIZATION (see *vaccination*) A method of preventing serious diseases such as polio, diphtheria and tetanus by injecting into the body a modified form of the organisms that cause the disease. Immunization is not offered in pregnancy because there is a risk of harming the unborn baby.

INCOMPETENT CERVIX (see *cervical incompetence*)

INCONTINENCE Partial or complete loss of control over the bladder or bowels. Forceps and ventouse deliveries and pushing for a long time in the second stage of labour can sometimes cause incontinence.

INDUCTION (see *pessary*; *prostaglandins*; *'sweep'*) Starting labour off by doing a 'sweep', inserting prostaglandin pessaries into the vagina, breaking the waters, or giving the mother a hormone drip.

INVOLUTION The process by which the womb shrinks after childbirth and returns to its pre-pregnancy size and position. Takes about six weeks.

ITCHING (see *obstetric cholestasis*) Itching during pregnancy should always be reported to a midwife or doctor as it may be a sign of a serious disease called obstetric cholestasis. However, localized itching, such as over the site of an old operation scar, is usually normal.

KEGEL EXERCISES (see *pelvic floor exercises*)

KETONES Produced when the body starts burning fat to meet its energy requirements. The mother's urine is tested for ketones during labour to check that she has enough energy to keep her contractions going.

KICK CHART A chart used during pregnancy for the mother to record the movements made by her baby. Too few movements in the space of 12 hours might mean that the baby is distressed.

LINEA NIGRA A dark line which appears down the middle of the abdomen during pregnancy. It fades after the baby is born.

LISTERIOSIS An infection caught from eating unwashed fruit and vegetables, or soft cheeses made from unpasteurized milk. Not dangerous for the pregnant woman, but can be life-threatening to her unborn baby, and may lead to premature delivery.

LITHOTOMY POSITION A position in which the woman's legs are raised and held apart in stirrups to enable medical procedures such as an internal examination, forceps delivery or stitching the perineum to be carried out.

LOCHIA The name given to the heavy period that occurs in the first weeks after birth. Some women bleed for as long as six weeks.

LOW BIRTHWEIGHT A baby who weighs under 2500g is considered to be of low birthweight. Low birthweight babies may be weak and are vulnerable to infection.

MASTITIS Infection of the breast treated with antibiotics. Breastfeeding women are often incorrectly diagnosed with mastitis when their problem is simply a blocked milk duct.

MECONIUM The baby's first bowel movement which is black, sticky and tar-like. If the baby opens his bowels in the womb during labour, the waters will be meconium stained. Meconium staining may be a sign that the baby is distressed.

MEMBRANES (see *amniotic sac*)

MENSTRUAL CYCLE The female cycle during which the womb is prepared for pregnancy, an egg is released from the ovary and is expelled from the body with the lining of the womb during menstruation. An average cycle lasts 28 days, but cycles lasting from 21 to 35 days are not uncommon.

MINERALS Substances such as iron, calcium, magnesium and zinc which are found in dark green vegetables, wholemeal bread, unrefined cereals, dairy products and fish. Important for a healthy pregnancy.

MOBILE EPIDURAL (see *epidural*) An anaesthetic injection into the spine which aims to remove the pain of contractions while leaving the mother some mobility. May involve a combination of drugs. Not available at all hospitals.

MOXIBUSTION A technique used in traditional Chinese medicine for turning breech babies into a head down position. A herb called 'moxa' is burned close to acupuncture points on the mother's feet. Success rates are reported to be as high as 90 per cent.

NAUSEA Feeling of sickness, common in the first three months of pregnancy. Can also be caused by drugs given for pain relief in labour, eg Pethidine.

NIPPLES May become sore when breastfeeding, but shouldn't if the baby is correctly positioned at the breast. There is no need to prepare the nipples during pregnancy for breastfeeding. In labour, stimulating the nipples may make contractions more effective.

NOSE BLEEDS Quite common during pregnancy because the increased volume of blood in the woman's circulation places extra pressure on the tiny vessels in the nose.

NUCHAL TRANSLUCENCY SCAN A screening test carried out at around 12 weeks of pregnancy. A high resolution ultrasound scanner measures the fold of skin behind the baby's neck. The thickness of the fold combined with the mother's age are used to estimate the risk of Down's syndrome.

OBSTETRIC CHOLESTASIS A serious complication of pregnancy involving the liver and bile duct. The main symptom is itching over the whole body. Both mother and baby are at risk, and the pregnancy needs careful monitoring in a consultant unit.

OBSTETRICIAN A highly trained doctor specializing in the care of women who have complications during pregnancy, labour and the early postnatal period.

OCCIPITO-ANTERIOR (OA) POSITION (see *anterior position*)

OEDEMA (see *fluid retention*; *pre-eclampsia*) Medical term for swelling in any part of the body.

OESTROGEN The female hormone which is responsible for growth of the uterine muscle during pregnancy, and for the development of the milk glands in the breasts. At the end of pregnancy, oestrogen levels increase, precipitating labour.

OPERCULUM (see *show*)

OPTIMAL FETAL POSITIONING (OFP) (see *anterior position*) Refers to positions the woman can use during pregnancy and labour to help her baby go down into the pelvis in an anterior position. The term was coined by a New Zealand midwife called Jean Sutton.

OVERDUE (see *induction*) Going beyond 40 weeks of pregnancy. Most hospitals induce labour when the mother has reached 40 weeks and 10 days of pregnancy.

OVULATION (see *menstrual cycle*) The release of an egg from the ovary; usually occurs 14 days before the start of menstruation.

OXYTOCIN The hormone that makes the womb contract during labour. It also causes milk to be squeezed out of the milk reservoirs in the breasts during breastfeeding.

PASSIVE IMMUNITY (see *antibodies*) The immunity a baby acquires from the antibodies passed to him by his mother during pregnancy and breast-feeding. Helps protect the baby against infection.

PELVIC FLOOR EXERCISES (see *incontinence*) Exercises designed to strengthen the muscles of the pelvic floor and so reduce the risk of incontinence and prolapse. Often taught at antenatal classes.

PERINEUM (see *episiotomy*) The tissue between the back of the vagina and the back passage. Some research shows that massaging the perineum with oil during pregnancy helps protect it from tearing during childbirth.

PESSARY (see *induction*; *prostaglandins*; *thrush*) A soluble tablet containing prostaglandin which is inserted into the vagina to induce labour when the cervix is not 'ripe' (ready for labour). Pessaries melt at body temperature and stimulate contractions. Pessaries are also used to treat thrush.

PETHIDINE Synthetic form of morphine used for pain relief in labour. Given by injection into the thigh. Side-effects include drowsiness and sickness; also passes to the baby and can affect his breathing at birth.

PHENYLKETONURIA (see *Guthrie test*) A metabolic disorder affecting 1 in 10,000 babies. The baby cannot break down proteins, and toxic substances accumulate in the brain causing mental disability. A special diet is prescribed to enable the baby to develop normally.

PILES (see *haemorrhoids*)

PLACENTA Large organ, weighing about half a kilogram by the end of pregnancy, which passes oxygen, food and antibodies from the mother to the baby. While it acts as a barrier to many harmful substances, it cannot stop drugs, nicotine and viruses from reaching the baby.

PLACENTA PRAEVIA Condition where the placenta is situated very close to, or lies across the cervix. May mean that the baby has to be born by caesarean section.

PRE-ECLAMPSIA (see *eclampsia*) A condition which is not well understood. It seems to be related to the early development of the placenta, although it does not cause a problem until the second half of pregnancy. The symptoms are high blood pressure, protein in the urine and sometimes swelling.

PREMATURE BIRTH Birth occurring before 37 completed weeks of pregnancy. Premature babies may have difficulty breathing, maintaining their body temperature and sucking and often have to be looked after in a special-care baby unit.

PRESENTATION (see *breech position*; *brow presentation*; *engagement*) The term midwives use to describe the part of the baby that is most deeply engaged in the pelvis and which will be born first. The most usual presentation is cephalic or vertex (head first).

PROGESTERONE Hormone which is vital to maintain pregnancy. Progesterone relaxes the muscles of the womb to prevent the baby from being born too early, and also the muscles of the gut and urinary tract which can sometimes lead to indigestion, constipation and urinary infections.

PROLACTIN Hormone which stimulates the breasts to make milk.

'PROM' (premature rupture of the membranes) When the 'waters' break early; can lead to premature birth.

PROSTAGLANDINS Hormones or chemical messengers that are produced in almost all tissues of the body, and have a variety of actions. They are used in obstetrics to induce labour and to control bleeding in the third stage.

PTYALISM Over production of saliva experienced by some women during pregnancy.

PUDENDAL BLOCK An anaesthetic injection given via the vagina or through the perineum to numb the lower part of the vagina and the perineum. May be used for a forceps delivery if the mother has not got an epidural in place.

PUERPERAL PSYCHOSIS Serious mental illness affecting 1 in 1000 women. Symptoms include hallucinations and insomnia. Sufferers lose touch with reality and may harm themselves or their babies. Treatment in a mother and baby unit is necessary.

PUERPERIUM The six weeks following the birth of a baby.

RASPBERRY LEAF The raspberry leaf plant has been used for centuries to tone up the uterus and shorten labour. It is usually taken as tea or in tablet form from about 36 weeks of pregnancy.

RELAXATION Relaxation techniques are often taught in antenatal classes. Being able to relax during labour helps conserve energy, and maximize the oxygen supply to the baby.

RELAXIN A hormone that, in animals, softens the pelvic ligaments and the cervix in readiness for labour. It's uncertain whether it plays any part in human pregnancy and labour.

RETAINED PLACENTA When the placenta remains in the womb after the baby has been born. Normally, it is delivered within quarter of an hour of the baby. If retained, surgery is required to remove it.

RHESUS POSITIVE/NEGATIVE If a person has the gene for the Rhesus factor, they are said to be Rhesus positive because their red blood cells have a special protein attached to them. Women who do not have this protein are Rhesus negative. If the baby they are carrying is Rhesus positive, there is a risk that their blood will attack the baby's blood cells and destroy them.

RUBELLA The medical term for German measles. If a woman catches rubella during early pregnancy, the development of her baby's heart, eyes and ears may be affected.

SALIVA Tests on saliva are used to diagnose whether someone is a carrier of the cystic fibrosis gene. If both the mother and father are carriers, there is a risk that their baby will have the disease.

SALMONELLA A bacteria often found in chickens that causes food poisoning. Infection is usually the result of eating contaminated food, poor kitchen hygiene and inadequate cooking.

SCREENING TEST (see *diagnostic test*) A test which assesses the baby's risk (eg 1 in 25 or 1 in 250) of having a condition such as spina bifida or Down's syndrome. It cannot say for certain that the baby is affected.

SECOND STAGE The middle part of labour from when the cervix is 10cm dilated to the birth of the baby.

SHIRODKAR SUTURE A stitch tied round the cervix to prevent it from opening too early in pregnancy. Can sometimes help women who have had repeated miscarriages because of a weak cervix. The stitch is inserted at 14 weeks and removed at 37 weeks.

SHOW (see *operculum*) When the mucus plug which seals the neck of the womb during pregnancy comes away, sometimes with a little blood. An early sign of labour.

SPINA BIFIDA A condition where the bones of the baby's spine have not closed properly around the spinal cord so that the nerves are damaged. In severe cases, the baby may be paralysed from the waist down; in other cases, there may be very few symptoms.

STILLBIRTH When a baby is born who shows no signs of life. The SANDS organization help people who have suffered this tragedy.

STITCHES (see *episiotomy*; *perineum*) Stitches may be used to repair a tear in the perineum or an episiotomy, or to close a caesarean section wound. Stitches need to be kept clean and dry. Some women find that taking arnica tablets helps them heal.

STRETCH MARKS Red lines which appear on the abdomen and thighs during pregnancy, due to tearing of the tissues beneath the surface of the skin as it stretches. After the baby is born, the marks fade and become silvery.

'SWEEP' (see *induction*; *membranes*) A method of induction. The midwife inserts a finger into the cervix and gently separates the membranes from the edge of the womb, triggering the release of hormones that initiate labour.

SYNTOCINON A synthetic form of oxytocin, the hormone which stimulates contractions. It is used in a drip to induce or speed up labour.

SYNTOMETRINE Drug given by injection into the thigh as the baby's shoulders are being born, to speed up the delivery of the placenta.

TENS Transcutaneous Electrical Nerve Stimulation. A method of relieving pain in labour. Pulses of electricity are channelled through four pads placed on the mother's back. These override the pain signals coming from the uterus and cervix, and stimulate the body to release its own pain-killing substances.

THALASSAEMIA A genetic abnormality of the blood affecting people from Africa, Asia, the Middle East and the Mediterranean. Symptoms include anaemia and attacks of severe pain. Regular blood transfusions are required. If both the mother and father are carriers of the thalassaemia gene, they will be offered an antenatal test to see if their baby has the disease.

THIRD STAGE The final part of labour when the placenta is delivered. A drug (syntometrine) can be given to speed the process, or the mother may prefer to wait for the placenta to be delivered naturally.

THRUSH Fungal infection that affects the mouth, vagina or nipples. Often a side-effect of taking antibiotics. Sometimes mothers pass thrush to their babies during breastfeeding. Both mother and baby then need treatment, but the mother should continue to breastfeed.

TOXAEMIA (see *eclampsia*)

TOXOPLASMOSIS Infection caused by a parasite which is endemic in the cat world. If a pregnant woman becomes infected, the development of her baby's eyes and brain may be affected. To minimize the risk, gloves should be worn to handle litter trays and vegetables and fruit should be washed thoroughly to remove any traces of soil.

TRANSITION The bridge between the first and second stages of labour when the cervix is almost fully dilated and the mother starts to feel the urge to push. Symptoms may include vomiting, shivering and aggressive behaviour.

TRANSVERSE LIE A term used by midwives to describe a baby who is lying across his mother's womb so that neither his head nor his bottom is in her pelvis. A caesarean section is necessary.

ULTRASOUND SCAN Reflected sound waves build up a picture of the organs inside the body. During pregnancy, scans are used to estimate the due date, to see whether the baby is developing normally and to show where the placenta is situated.

UMBILICAL CORD The lifeline linking the baby to the placenta. Average length 50cm. Contains two arteries and one vein and is covered in a jelly-like substance (Wharton's jelly) to prevent it from getting tangled.

URINE TESTING (see *diabetes*) An important part of pregnancy care. Protein in the urine may point to pre-eclampsia, or a urinary infection. Sugar in the urine could indicate gestational diabetes.

VACCINATION (see *immunization*)

VACUUM EXTRACTION (see *second stage*) A way of helping the baby to be born if the mother is having a difficult second stage. Involves putting a silicone plastic cup on the baby's head, sucking the air out and then pulling on the cup to deliver the baby.

VAGINA (see *vulva*) The passage from the womb to the outside world. Its walls are elastic so that they can stretch to accommodate the baby.

VARICOSE VEINS (see *haemorrhoids*) Painful distended veins in the legs or back passage. Common in pregnancy because the weight of the baby obstructs the circulation of blood around the body.

VENTOUSE (see *vacuum extraction*)

VERNIX The white coating that covers the baby during the last months of pregnancy. Helps protect the baby's skin, and makes him slippery so that he can travel more easily down the birth canal during labour. Vernix is absorbed into the baby's body after birth.

VITAMIN A Important for night-time vision and for healing. The best source for pregnant women is from vegetables. Too much can be toxic, so only take vitamin supplements if recommended by a doctor.

VITAMIN K Essential to make the blood clot. It used to be given by injection to all new babies. Research carried out in the 1990s questioned whether this was safe and some hospitals and parents now prefer it to be given by mouth.

VULVA The external genital area, composed of thick layers of skin which form outer and inner lips or labia. The colour of the vulva changes from pink to purple during pregnancy.

ZINC A mineral that is important for the normal development of the baby in the womb, and to help strengthen the uterine muscles. Found in high-fibre foods such as bran cereals, hard cheese and meat.

ZYGOTE The name given to the unborn baby in the very earliest stage of his development.

useful organizations

Exercise and therapies in pregnancy

The Aquanatal Register
Tel: 01628 661961
www.aquanatal.co.uk
Safe exercise in water during and after
pregnancy. Classes are run locally.

Body Control Pilates Association
Tel: 020 7379 3734
www.bodycontrol.co.uk

The British Acupuncture Council
Tel: 020 8735 0400
www.acupuncture.org.uk

British Homeopathic Association
Tel: 0870 444 3950
www.trusthomeopathy.org

British Wheel of Yoga
Tel: 01529 306851
www.bwy.org.uk

**The International Federation of
Professional Aromatherapists**
Tel: 01455 637987
www.ifparoma.org

Pilates Foundation UK Ltd
Tel: 07071 781859
www.pilatesfoundation.com

The Pilates Institute
Tel: 020 7253 3177
www.pilates-institute.co.uk

Problems in pregnancy

Action on Pre-Eclampsia (APEC)
Tel: 020 8863 3271
www.apec.org.uk
A UK charity set up to prevent suffering
from pre-eclampsia.

Antenatal Results and Choices (ARC)
Tel: 020 7631 0285 (Helpline)
www.arc-uk.org
Non-directive support and information.

BackCare
Tel: 020 8977 5474
www.backpain.org

BLISS (Baby Life Support Systems)
Tel: 0500 618140 (Parent Support Helpline
Freephone)
www.bliss.org.uk
Making sure that more babies born
prematurely or sick in the UK survive.

General Osteopathic Council
Tel: 020 7357 6655
www.osteopathy.org.uk
Find a registered osteopath.

**Hyperemesis Gravidarum Support
Group (Blooming Awful)**
Tel: 07050 655 094
www.hyperemesis.org.uk
Information for those with very severe
pregnancy nausea, and their families

Obstetric Cholestasis Support
Tel: 0121 353 0699

PETS
Tel: 01286 882685
www.dawnjames.clara.net
Support and information for women,
who themselves have suffered from pre-
eclampsia.

Symphysis Pubis Dysfunction
Tel: 01235 820921
www.pelvicpartnership.org.uk
www.spd-uk.org

Toxoplasmosis and pregnancy
Tel: 020 7620 0188
www.tommys.org
Informtion on toxoplasmosis

Expecting more than one baby

The Multiple Births Foundation
Tel: 020 8383 3519
www.multiplebirths.org.uk

**Twins and Multiple Births Association
(TAMBA)**
Tel: 0800 138 0509
www.tamba.org.uk

Planning your birth

Active Birth Centre
Tel: 020 7281 6760
www.activebirthcentre.com
Pre- and postnatal yoga classes,
preparation for birth and pool hire.

**Association for Improvements in the
Maternity Services**
Tel: 0870 765 1433
www.aims.org.uk
Working to get women the best care.

Association of Radical Midwives
Tel: 01695 572776
www.radmid.demon.co.uk
Supporting midwifery.

BirthChoiceUK
www.birthchoiceuk.com
Helping you make choices about where to
have your baby.

British Doula Association
Tel: 020 7244 6053
www.topnotchnannies.com
Sets professional standards of practice.

Caesarean Support Network
Tel: 01624 661269
www.findsupport.co.uk

Find a doula
www.doula.org.uk
Provides a UK-wide database of local
doula services.

Gentle Water Birthing Pools
Tel: 01273 474927
www.gentlewater.co.uk
Water birth and pool hire.

Home Birth Reference site
www.homebirth.org.uk
Information about home birth.

Independent Midwives Association
Tel: 01483 821104
www.independentmidwives.org.uk
Information about, and support for,
independent midwives.

Splashdown Water Birth Services
Tel: 0870 44 44 403
www.splashdown.org.uk
Information on water birth and pool hire.

Breastfeeding

The NCT Breastfeeding Line 0870 444 8708 can put you straight through to an NCT Breastfeeding Counsellor any day of the week, from 8am to 10pm.

Association of Breastfeeding Mothers (ABM)
Tel: 020 7813 1481
www.abm.me.uk
Counselling and telephone support for breastfeeding mothers.

La Leche League (Great Britain)
Tel: 0845 120 2918
www.laleche.org.uk
They aim to help mothers to breastfeed through mother-to-mother support.

Postnatal

The National Childbirth Trust runs local postnatal groups in all areas where new parents can get to know each other.

Association for Post-Natal Illness
Tel: 020 7386 0868
www.apni.org
Aims to provide support to mothers who are suffering from postnatal illness.

Birth Crisis Network
Tel: 020 7485 4725
www.sheilakitzinger.com
A telephone helpline that women can ring if they want to talk about a traumatic birth.

Depression Alliance
Tel: 020 8768 0123
www.depressionalliance.org
The DAPeND helpline offers telephone support nationally to mothers suffering from perinatal depression (postnatal or antenatal) and their families.

Home-Start
Tel: 0800 0686 368
www.home-start.org.uk
Trained volunteers visit families regularly.

MAMA (Meet-A-Mum Association)
www.mama.org.uk
Provides friendship and support.

Positively Women
Tel: 020 7713 0222
www.positivelywomen.org.uk
Support for women with HIV and AIDS and their families.

Samaritans
Tel: 08457 90 90 90
www.samaritans.org.uk
A UK charity offering support to people who are suicidal or despairing.

TABS (Trauma and Birth Stress after Childbirth)
www.tabs.org.nz
A New Zealand-based organization supporting parents with post-traumatic stress disorder after birth.

Working parents

Daycare Trust
Tel: 020 7840 3350
www.daycaretrust.org.uk
National childcare charity, campaigning for quality affordable childcare.

The Maternity Alliance
Tel: 020 7490 7638
www.maternityalliance.org.uk
Information and support on the rights for women at work before and after childbirth.

Parents at Work
Tel: 020 7253 7243
www.parentsatwork.org.uk
Helps children, working parents and their employers find a better balance between responsibilities at home and work.

Baby loss

Ectopic Pregnancy Trust
Tel: 01895 238025
www.ectopic.org
UK charity providing information about symptoms, diagnosis and treatment.

Foundation for the Study of Infant Deaths (FSID)
Tel: 0870 787 0554 (Helpline)
www.sids.org.uk/fsid
Charity working to prevent infant deaths and promote baby health.

The Miscarriage Association
Tel: 01924 200799
www.miscarriageassociation.org.uk

Stillbirth and Neonatal Death (SANDS)
Tel: 020 7436 5881
www.uk-sands.org
Support for parents and families whose baby is stillborn or dies soon after birth.

Support for babies with problems

Association for Spina Bifida and Hydrocephalus (ASBAH)
Tel: 01733 555988
www.asbah.org
ASBAH provides advice and practical support to people with spina bifida and hydrocephalus, their families and carers.

Birth Defects Foundation
Tel: 01543 468888
www.birthdefects.co.uk

Cleft Lip and Palate Association (CLAPA)
Tel: 020 7431 0033
www.clapa.com

Contact a Family
Tel: 020 7608 8700
www.cafamily.org.uk
Helping families of disabled children.

Cystic Fibrosis Trust
Tel: 020 8464 7211
www.cftrust.org.uk

Disabled Parents Network
Tel: 08702 410450
www.disabledparentsnetwork.org.uk
National organization of and for disabled people who are parents or who hope to become parents, and their families.

Down's Syndrome Association
Tel: 020 8682 4001
www.downs-syndrome.org.uk

REACH
Tel: 0845 130 6225
www.reach.org.uk
Working with children with hand or arm deficiency.

SCOPE
Tel: 0808 800 3333
www.scope.org.uk
Scope is a UK disability organization whose focus is people with cerebral palsy and their carers.

Sickle Cell Society
Tel: 020 8961 7795
www.sicklecellsociety.org
Information, counselling and caring for those with sickle cell disorders and their families.

SoftUK
Tel: 0121 351 3122
www.soft.org.uk
SoftUK provides support for families affected by Patau's syndrome and Edwards' syndrome and related disorders.

UK Thalassaemia Society
Tel: 020 8882 0011
www.ukts.org

all about the NCT

Since it started in the mid-1950s, The National Childbirth Trust has worked successfully to improve the experience of childbirth in the UK in so many ways. Through its antenatal classes, postnatal groups, support for breastfeeding and national campaigning, the charity has furthered its goal of ensuring that all parents have an experience of pregnancy, birth and early parenthood that enriches their lives and gives them confidence in being a parent.

Powerful at a local, national and UK level, The National Childbirth Trust has over 350 branches across the UK, run by parents for parents. There's bound to be a local branch near you, offering:

- antenatal classes
- breastfeeding counselling
- new baby groups
- open house get-togethers
- support for dads
- working parents' groups
- nearly-new sales of baby clothes and equipment

as well as many events where parents can meet others going through the same changes for mutual support and friendship. You can also hire a breast pump or a Valley Cushion locally, after birth.

To find the contact details of your local branch, ring the NCT Enquiry Line: 0870 444 8707 or check the branch details on **www.nctpregnancyandbabycare.com**

To get support with feeding your baby, ring the NCT Breastfeeding Line: 0870 444 8708

To find answers to pregnancy and parenting queries, ring the Enquiry Line or log on to: **www.nctpregnancyandbabycare.com**

To buy excellent baby goods, maternity bras, toys and gifts from NCT Maternity Sales, look at: **www.nctms.co.uk** or telephone 0870 112 1120.

To join the NCT, just call 0870 990 8040.
Although it's not essential to become a member to enjoy the services and support of The National Childbirth Trust, membership is encouraged because it helps to fund the charity's work – supporting all parents.

National Childbirth Trust, Alexandra House, Oldham Terrace, London W3 6NH.
Tel 0870 770 3236 Fax 0870 770 3237

'Join us and help make the UK a better place for all new parents.'
Gillian Fletcher, President, The National Childbirth Trust

references

Page 29
Importance of support during labour:
Hodnett ED. *Continuity of Caregivers for Care during Pregnancy and Childbirth* (Cochrane Review). In: *The Cochrane Library*, Issue 3, 2003a. Oxford: Update Software. www.nelh.nhs.uk/cochrane.asp

Hodnett ED. *Caregiver Support for Women during Childbirth* (Cochrane Review). In: *The Cochrane Library*, Issue 3, 2003b. Oxford: Update Software. www.nelh.nhs.uk/cochrane.asp

Most women with the right support can give birth without medical assistance: World Health Organization: Care in Normal Birth: a Practical Guide. Report of a Technical Working Group. Geneva: WHO, 1996.

Page 32
Hodnett ED (2003b) ibid.

Page 36
Hodnett ED (2003b) ibid.

MIDIRS. *Support in Labour – Informed Choice for Professionals*. MIDIRS, 2003. www.infochoice.org

Breart G, Mlika-Cabane N, Kaminski M *et al*. Evaluation of Different Policies for the Management of Labour. *Early Hum Dev*. 1992; 29: 309–12.

'The continuous presence of an experienced support person... beneficial effects on childbirth.' Enkin M, Keirse MJNC, Neilson J, *et al*. *A Guide to Effective Care in Pregnancy and Childbirth* (3rd edition). Oxford: Oxford University Press 2000, p253.

Page 38
Robertson A. *The Midwife Companion – The Art of Support During Birth*. Camperdown: ACE Graphics, 1997, p62.

Page 39
A woman 'labours best when she's undisturbed and has privacy': Robertson A. (ibid) p26.

Most women simply want their birth partner 'to be there': Singh D, Newburn M. *Access To Maternity Information and Support. The Experiences and Needs of Women Before and After Giving Birth*. London: National Childbirth Trust, 2000.

Support acts as a buffer against stress: Cobb S. 1976. Cited McCourt C, Percival P. Chapter 12: Social Support in Childbirth. In: Page LA, Percival P (eds) *The New Midwifery – Science and Sensitivity in Practice*. Edinburgh: Churchill Livingstone, 2000, pp245–68.

What is a doula?
WHO (1996) ibid.
Hodnett ED (2003b) ibid.

Page 42
Campbell R, McFarlane A.*Where to be Born?* Oxford: National Perinatal Epidemiology Unit, 1994.

Page 43
Hodnett ED (2003a) ibid.

Page 44
Campbell, McFarlane (1994) ibid.
Hodnett ED (2003a) ibid.

Page 45
First labour is particularly suitable for home birth: Dr Rick Porter, *Pregnancy and Birth magazine*, Sept 1998; p77.

Transfer rates from home to hospital: *Home Births – The report of the 1994 Confidential Enquiry by the National Birthday Trust Fund*, The Parthenon Publishing Group, 1997.

Women rate home birth as less painful: Home birth and hospital deliveries. *Res Nurs Health June 1988*; 11(3): 175–81.

Page 46
Home birth at least as safe as hospital for healthy women with normal pregnancies: National Birthday Trust Fund (1997) ibid.

BMJ 23 Nov1996; 313 (7068).

Campbell, McFarlane (1994) ibid.

Page 48
Very few home-hospital transfers are due to real emergencies: National Birthday Trust Fund (1997) ibid.

Study of 29 midwifery practices in the US: Murphy PA, Fullerton J (Department of Obstetrics and Gynaecology, Columbia University College of Physicians and Surgeons, New York, NY10032).

Page 49
In an earlier UK study of 285 women... 9.4 per cent were transferred during labour: Ford C, Iliffe S, Franklin O. *BMJ*;14 Dec1991; 303(6816):1517-19.

Transfer rate of 16 per cent: National Birthday Trust Fund (1997) ibid.

Page 50
Warm water helps pain of labour: The Royal College of Midwives Position Paper no. 1a: The Use of Water in Labour and Birth, Oct 2000. www.rcm.org.uk

Study showing fewer babies born in water admitted to special care: Gilbert R, Tookey P. Perinatal mortality and morbidity among babies delivered in water: a surveillance study and postal survey. *BMJ*; 21 Aug 1999 319: 483-87.

Page 51
Babies less stressed at water birth: Geissbuhler V, Eberhard J. Waterbirths. *Fetal Diagnosis and Therapy* 2000; 15(5): 291–300.

Beneficial effects of water: RCM Position Paper no. 1a, ibid.

Page 52
Water must be kept at or below 37°C: Garland D, Jones K. Waterbirth:

supporting practice with clinical audit. *MIDIRS Midwifery Digest* 2000; 10(3): 333–6.
Royal College of Obstetricians and Gyneacologists Statement no. 1 Jan 2001. www.rcog.org.uk

Page 56
Benefits of continuity of care:
Hodnett ED (2003a) ibid.

World Health Organization (1996) ibid.

The Edgware Birth Centre:
Saunders D, Boulton M, Chapple J, Ratcliffe J *et al. Evaluation of the Edgware Birth Centre.* London: Commissioned by Barnet Health Authority, 2000.

Women giving birth at home were more satisfied with their care:
Singh D, Newman M, 2000. Cited NCT *All-Party Parliamentary Group on Maternity Briefing.* London: NCT, 2001.

Page 60
Monitoring in labour:
National Institute for Clinical Excellence. *The use of electronic fetal monitoring.* London: NICE, 2001:
www.nice.org.uk/pdf/efmguidelinenice.pdf

Page 79
Evidence to support perineal massage:
Eason E, Labreque M, Wells G. Feldman P. Preventing perineal trauma during childbirth: a systematic review. *Obstet Gynaecol,* 2000; 5(3):464–71

Water birth and perineum:
Brown L. The tide has turned: audit of water birth. *BJM* 1998; 6(4): 236–43.

Page 84
Squier *et al.* 2000.

Page 87
Air travel in pregnancy:
Kingman CE, Economides DL. Air travel in pregnancy. *The Obstetrician and Gynaecologist* 2002; 4: 188–92.

Air travel and deep vein thrombosis:
Royal College of Obstetricians and Gynaecologists. Advice on Preventing Deep Vein Thrombosis for Pregnant Women Travelling by Air. Scientific Advisory Committee Opinion Paper 1 Oct 2001.

Page 92
Alcohol in pregnancy:
MIDIRS. *Alcohol and pregnancy – Informed Choice for Professionals.* MIDIRS, 2003. www.infochoice.org

Page 93
Caffeine intake during pregnancy:
Food Standards Agency.
www.foodstandards.gov.uk

Page 94
Pregnancy nausea linked to a larger placenta and lower rate of miscarriage:
Huxley RR. Nausea and vomiting in early pregnancy. *Obstet Gynecol* 2000; 95: 779–82.

Page 108
See the Bliss Parent Information Guide and their website: www.bliss.org.uk

Page 110
Conde-Agudelo et al Kangaroo Mothercare. (Cochrane Review) In: *The Cochrane Library,* Issue 2, 2003.

Page 115
Nolan M. Modern Midwife, January 1997, Vol7 No.1

Page 116
Success rate for moxibustion:
Francesco Cardini MD; Huang Weixin, MD. Moxibustion for Correction of Breech Presentation A Randomised Controlled Trial. *J Am Med Assoc* 1998; 280(18): 1580–4.

External cephalic version, success rate:
Hofmeyr GJ, Kulier R. External cephalic version for breech presentation at term (Cochrane Review). In: *The Cochrane Library,* Issue 2, 2003. Oxford: Update Software.

Bewley S, Robson SC *et al.* Introduction of external cephalic version at term into routine clinical-practice. *Eur J Obstet Gynaecol Reprod Biol* 1993; 52: 89–93.

Zhang J, Bowes WA *et al.* Efficacy of external cephalic version – A review. *Obstet Gynaecol* 1993; 82: 306–12.

Page 117
Caesarean birth considered safer than vaginal birth for a breech baby, according to international trial:
Term Breech Trial Collaborative Group. *Lancet* 2000; 356: 1375–83.

Page 119
Guidelines on induction from the National Institute for Clinical Excellence:
NICE 2001: About Induction of Labour – Information for pregnant women, their partners and their families.
www.nice.org.uk/pdf/inductionoflabourin-foforwomen.pdf

Page 124
Statistics on birth intervention:
Department of Health: NHS Maternity Statistics, England: 2001–2002. Statistical Bulletin 2003/09.
www.doh.gov.uk/public/sb0309.htm

Women giving birth at home half as likely to have medical intervention:
Home Births – The report of the 1994 Confidential Enquiry by the National Birthday Trust Fund, The Parthenon Publishing Group, 1997.

Page 126
Induction of labour is best used only when medically indicated:
Enkin M *et al* (2000) ibid., p375, p495.

Induction after waters have broken:
Royal College of Obstetricians and Gynaecologists: Induction of labour. RCOG Press, 2001.
www.rcog.org.uk/resources/public/rcog_i nduction_of_labour.pdf

Page 127
Recommended alternatives to induction:
RCOG (2001) ibid.

Increased risks for baby after 42 weeks:
Crowley P. Interventions for preventing or improving the outcome of delivery at or beyond term (Cochrane Review). In: *The Cochrane Library,* Issue 2, 2003. Oxford: Update Software.
www.nelh.nhs.uk/cochrane.asp

Induction is strongly recommended after four days: RCOG (2001) ibid.

Page 128
Recommendations for EFM:
National Institute for Clinical Excellence: The use of electronic fetal monitoring. London NICE 2001.
www.nice.org.uk/pdf/efmguidelinenice.pdf

Page 129
Fetal distress and electronic fetal monitoring: NICE (2001) ibid.

Use of EFM increases the caesarean rate:
Enkin M *et al.* (2000) ibid., p279.

Page 130
Howell CJ: Epidurals versus non-epidural analgesia for pain relief in labour: (Cochrane Review). In: *The Cochrane Library,* Issue 2, 2003. Oxford: Update Software. www.nelh.nhs.uk/cochrane.asp

Page 131
Try to get your baby into the best position:
Sutton J *et al. Understanding and teaching*

optimal foetal positioning. New Zealand: Birth Concepts, 1996.

The benefits of support in labour: Hodnett ED (2003a) ibid.

Hodnett ED (2003b) ibid.

Page 133
Ventouse rather than forceps: Enkin M *et al.* (2000) ibid., p401.

Less postnatal pain with ventouse: Johanson RB, Menon V. Vacuum extraction versus forceps for assisted vaginal delivery (Cochrane Review). In: *The Cochrane Library*, Issue 3, 2003. Oxford: Update Software. www.nelh.nhs.uk/cochrane.asp

Page 135
The urgency of a caesarean is graded into four categories: Thomas J, Paranjothy S. The National Sentinel Caesarean Section Audit. London: RCOG Press, 2001.

Vaginal birth is safer for the mother: Lilford RJ *et al.* The relative risks of caesarean section (intrapartum and elective) and vaginal delivery. *Br J Obstet Gynaeco* 1990; 97(10): 883–92.

An elective caesarean is thought to be safer than an emergency caesarean: Lilford RJ *et al.* (1990) ibid.

Page 136
Use of EFM increases the caesarean rate: Enkin M *et al.* (2000) ibid., p279.

Waiting until at least 39 weeks: Morrison JJ *et al.* Neonatal respiratory morbidity and mode of delivery at term: influence of timing of elective caesarean section. *Br J Obstet Gynaecol* 1995; 102: 101–6.

Page 137
Department of Health: NHS Maternity Statistics, England: 2001–2002. Statistical Bulletin 2003/09. www.doh.gov.uk/public/sb0309.htm

Page 146
Odent, M. *The Scientification of Love.* London: Free Association Books 1999.

Page 149
Taking painkillers too early may increase chance of caesarean: Ontario Women's Health Council. Attaining and maintaining best practices in the use of caesarean section. Ontario: Ontario Women's Health Council (caesarean section working group), 2000.

www.womenshealthcouncil.com
Page 151
Labour pain stimulates hormones: Page LA. *The New Midwifery: Science and Sensitivity in Practice.* Edinburgh: Churchill Livingstone, 2000.

Endorphins in mother-baby bonding: Odent M (1999) ibid.

Page 152
Enkin M *et al.* (2000) ibid., p486.

Page 158
Enkin M *et al* .(2000) ibid., p319.

Page 159
Beneficial effects of water: RCM Position Paper, No.1a (2000) ibid.

Benefits of a birth pool in labour: Garland D. *Waterbirth: An Attitude to Care* (2nd edition). Oxford: Books for Midwives, 2002.

Page 160
Getting too hot in a pool can cause fetal distress: Garland D. (2002) ibid.

Use of Entonox during labour: Garcia J, Redshaw M, Fitzsimons B *et al. First Class Delivery: A National Survey of Women's Views of Maternity Care.* London: Audit Commission/National Perinatal Epidemiology Unit,1998.

Page 162
Taking painkillers too early may increase the chance of a caesarean: Ontario Women's Health Council (2000) ibid.

Women's views of Pethidine: Fairlie F, Walker J, Marshall L, *et al.* Intramuscular opioids for maternal pain relief in labour. *Br J Obstet Gynaecol* 1999; 106: 1181–7.

How Pethidine compares with other opioid drugs in labour: Jordan S. *Pharmacology for Midwives: The Evidence Base for Safe Practice.* Basingstoke: Palgrave, 2002.

Effect of Pethidine on baby after birth: Crowell MK, Hill P, Humenick S. Relationship between obstetric analgesia and time of effective breastfeeding. *J Nurse-Midwifery* 1994; 39(3): 150–6.

Nissen E, Lilja G, Matthiesen A, *et al.* Effects of maternal pethidine on infants' developing breastfeeding. *Acta Paediatrica* 1995; 84(2): 140–5.

Clyburn P, Rosen M. The effects of opioid and inhalational analgesia on the

newborn. In: Reynolds F. *Effects on the Baby of Maternal Analgesia and Anaesthesia.* London: Saunders, 1993.

Page 163
Pethidine and Sickness: Jordan S. *Pharmacology for Midwives: The Evidence Base for Safe Practice.* Basingstoke: Palgrave, 2002.

Complementary therapies in labour: Smith et al Complementary and alternative therapies (Cochrane Review). In: *The Cochrane Library*, Issue 2, 2003.

Page 165
Length of stage two: Janni W, Schiessl B, Pescherrs U, *et al.* The prognostic impact of a prolonged second stage of labor on maternal and fetal outcome. *Acta Paediatrica et Scandinavia* 2002; 81(3): 214–21.

Midwife's role during 'crowning': McCandlish R, Bowler U, van Asten H, *et al.* A randomised controlled trial of care of the perineum during second stage of normal labour. *Br J of Obstet Gynaecol* 1998; 105(2): 1262–72.

Page 167
Breastfeeding immediately a good idea: De Chateau P, Wilberg B. Long-term effect on mother-infant behaviour of extra contact during the first hour postpartum. *Acta Paediatrica et Scandinavia* 1997; 66; 145–51.

Righard L, Alade MO. Effect of delivery room routines on success of first breastfeed. *Lancet* 1990; 336: 1105–7.

Widstrom A-M, *et al.* Short-term effects of early suckling and touch of the nipple on maternal behaviour. *Early Human Dev*, 1990; 21: 153–63.

Most babies wait an hour before seeking the nipple: Widstrom AM. *Breastfeeding: The Baby's Choice.* (video) 1996.

Page 170
Syntometrine and vomiting: Rogers J, Wood J, McCandlish R, *et al.* Active versus expectant management of third stage of labour. *Lancet Mar 7* 1998; 351: 693–9.

Syntometrine and blood pressure: British National Formulary (no 40). London: British Medical Association/Royal Pharmaceutical Society of Great Britain, 2000.

Syntometrine versus syntocinon:

McDonald S, Prendiville WJ, Elbourne DA. Prophylactic syntometrine versus oxytocin for delivery of the placenta (Cochrane Review). In: *The Cochrane Library*, Issue 2. Oxford: Update Software.

Comparison of third stage:
Rogers *et al.* (1998) ibid.

Page 171
Iron levels in mother after birth:
Thilaganathan B, Cutner A, Latimer J, *et al.* Management of the third stage of labour in women at low risk of postpartum haemorrhage. *Eur J Obstet Gynaecol Reprod Biol* 1993; 48(1): 19-22.

Page 176
For more about traditions of care:
Jackso D. *Baby Wisdom*. London: Hodder Mobius, 2002.

Page 194
Skin-to-skin stimulates milk supply:
World Health Organization. *Evidence for the Ten Steps to Successful Breastfeeding*, 1998. www.babyfriendly.org.uk

Page 195
How skin-to-skin contact after birth enhances breastfeeding:
Righard Alade. Effect of delivery room routines on success of first breastfeed. *Lancet* 1990; 336: 1105-7 In: Mohrbacher N, Stock J. *The Breastfeeding Answer Book*. La Leche League, 2003.

Elliot L. *Early Intelligence*. London: Penguin, 1999 – cites several studies to support bonding enhanced by smell and skin-to-skin contact. See in particular p166.

Page 196
Show your baby that night-time is not for playing:
Nikolopoulou M, James-Roberts I. Preventing sleeping problems in infants who are at risk of developing them. *Arch Dis Child* 2003; 88(2): 108–11.

Pinella T, Birch L. Help me make it through the night: behavioural entrainment of breastfed infants' sleep patterns *Pediatrics* Feb 1993; 91(2): 436–44.

At first your baby will feed little and often:
Frantz 1985: Frantz 1983: In: Mohrbacher N, Stock J. (2003) ibid.

Page 197
Breastfeeding helps jaundice pass:
Yamauchi,Yamanouchi. Breastfeeding frequency during the first 24 hours after birth in fullterm neonates *Pediatrics* 1990; 86: 171–75. In: Mohrbacher N, Stock J. (2003) ibid.

Effect of Pethidine on breastfeeding:
Nissen E *et al.* Effects of routinely given pethidine during labour on infants' developing breastfeeding behaviour. *Acta Paediatr* 1997; 16(2): 201-8, In: Mohrbacher N, Stock J. (2003) ibid.

Page 200
Stanway P, Stanway A. *Breast is Best*. Pan, 1996 p17.

Page 202
Comparison of iron levels in formula milk and breastmilk: Inch S; No Contest. *New Generation*, NCT, December 1997, p6.

Page 203
Breastfeeding in hot weather:
Nylander. Unsupplemented breastfeeding in the maternity ward. *Acta Obst Gyn Scand* 1991; 70: 205-9, In: Mohrbacher N, Stock J. (2003) ibid.

The World Health Organization recommends:
See www.who.int

Page 207
Renfrew M, Fisher C, Arms S. *The New Breastfeeding*. Celestial Arts, 2000, p67.

Page 208
For more about feeding as the first social relationship, see:
Trevarthen C. Communication and co-operation in early infancy: a description of primary intersubjectivity. In: Bullowa M. (ed.) *Before Speech*. Cambridge: Cambridge University Press ,1979.

For more on breastfeeding multiples:
Multiple Births Foundation. *Feeding Twins, Triplets and More*. 1979, p1.

Page 214
Babies whose cries are answered, cry less:
Bell SM, Ainsworth MDS. Infant crying and maternal responsiveness. *Child Dev* 1972; 43: 1171–90.

Babies remember music from the womb:
Hepper PG. Fetal soap addiction. *Lancet* 11 June 1988; 1347–48.

Playing your favourite music can sometimes help soothe a crying baby:
Frederic GF, *et al. Music Therapy and Pregnancy*. MIDIRS June 2002; 12:2;197–201.

Page 215
Nikolopoulou M, James-Roberts I. Preventing sleeping problems in infants who are at risk of developing them. *Arch Dis Child* 2003; 88(2): 108–11.

Page 216
Cranial osteopathy research:
Hayden CJ. Towards an understanding of osteopathy in the treatment of infantile colic. *J Manual and Manipulative Therapy*. 2002, p162.

Cycles of arousal and sleep come together:
McKenna J, *et al.* Experimental studies of infant-parent co-sleeping. *Early Hum Dev* 1994; 38:187–201.

Bedsharing mothers disturbed less:
McKenna J, *et al.* (1994) ibid.

Baby sleeping in a separate room cries more and gets more upset: Cory A. Mermer response to Blair *et al.* 1999. http://bmj.com/cgi/eletters/319/7223/1457

Keeping your baby's cot in your room halves the risk of cot death: Blair *et al.* *BMJ* Babies sleeping with parents: case-control study 1999; 319: 1457–62.

Page 217
Gatts JD, *et al.* Reducing crying and irritability in neonates. *J Perinatol.* May/June 1995; 15(3): 215–21.

Page 221
A health visitor can help:
Seeley S, Murray L, Cooper PJ. The outcome for mothers and babies of health visitor intervention. *Health Visitor*, April 1996.

Page 222
Ballard CG, *et al.* Prevalence of postnatal psychiatric morbidity in mothers and fathers. *BJP*, June 1994.

Page 224
Onozawa K, Glover V, Kumar C, *et al.* Infant massage improves mother-infant interaction for mothers with postnatal depression, *J Affect Disord* 2001; 63: 201-207.

Proven benefits of massage:
Field T. Interventions for premature infants *J Paediatr.* 1986; 109.
Field T, *et al.* Massage stimulates growth in preterm infants: A replication. *Infant Behaviour and Development* 1990; 13.

Page 229
Olson, Fournier, Druckman. The Enrich Couple Inventory. Psychology Today magazine, May/June 2002.

index

Acknowledgements

Photographs

Andrew Florides 21, 26, 33, 37, 47, 55, 150, 153, 188, 231
Michael Bassett 90, 195, 196, 212, 225–7
Jackie Chapman 193, 201, 206, 209, 217, 221, 230
Independent midwives 46, 161, 165, 169, 178, 181
Anne Green-Armytage 30, 122, 187, 203, 215
Saskia van Rees 23, 38, 142
Hannah Clements 136, 139, 170
Tracy Grant 81, 167, 190
Lynn Walford 91, 101
Persil 119, 149
MIDIRS Photo Library 128, 131
Daniel Ward 8, 69
George Williams 13, 15
Victoria Smith 48
Antonia Robinson 51
Victoria Dick 54
Megan Oxberry 59
Louise O'Gorman 64
Corbis Photo Library 75, 95
Bubbles Photo Library 76
Jo Lovell 111
Prima Baby magazine 205
Photodisc 6, 174

Illustrations
All drawings by Kenny Grant except those on pp154–157, 164 which are by Helen Chown.

About the authors

Sue Allen-Mills, long-time NCT antenatal teacher, wrote on self-care in pregnancy. **Tricia Anderson**, currently a Senior Lecturer in Midwifery at Bournemouth University and independent midwife, read manuscripts and contributed the introductions. **Anna Berkley** registered midwife wrote about choices for your care. **Suzy Colebeck**, NCT antenatal teacher, collected and edited NCT members' birth stories. **Caroline Deacon**, journalist and NCT breastfeeding tutor contributed the practical information on breastfeeding and baby-soothing. **Miranda Dodwell**, who wrote on medical intervention, has a Ph.D. in Genetics and is an NCT antenatal teacher. **Hannah Hulme Hunter** is a practising midwife and supervisor of midwives. She wrote the information on straightforward birth and early days with a new baby. **Penny Lane** contributed the section on from girl to mother and information on the role of hormones in birth and breastfeeding. **Mary Nolan** read the manuscript and wrote the A to Z glossary. She is a long-time NCT antenatal tutor and writer on childbirth issues, with a PhD in antenatal education.

Grateful thanks are due to Julie Frohlich, midwife, and to the following members of The National Childbirth Trust who assisted by reading and commenting on manuscripts: Debbie Chippington-Derrick, NCT caesarean and VBAC co-ordinator; Cynthia Clarkson, Chair of NCT Research Networkers Panel; Rosemary Dodds, NCT Policy Research Officer; Juliet Goddard, NCT postnatal tutor; Linda Griffiths, NCT information officer and librarian; Gina Lowdon NCT caesarean and VBAC co-ordinator; Heather Neil, NCT breastfeeding counsellor; Louise Pengelley, NCT antenatal tutor.

For help with information about premature birth and the early days with a new baby: Bonnie Green and Shanit Marshall of Bliss; Nicola Jones; Bridie Keyse, Health Visitor. For help with information on antenatal testing, Elizabeth Dormandy, King's College, London University.

Your Birth Year
First published in 2004 by Mitchell Beazley, an imprint of Octopus Publishing Group Ltd, 2–4 Heron Quays, London, E14 4JP

Text copyright © NCT Publishing 2004
Design copyright © Octopus Publishing Group Ltd

Publisher's note: Before following any information or exercises contained in this book, it is recommended that you consult your doctor. The publishers cannot accept responsibility for any injuries or damage incurred as a result of following the information given in this book.

ISBN 1 84000 890 3
A CIP catalogue copy of this book is available from the British Library.

Printed and bound by Toppan Printing Company, China

For Mitchell Beazley
Executive Editor Vivien Antwi
Executive Art Editor Christine Keilty
Production Gary Hayes

For NCT
Content consultant Roz Collins

For NCT Publishing
Managing Editor Sonia Leach
Production Manager Michelle Williams
Production Assistant/Picture Research Karen Weaver
Design Tim McPhee, Jim Reader
Illustrations Kenny Grant, Helen Chown